STUDY GUIDE

FUNDAMENTALS OF FINANCIAL MANAGEMENT: THE CONCISE EDITION

STUDY GUIDE
FUNDAMENTALS OF FINANCIAL MANAGEMENT: THE CONCISE EDITION

EUGENE F. BRIGHAM

JOEL F. HOUSTON

DANA ABERWALD CLARK

UNIVERSITY OF FLORIDA

The Dryden Press
Harcourt Brace College Publishers

Fort Worth   Philadelphia   San Diego   New York   Orlando   Austin   San Antonio
Toronto   Montreal   London   Sydney   Tokyo

Requests for permission to make copies of any part of the work should be mailed to: Permissions Department, Harcourt Brace & Company, 6277 Sea Harbor Drive, Orlando, Florida 32887-6777.

Some material in this work previously appeared in *Fundamentals of Financial Management*, Seventh Edition, Study Guide, copyright ©1995, 1989, 1986 by the Dryden Press. All rights reserved.

Address for Orders
The Dryden Press
6277 Sea Harbor Drive
Orlando, Florida 32887-6777
1-800-782-4479 or 1-800-433-0001 (in Florida)

Address for Editorial Correspondance
The Dryden Press
301 Commerce Street, Suite 3700
Fort Worth, TX 76102

ISBN: 0-03-0159628

Printed in the United States of America

 6 7 8 9 0 1 2 3 4 095 9 8 7 6 5 4 3

The Dryden Press
Harcourt Brace College Publishers

PREFACE

This *Study Guide* is designed primarily to help you develop a working knowledge of the concepts and principles of financial management. Additionally, it will familiarize you with the types of true/false and multiple-choice test questions that are being used with increasing frequency in introductory finance courses.

The *Study Guide* follows the outline of *Fundamentals of Financial Management: The Concise Edition*. You should read carefully the next section, "How to Use This *Study Guide*," to familiarize yourself with its specific contents and to gain some insights into how it can be used most effectively.

We would like to thank Lou Gapenski, Carol Stanton, and Susan Sternberg for their considerable assistance in the preparation of this edition and Bob LeClair for his helpful ideas in prior editions which we carried over to this one.

We have tried to make the *Study Guide* as clear and error-free as possible. However, some mistakes may have crept in, and there are almost certainly some sections that could be clarified. Any suggestions for improving the *Study Guide* would be greatly appreciated and should be addressed to Joel Houston. Since instructors almost never read study guides, we address this call for help to students!

Eugene F. Brigham
Joel F. Houston
Dana Aberwald Clark

College of Business Administration
University of Florida
PO Box 117160
Gainesville, FL 32611-7160

May 1995

HOW TO USE THIS STUDY GUIDE

Different people will tend to use the *Study Guide* in somewhat different ways. This is natural because both introductory finance courses and individual students' needs vary widely. However, the tips contained in this section should help all students use the *Study Guide* more effectively, regardless of these differences.

Each chapter contains (1) an overview, (2) an outline, (3) definitional self-test questions, (4) conceptual self-test questions, (5) self-test problems, and (6) answers and solutions to the self-test questions and problems. You should begin your study by reading the overview; it will give you an idea of what is contained in the chapter and how this material fits into the overall scheme of things in financial management.

Next, read over the outline to get a better fix on the specific topics covered in the chapter. It is important to realize that the outline does not list every facet of every topic covered in the textbook—the *Study Guide* is intended to highlight and summarize the textbook, not to supplant it. Also, note that appendix material is clearly marked as such within the outline. Thus, if your instructor does not assign a particular appendix, you may not want to study that portion of the outline.

The definitional self-test questions are intended to test your knowledge of, and also to reinforce your ability to work with, the terms and concepts introduced in the chapter. If you do not understand the definitions thoroughly, review the outline prior to going on to the conceptual questions and problems.

The conceptual self-test questions focus on the same kinds of ideas that the textbook end-of-chapter questions address, but in the *Study Guide*, the questions are set out in a true/false or multiple-choice format. Thus, for many students these questions can be used to practice for the types of tests that are being used with increasing frequency. However, regardless of the types of tests you must take, working through the conceptual questions will help drive home the key concepts of financial management.

The numeric problems are also written in a multiple-choice format. Generally, the problems are arranged in order of increasing difficulty. Also, note that some of the *Study Guide* problems are convoluted in the sense that information normally available to financial managers is withheld and information normally unknown is given. Such problems are designed to test your knowledge of a subject, and you must work "backwards" to solve them. Furthermore, such problems are included in the *Study Guide* in part because they provide a good test of how well you understand the material and in part because you may well be seeing similar problems on your exams.

Finally, each *Study Guide* chapter provides the answers and solutions to the self-test questions and problems. The rationale behind a question's correct answer is explained where necessary, but the problem solutions are always complete. Note that the problems in the early chapters generally provide both "table-based" and "financial calculator" solutions. In later chapters, only calculator solutions are shown. You should not be concerned if your answer differs from ours by a small amount which is caused by rounding differences.

Of course, each student must decide how to incorporate the *Study Guide* in his or her overall study program. Many students begin an assignment by reading the *Study Guide* overview and outline to get the "big picture," then read the chapter in the textbook. Naturally, the *Study Guide* overview and outline is also used extensively to review for exams. Most students work the textbook questions and problems, using the latter as a self-test and review tool. However, if you are stumped by a text problem, try the *Study Guide* problems first because their detailed solutions can get you over stumbling blocks.

WANT TO DO WELL ON EXAMS? THEN READ THIS!

The goals of a good testing system are (1) to give students direction as to the most important material, (2) to motivate them to study properly, and (3) to determine how much they have learned. In finance, it is easy to construct a combination problem/essay exam which accomplishes these goals, but if essay questions are ruled out by class size, then instructors have a more difficult job. They must then develop complex, unambiguous questions and problems which require students to think through the issues and determine which of several plausible-looking statements is most correct. A good exam will require students to recall how to use a number of equations, graphs, and problem set-ups, to actually set up examples or draw graphs to determine the required answers, and to understand how the results are used in the decision-making process. It is not easy to accomplish these goals in a multiple-choice exam, but it can be done.

Many students in the introductory finance course have never faced this type of an exam, and they are "thrown for a loop" by our questions. Eventually, they catch on to our examination process, and when they do, they think it is both fair and reasonable. Still, learning how to take multiple-choice finance exams can be traumatic and stressful. *The purpose of this section is to try to reduce your stress if you will be faced with multiple-choice exams.* If you will be taking "regular" problem/essay exams, the section will stiil be useful, but if you will be taking multiple-choice exams, you simply cannot afford to skip it!

How to Take Multiple-Choice Finance Tests

Like it or not, testing is inherently competitive--students compete against one another and also against the instructor. Of course, the instructor wants the students to do well, but he or she also wants to challenge students and to see just how well they understand the material.

You should understand how your instructor makes up his or her exams because this will help you to prepare for them. Obviously, we don't know how your specific instructor will construct exams, but chances are that he or she will do something similar to what we and most other instructors do. So, here are some pointers that will help you as you study finance and prepare for exams.

1. Recognize that finance is inherently quantitative--it deals with numbers and relationships between numbers. It is less intuitive than management or marketing but more intuitive than accounting or statistics. For example, accountants are primarily interested in reporting *historical* data, but in finance we want to know how different actions will affect *future* data. Therefore, as they write out exams, instructors will ask you to do lots of calculations, but to do more than just crank out numerical answers--they will also expect you to know how your answer would tend to change if the data were changed and how the very possibility of such changes might influence actual decisions.

2. You will probably have to answer two types of questions on finance exams: (1) numerical problems and (2) conceptual true/false or multiple-choice questions. You are probably used to taking courses where you can cram just before the exams, memorize some equations and

facts, then regurgitate them on the exam and do fine. That won't work in finance--you obviously will need to learn some facts, but you must also learn how to set up and solve relatively complex problems and reason out difficult conceptual multiple-choice questions.

3. You can study for problems in two ways: work all the problems you can find and hope you will get recognizably similar ones on the exam, or, preferably, think about the various types of problems in a generic sense, and try to understand what each type of problem is all about; that is, think about why the particular problem is important, what type of decision it deals with, and why the solution is laid out as it is.

4. The worst way to study homework problems is to just work on each problem until you get the right answer, pat yourself on the back for getting it, and then move on to the next problem. The best way to study problems is to consciously and systematically go through these four steps: (1) Begin by asking yourself what the purpose of the problem is; for example, if the problem deals with a ratio analysis by a banker considering whether or not to make a loan to a company, make note of that fact. (2) Next, ask yourself what formula, table set-up, or what-have-you is necessary to get a solution; in a ratio analysis, you might at this point list the ratios that would be most relevant. (3) Then insert the data to get the required answer. (4) Finally, conclude by asking yourself two sets of questions:

(a) If my instructor were to give us a problem like this on the exam, how might he or she change it to make up a good exam problem? Obviously the numbers could be changed, but could we be required to solve for a different variable? For example, if the problem gave us balance sheet data and then required us to determine the current ratio, could we be given the current ratio plus some balance sheet data and then be required to complete the balance sheet?

(b) If our instructor wants to see if we understand the implications of the answer for decision making, what kind of conceptual question might we be asked? For example, if we calculated a current ratio of 2.3x, how could we tell if that ratio was good, bad, or indifferent, and who might use the current ratio, and for what purposes?

We let our students bring to the exams one 8 1/2" by 11" sheet of paper with as much written on the two sides as they can squeeze on it. We do this partly to reduce their tendency to try to memorize things, but we also want them to think about problems generically, and having them list formulas and prototype examples of each type of problem on their "cheat sheet" helps in this regard.

5. Except for a few definitional questions, most non-numeric (conceptual) exam questions are actually based on problems. When we and most other finance professors make up regular problem/essay exams as opposed to multiple-choice exams, we often ask for the solution to a problem and then ask for an essay explanation of how changes in various factors would affect the answer. Or, we might just skip the numerical problem part and simply ask you to explain how changes in different input variables would affect some output variable.

For example, we might give you the following partial balance sheet and then ask you to calculate the current ratio:

Inventory	$ 50	Accounts payable	$ 50
Other current assets	45	Short-term bank loans	50
Total current assets	$ 95	Total current liabilities	$100

You would find the current ratio to be 95/100 = 0.95. Then, on an essay exam, we might ask you three additional questions:

(a) Would the current ratio be improved (increased) if the company took out a 6-month loan for $100 and used the proceeds to increase inventory?

(b) Would your answer in Part a have been the same if the company's original current ratio had been 1.5 rather than 0.95? Explain.

(c) What general conclusions can you reach regarding the effects on the current ratio of adding equal dollar amounts to both current assets and current liabilities?

To answer Part a, you would make the necessary changes in the balance sheet, calculate the new current ratio of ($95 + $100)/($100 + $100) = $195/$200 = 0.975, and answer, "Yes, the current ratio would be improved--it would increase from 0.95 to 0.975." To answer Part b, you would increase Other current assets (or Inventory) by $55 to produce a situation where the original current ratio was 1.5, then add $100 to both inventories and bank loans, and get this new current ratio:

$$\text{Current ratio} = (\$150 + \$100)/(\$100 + \$100) = \$250/\$200 = 1.25.$$

Then you would answer Part b as follows: "No. In this case, adding an equal amount to both current assets and current liabilities will cause the current ratio to decrease from 1.5 to 1.25."

To answer Part c, you should first suspect that whether the current ratio increases or decreases depends on whether or not the initial current ratio is above or below 1.0. You might then go back to the original data, add $5 to other current assets to bring the current ratio up to 1.0, and then add $100 to both inventories and bank loans to confirm your hunch. Then you would answer Part c as follows: "If the current ratio is initially below 1.0, then adding equal dollar amounts to current assets and current liabilities will improve the current ratio, while if the initial ratio is greater than 1.0, the current ratio will be reduced. If the initial current ratio is 1.0, then the change will have no effect on the current ratio--it will remain constant at 1.0."

6. The essay questions in Point 5 were derived directly from the problem, and we answered the questions by modifying the data in the problem. Thus, the questions were based on the problem. *Now note that we could have skipped the problem and gone directly to the conceptual questions.* For example, we could have given you a question like this:

"If a company whose current ratio is 0.95 takes out a 6-month loan from its bank and uses the cash to increase inventory, how would this affect its current ratio?"

Now you would probably approach the question by writing out the formula for the current ratio, making up some data where the current ratio is 0.95, then adding some amount to current assets and current liabilities, and finally calculating a new current ratio. Some people can think such questions through abstractly, but most of us find it easier to work out some numbers, get the picture of what's happening, and then reach general conclusions. *Therefore, for most of us it is most efficient to approach conceptual questions that test our knowledge of relationships by first asking what generic problem the question is based on by thinking about the question within the framework of a problem,* in this case the calculation of a current ratio.

7. When we make up multiple-choice exams, we put several false statements plus one true statement into a question and then ask you to identify the correct statement. For example, we might ask you the following question:

If a firm takes out a 6-month loan and uses the proceeds to build inventory, then, other things held constant, its current ratio will
a. Increase.
b. Decrease.
c. Remain constant.
d. Fluctuate.
e. Increase, decrease, or remain constant, depending on the level of the initial current ratio.

As we saw above, the correct answer is "e," but if we had not just gone through the example, how would you have approached the question? You could try guessing, but a better approach would be to set up a partial balance sheet, put some numbers in, and see what happens to the current ratio. That is the best way for most of us to attack many of the conceptual questions you will face.

8. You should realize that when professors make up conceptual questions, they often start with numerical problems and then frame "word" questions as they look at the details of a problem. For example, we might be looking at a balance sheet and the calculations for the current ratio and then come up with the question posed in Point 7.

9. To take this a step further, many professors write a multiple-choice exam problem and then ask a multiple-choice conceptual question which is related to the problem, *but does not tie the two together* physically on the exam. Thus, you might be asked to calculate some ratios as a problem and then, separately, be asked to answer a conceptual question about ratios which would be easier to answer if you make the connection between the problem and the question.

10. At Florida, we generally give two midterms plus a final exam, and each is a 2-hour exam. We have about 10 multiple-choice conceptual questions first, then about 10 multiple-choice problems. Initially, most students worked straight through the exam, front to back. However, some of the more astute students figured out that if they worked the problems first, they would get some clues that would help with the questions. Now our students generally work

the problems first, regardless of their order of appearance on the exams. Note, though, that we and many other instructors include a number of relatively easy questions and problems, along with some difficult ones designed to separate the best students from the rest. Further, the most difficult problems are placed toward the end of the problem set. We warn our students not to spend too much time on any one problem and, if they don't have a clue as to how to handle it, to go on and then come back to it later if they have time.

11. One final comment about studying is appropriate. Some of our less astute students tend to tackle a given problem, not see how to work it, look up the solution or get someone to explain it to them, and then say to themselves, "Oh yes, I see how to work it, and I could work one like it on the exam. Now let's finish the rest of the problems." Too often, this is pure self-deceit: The student really doesn't understand the problem and could not work one like it unless it was virtually identical. Slowing down and going through our checklist will help avoid this problem.

CONTENTS OF THE STUDY GUIDE

CHAPTER 1
AN OVERVIEW OF FINANCIAL MANAGEMENT

OVERVIEW

This chapter provides an overview of financial management and should give you a better understanding of the following: (1) what forces will affect financial management in the future, (2) how businesses are organized, (3) how finance fits into the structure of a firm's organization, (4) how financial managers relate to their counterparts in other departments, and (5) what the goals of a firm are and how financial managers can contribute to the attainment of these goals.

OUTLINE

Finance consists of three interrelated areas: money and capital markets, investments, and financial management. Career opportunities within each field are varied and numerous, but financial managers must have a knowledge of all three areas.

- Many finance majors go to work for financial institutions, including banks, insurance companies, investment companies, savings and loans, and credit unions. The bank officer trainee is the most common initial job in this area.

- Finance graduates who go into investments generally work for a brokerage house in sales or as a security analyst; for a bank, a mutual fund, or an insurance company in the management of investment portfolios; or for a financial consulting firm, advising individual investors or pension funds on how to invest their funds.

- Financial management, the broadest of the three areas, and the one with the greatest number of job opportunities, is important to all types of businesses. The types of jobs one encounters in this area range from decisions regarding plant expansions to the choice of stocks or bonds to finance expansion.

The two most important trends for financial management during the 1990s are likely to be the continued globalization of business and the increased use of computer technology.

- Four factors have made the trend toward globalization mandatory for many businesses.
  - ☐ Transportation and communications improvements have lowered shipping costs, lowered trade barriers, and increased competition.
  - ☐ Increased political clout of consumers has also helped lower trade barriers.
  - ☐ Due to increased technology, higher development costs have resulted, necessitating increased unit sales.
  - ☐ Competitive pressures have forced companies to shift manufacturing operations to lower-cost countries.

- Continued advances in computer technology are revolutionizing the way financial decisions are made. Thus, the new generation of financial managers will need stronger computer and quantitative skills than were required in the past.

Historical trends discussed above have greatly increased the importance of financial management. Today the financial manager must make decisions in a much more coordinated manner, and he or she generally has direct responsibility for the control process. Because there are financial implications in virtually all business decisions, nonfinancial executives simply must know enough finance to work these implications into their own specialized analyses.

The financial staff's task is to acquire and use funds so as to maximize the firm's value. Some specific activities follow.

- The financial staff uses *forecasting and planning* to shape the firm's future position.

- The financial staff makes *major investment and financing decisions*.

- The financial staff *coordinates and controls* when interacting with other departments so that the firm operates as efficiently as possible.

- The financial staff must *deal with the financial markets*.

The three main forms of business organization are the sole proprietorship, the partnership, and the corporation. About 80 percent of businesses operate as sole proprietorships, but when based on dollar value of sales, 80 percent of all business is conducted by corporations.

- A *sole proprietorship* is an unincorporated business owned by one individual.

- ☐ Advantages are: (a) it is easily and inexpensively formed, (b) it is subject to few government regulations, and (c) it pays no corporate income taxes (however, all business earnings are taxed as personal income to the owner).
- ☐ Disadvantages are: (a) it is limited in its ability to raise large sums of capital, (b) the proprietor has unlimited personal liability for business debts, and (c) it has a life limited to the life of the individual who created it.

■ A *partnership* exists when two or more persons associate to conduct a noncorporate business.
   - ☐ Its major advantage is its low cost and ease of formation.
   - ☐ Disadvantages are: (a) unlimited liability, (b) limited life, (c) difficulty in transferring ownership, and (d) difficulty of raising large amounts of capital.

■ A *corporation* is a legal entity created by a state, and it is separate and distinct from its owners and managers.
   - ☐ Advantages are: (a) unlimited life, (b) ownership which is easily transferred through the exchange of stock, and (c) limited liability. Because of these three factors, it is much easier for corporations to raise money in the capital markets.
   - ☐ Disadvantages are: (a) corporate earnings are subject to double taxation and (b) setting up a corporation and filing required state and federal reports are more complex than for a sole proprietorship or partnership.
   - ☐ A charter must be filed with the state where the firm is incorporated, and bylaws which govern the management of the company must be prepared.

■ The value of any business, other than a very small one, will probably be maximized if it is organized as a corporation.

Maximizing the price of the firm's common stock is the most important goal of most corporations.

■ Other objectives, such as personal satisfaction, employee welfare, and the good of the community, also have an influence, but for publicly-owned companies, they are less important than stock price maximization.

■ Hostile takeovers and proxy fights have also stimulated management to maximize share price.

■ Social responsibility raises the question of whether businesses should operate strictly in their stockholders' best interests or also be responsible for the welfare of their employees, customers, and the communities in which they operate.
   - ☐ Any voluntary, socially responsible acts that raise costs will be difficult, if not impossible, in industries that are subject to keen competition.

- ☐ Even firms with above-average profits will be constrained in exercising social responsibility by capital market forces because investors will normally prefer a firm that concentrates on profits over one excessively devoted to social action.
- ☐ Socially responsible actions that increase costs may have to be put on a mandatory, rather than a voluntary, basis to insure that the burden falls uniformly on all businesses.
- ☐ Industry and government must cooperate in establishing rules for fair hiring, product safety, environmental protection, and other programs that affect all businesses.

- ■ The same actions that maximize stock price also benefit society. To maximize stock price, a firm must provide a low-cost, high-quality product to consumers. This, in itself, is a benefit to society.

Business ethics can be thought of as a company's attitude and conduct toward its employees, customers, community, and stockholders. Most firms today have in place strong codes of ethical behavior; however, it is imperative that top management be openly committed to ethical behavior and that they communicate this commitment through their own personal actions as well as company policies.

An agency relationship exists when one or more persons (the principals) hire another person (the agent) to act on their behalf, delegating decision-making authority to that agent. Agency relationships exist (1) between stockholders and managers and (2) between stocholders and creditors (debtholders).

- ■ A potential *agency problem* exists whenever a manager owns less than 100 percent of the firm's common stock.
  - ☐ Since the firm's earnings do not go solely to the manager, he or she may not concentrate exclusively on maximizing shareholder wealth.
  - ☐ Another potential conflict between management and stockholders arises in a leveraged buyout because management might attempt to *minimize* the firm's stock price just prior to the buyout. However, the Securities and Exchange Commission (SEC) now requires disclosure of material information relating to proposed deals where a conflict of interest exists.
- ■ Several mechanisms are used to ensure that managers act in shareholders' best interests: (1) the threat of firing, (2) the threat of takeover, and (3) the proper structuring of managerial compensation.

- ■ Another agency problem involves conflicts between stockholders and creditors (debtholders).
  - ☐ Conflicts arise if (a) management, acting for its stockholders, takes on projects that have greater risk than was anticipated by creditors or (b) the firm increases debt to a level higher than was anticipated. Both of these actions decrease the value of the debt outstanding.

☐ It is in the firm's best interest to deal fairly with its creditors in order to assure future access to debt markets at reasonable interest costs.

The financial manager can affect the firm's stock price by influencing the following factors: (1) projected earnings per share, (2) timing of the earnings stream, (3) riskiness of these projected earnings, (4) use of debt, and (5) dividend policy. Every significant corporate decision should be analyzed in terms of its effects on these factors and, through them, on the price of the firm's stock.

Although managerial actions affect the value of a firm's stock, external factors also influence stock prices. Included among them are legal constraints, the general level of economic activity, tax laws, and conditions in the stock market.

SELF-TEST QUESTIONS

Definitional

1. Finance consists of three interrelated areas: (1) _money_ & _capital markets_ which deals with many of the topics covered in macroeconomics; (2) _investments_, which focuses on the decisions of individuals and financial institutions as they choose securities for their investment portfolios; and (3) _financial management_ or "business finance."

2. In the 1990s, two of the most important trends affecting financial management are likely to be the continued _globalization_ of business and the increased use of _computer technology_.

3. Sole proprietorships are easily formed, but often have difficulty raising _capital_, they subject proprietors to unlimited _liability_, and they have a limited _life_.

4. Partnership profits are taxed as _personal_ income in proportion to each partner's proportionate ownership.

5. A partnership is dissolved upon the withdrawal or _death_ of any one of the partners. In addition, the difficulty in _transferring_ ownership is a major disadvantage of the partnership form of business organization.

6. A(n) _Corporation_ is a legal entity created by a state, and it is separate from its owners and managers.

7. The concept of limited liability means that a firm's stockholders are not personally liable for the debts of the business.

8. Modern financial theory operates on the assumption that the goal of management is the maximization of shareholder wealth. This goal is accomplished if the firm's stock price is maximized.

9. Socially responsible activities that increase a firm's costs will be most difficult in those industries where competition is most intense.

10. Firms with above-average profit levels will find social actions constrained by capital market factors.

11. A(n) agency relationship exists when one or more persons (the principals) hire another person (the agent) to act on their behalf.

12. Potential agency problems exist between a firm's shareholders and its managers and also between shareholders and creditors.

13. A firm's stock price depends on several factors. Among the most important of these are the level of projected earnings per share and the riskiness of these projections.

Conceptual

14. The primary objective of the firm is to maximize EPS.

     a. True   **b.** False

15. The types of actions that help a firm maximize stock price are generally not directly beneficial to society at large.

    a. True   **b.** False

16. There are factors that influence stock price over which managers have virtually no control.

    a. True   **b.** False

17. Which of the following factors affect stock price?

    a. Level of projected earnings per share.
    b. Riskiness of projected earnings per share.

c. Timing of the earnings stream.
d. The manner of financing the firm.
e. All of the above factors.

18. Which of the following factors tend to encourage management to pursue stock price maximization as a goal?

a. Shareholders link management's compensation to company performance.
b. Managers' reactions to the threat of tender offers and proxy fights.
c. Managers do not have goals other than stock price maximization.
d. Statements a and b are both correct.
e. Statements a, b, and c are all correct.

19. The primary contribution of finance to total social welfare is its

a. Function as a productive resource.
b. Contribution to the efficient allocation and use of resources.
c. Role as an exogenous variable.
d. Positive impact on the externalities of "other variables."
e. Contribution to environmental protection.

20. Shareholder agency costs include

a. Expenditures to monitor managerial actions.
b. Managerial salaries.
c. Opportunity costs associated with managerial restrictions.
d. All of the above.
e. Answers a and c.

21. Which of the following represents a significant *disadvantage* to the corporate form of organization?

a. Difficulty in transferring ownership.
b. Exposure to taxation of corporate earnings and stockholder dividend income.
c. Degree of liability to which corporate owners and managers are exposed.
d. Level of difficulty corporations face in obtaining large amounts of capital in financial markets.

ANSWERS TO SELF-TEST QUESTIONS

1. money and capital markets; investments; financial management
2. globalization; computer technology
3. capital; liability; life
4. personal
5. death; transferring
6. corporation
7. limited liability
8. maximization; wealth; stock price
9. competition
10. constrained
11. agency
12. managers; creditors (or debtholders)
13. earnings per share

14. b. An increase in earnings per share will not necessarily increase stock price. For example, if the increase in earnings per share is accompanied by an increase in the riskiness of the firm, stock price might fall. *The primary objective is the maximization of stock price.*

15. b. The actions that maximize stock price generally also benefit society by promoting efficient, low-cost operations; encouraging the development of new technology, products, and jobs; and requiring efficient and courteous service.

16. a. Managers have no control over factors such as (1) external constraints (for example, antitrust laws and environmental regulations), (2) the general level of economic activity, (3) taxes, and (4) conditions in the stock market, all of which affect the firm's stock price.

17. e. The firm's stock price is dependent on all the factors mentioned. One additional factor not mentioned is dividend policy.

18. d. Mechanisms which tend to force managers to act in the shareholders' best interests include (1) the threat of firing, (2) the threat of takeover, and (3) the proper structuring of managerial compensation.

19. b. Financial management plays a crucial role in the operation of successful firms because of finance's contribution to the efficient allocation and use of resources. Successful firms are absolutely necessary for a healthy, productive economy.

20. e. Shareholder agency costs include expenditures to monitor managerial actions and the opportunity costs associated with restrictions placed on managers.

21. b. The double taxation of corporate earnings is a significant disadvantage of the corporate form of organization. The corporations' earnings are taxed, and then any earnings paid out as dividends are taxed again as income to the stockholders.

CHAPTER 2
FINANCIAL STATEMENTS, CASH FLOW, AND TAXES

OVERVIEW

Financial management requires the consideration of the types of financial statements firms must provide to investors, and the individuals from which debt and equity capital are obtained. Thus, this chapter begins with a discussion of the basic financial statements, how they are used, and what kinds of financial information users need. Because the value of any asset depends on the usable, or after-tax, cash flows the asset is expected to produce, the chapter also explains the difference between accounting income versus cash flow, and how cash flows through the firm. Finally, since it is the after-tax income that is important, the chapter provides an overview of the federal income tax system.

OUTLINE

Although the economic system has grown enormously since the early days of the barter system, the original reasons for accounting and financial statements still apply. Investors need them to make intelligent decisions, managers need them to see how effectively their enterprises are being run, and taxing authorities need them to assess taxes in a reasonable manner.

A firm's annual report to shareholders presents two important types of information. The first is a verbal statement of the company's recent operations and its expectations for the coming year. The second is a set of quantitative financial statements which report what actually happened to the firm's financial position, earnings, and dividends over the past few years.

The balance sheet shows the firm's assets and the claims against those assets. Assets, found on the left-hand side of the balance sheet, are typically shown in the order of their liquidity. Claims, found on the right-hand side, are generally listed in the order in which they must be paid.

■ Only cash represents actual money. Noncash assets should produce cash flows eventually, but they do not represent cash in hand.

■ Claims against the assets consist of liabilities and stockholders' equity. Thus, Assets − Liabilities − Preferred stock = Common stockholders' equity (Net worth).

■ The common equity section of the balance sheet is divided into two accounts: common stock and retained earnings. The common stock account arises from the issuance of stock to raise capital. Retained earnings are built up over time as the firm "saves" a part of its earnings rather than paying all earnings out as dividends.

■ Different methods, such as FIFO and LIFO, can be used to determine the value of inventory. These methods, in turn, affect the reported cost of goods sold, profits, and EPS.

■ Companies often use the most accelerated method permitted under the law to calculate depreciation for tax purposes but use straight line depreciation, which results in a lower depreciation expense, for stockholder reporting.

■ The balance sheet may be thought of as a snapshot of the firm's financial position *at a point in time* (for example, end of year). The balance sheet changes every day as inventory is increased or decreased, as fixed assets are added or retired, as bank loans are increased or decreased, and so on.

The income statement summarizes the firm's revenues and expenses over a period of time (for example, the past year). Earnings per share (EPS) is called "the bottom line," denoting that of all the items on the income statement, EPS is the most important.

The statement of retained earnings reports changes in the equity accounts between balance sheet dates. The balance sheet account "retained earnings" represents a claim against assets, not assets per se. Retained earnings as reported on the balance sheet do not represent cash and are not "available" for the payment of dividends or anything else. Retained earnings represent funds which have already been reinvested in the firm's operating assets.

In finance the emphasis is on the cash flow which the company is expected to generate. The firm's net income is important, but cash flows are even more important because dividends must be paid in cash, and cash is also necessary to purchase the assets required to continue operations.

■ A firm's operating cash flows are generally equal to cash from sales, minus cash operating costs, minus interest charges, and minus taxes.

■ Depreciation is a noncash charge, so it must be added back to net income to obtain an estimate of the cash flow from operations.

■ A stock's value is based on the *present value of the cash flows* which investors expect it to provide in the future. The cash flow provided by the stock itself is the expected future dividend stream, and that expected dividend stream provides the fundamental basis for the stock's value. There are two classes of cash flows:
  □ Operating cash flows arise from normal operations.
  □ Other cash flows arise from the issuance of stock, from borrowing, or from the sale of fixed assets.

■ To understand how the timing of cash flows influences the financial statements, one must understand the *cash flow cycle* within a firm. It shows the way in which actual net cash, as opposed to accounting net income, flows into or out of the firm during some specified period.

The statement of cash flows reports the impact of a firm's operating, investing, and financing activities on cash flows over an accounting period.

■ In general, *free cash flow* is the cash flow that remains after considering all operating cash inflows and the required expenditures necessary to maintain operating cash flows in the future.

■ The bottom line of the statement of cash flows reflects the net increase (decrease) in cash and marketable securities. This can be viewed as the firm's basic free cash flow.

Individuals pay taxes on wages and salaries, on investment income (dividends, interest, and profits from the sale of securities), and on the profits of proprietorships and partnerships.

■ U.S. income taxes are *progressive*; that is, the higher the income, the larger the percentage paid in taxes. *Marginal tax rates* begin at 15 percent and can go up to 39.6 percent.
  □ The marginal tax rate is the tax applicable to the last unit of income.
  □ The *average tax rate* is calculated as taxes paid divided by taxable income.

■ Because dividends are paid from corporate income that has already been taxed (at rates going up as high as 39 percent), there is double taxation of corporate income. Interest on most state and local government securities, which are often called "municipals," is not subject to federal income taxes. This creates a strong incentive for individuals in high tax brackets to purchase such securities.

■ Gains and losses on the sale of *capital assets* such as stocks, bonds, and real estate have historically received special tax treatment. Currently, *all long-term capital gains* income is taxed as if it were ordinary income, with a maximum tax rate capped at 28 percent.

Corporations pay taxes on profits.

Corporate tax rates are also progressive up to $18,333,333 of taxable income, but are constant thereafter. Marginal tax rates range from 15 to 39 percent.

Interest and dividend income received by a corporation are taxed.
☐ Interest is taxed as ordinary income at regular corporate tax rates.
☐ However, 70 percent of the dividends received by one corporation from another is excluded from taxable income. The remaining 30 percent is taxed at the ordinary rate. Thus, the effective tax rate on dividends received by a 35 percent marginal tax bracket corporation is 0.30(35%) = 10.5%.

■ The tax system favors debt financing over equity financing.
☐ Interest paid is a tax-deductible business expense.
☐ Dividends on common and preferred stock are not deductible. Thus, a 40 percent federal-plus-state tax bracket corporation must earn $1/(1.0 − 0.40) = $1/0.60 = $1.67 before taxes to pay $1 of dividends, but only $1 of pretax income is required to pay $1 of interest.

Before 1987, long-term corporate capital gains were taxed at lower rates than ordinary income. However, at present, long-term capital gains are taxed as ordinary income.

Ordinary corporate operating losses can be carried back to each of the preceding 3 years and forward for the next 15 years in the future to offset taxable income in those years. The purpose of permitting this loss treatment is to avoid penalizing corporations whose incomes fluctuate substantially from year to year.

■ The Internal Revenue Code imposes a penalty on corporations that improperly accumulate earnings if the purpose of the accumulation is to enable stockholders to avoid personal income tax on dividends.

■ If a corporation owns 80 percent or more of another corporation's stock, it can aggregate profits and losses and file a consolidated tax return. Thus, losses in one area can offset profits in another.

■ Small businesses which meet certain restrictions may be set up as *S corporations* which receive benefits of the corporate form—especially limited liability—yet are taxed as proprietorships or partnerships rather than as corporations. This treatment would be preferred by owners of small corporations in which all or most of the income earned each year is distributed as dividends because the income would be taxed only once at the individual level.

SELF-TEST QUESTIONS

Definitional

1. Of all its communications with shareholders, a firm's _annual_ report is generally the most important.

2. The income statement reports the results of operations during the past year, the most important item being _earnings per share_.

3. The _balance sheet_ lists the firm's assets as well as claims against those assets.

4. Typically, assets are listed in order of their _liquidity_, while liabilities are listed in the order in which they must be paid.

5. Assets − Liabilities − Preferred stock = _net_ worth, or _Common stockholders'_ equity.

6. The two accounts which normally make up the common equity section of the balance sheet are _common stock_ and _retained earnings_.

7. _Retained earnings_ as reported on the balance sheet represent income earned by the firm in past years that has not been paid out as dividends.

8. Retained earnings are generally reinvested in _operating assets_ and are not held in the form of cash.

9. The _statement of cash flows_ is designed to show how the firm's operations have affected its cash position.

10. The three major categories of the Statement of Cash Flows are cash flows associated with _operating_ activities, _long-term investing_ activities, and _financing_ activities.

11. The _Common stock_ account arises from the issuance of stock to raise capital.

12. The _statement of retained earnings_ reports changes in the equity accounts between balance sheet dates.

13. In finance the emphasis is on the _cash flows_ which the company is expected to generate.

14. A firm's _operating cash flow_ are generally equal to cash from sales, minus cash operating costs, minus interest charges, and minus taxes.

15. The _cash flow cycle_ shows the way in which actual net cash, as opposed to accounting net income, flows into or out of the firm during some specified period.

16. A(n) _progressive_ tax system is one in which tax rates are higher at higher levels of income.

17. A progressive tax structure, which when combined with inflation increases the government's share of GDP without any change in tax rates, is called _bracket creep_.

18. The marginal tax rate on the largest corporations, those with taxable incomes exceeding $18,333,333, is _35_ percent, while that on the wealthiest individuals can go up as high as _39.6_ percent.

19. Interest received on _municipal_ bonds is generally not subject to federal income taxes. This feature makes them particularly attractive to investors in _high_ tax brackets.

20. In order to qualify as a long-term capital gain or loss, an asset must be held for more than _12_ months.

21. Gains or losses on assets held less than one year are referred to as _short - term_ transactions.

22. Interest income received by a corporation is taxed as _ordinary_ income. However, only _30_ percent of dividends received from another corporation is subject to taxation.

23. Another important distinction exists between interest and dividends paid by a corporation. Interest payments are _tax deductible_, while dividend payments are not.

24. Ordinary corporate operating losses can first be carried back _3_ years and then forward _15_ years.

25. A firm that refuses to pay dividends in order to help stockholders avoid personal income taxes may be subject to a penalty for improper accumulation of earnings.

26. A corporation that owns 80 percent or more of another corporation's stock may choose to file consolidated tax returns.

27. The Tax Code permits a corporation (that meets certain restrictions) to be taxed at the owners' personal tax rates and to avoid the impact of duplicate taxation of dividends. This type of corporation is called a(n) S corporation. (double)

Conceptual

28. The fact that 70 percent of intercorporate dividends received by a corporation is excluded from taxable income has encouraged debt financing over equity financing.

     a. True   **b.** False

29. An individual with substantial personal wealth and income is considering the possibility of opening a new business. The business will have a relatively high degree of risk, and losses may be incurred for the first several years. Which legal form of business organization would probably be best?

    a. Proprietorship   **c.** Partnership   **e.** Limited partnership
    b. Corporation   **d.** S corporation

30. Which of the following statements is most *correct*?

    a. In order to avoid double taxation and to escape the frequently higher tax rate applied to capital gains, stockholders generally prefer to have corporations pay dividends rather than to retain their earnings and reinvest the money in the business. Thus, earnings should be retained only if the firm needs capital very badly and would have difficulty raising it from external sources.
    b. Under our current tax laws, when investors pay taxes on their dividend income, they are being subjected to a form of double taxation.
    c. The fact that a percentage of the interest received by one corporation, which is paid by another corporation, is excluded from taxable income has encouraged firms to use more debt financing relative to equity financing.
    d. If the tax laws stated that $0.50 out of every $1.00 of interest paid by a corporation was allowed as a tax-deductible expense, this would probably encourage companies to use more debt financing than they presently do, other things held constant.
    e. Statements b and d are both correct.

SELF-TEST PROBLEMS

1. Wayne Corporation had income from operations of $385,000, it received interest payments of $15,000, it paid interest of $20,000, it received dividends from another corporation of $10,000, and it paid $40,000 in dividends to its common stockholders. What is Wayne's federal income tax?

   a. $122,760   **b.** $130,220   **c.** $141,700   **d.** $155,200   **e.** $163,500

2. A firm purchases $10 million of corporate bonds which paid a 16 percent interest rate, or $1.6 million in interest. If the firm's marginal tax rate is 35 percent, what is the after-tax interest yield?

   a. 7.36%   **b.** 8.64%   **c.** 10.40%   **d.** 13.89%   **e.** 14.32%

3. Refer to Self-Test Problem 2. The firm also invests in the common stock of another company having a 16 percent before-tax dividend yield. What is the after-tax dividend yield?

   a. 7.36%   **b.** 8.64%   **c.** 10.40%   **d.** 13.89%   **e.** 14.32%

4. The Carter Company's taxable income and income tax payments are shown below for 1992 through 1995:

Year	Taxable Income	Tax Payment
1992	$10,000	$1,500
1993	5,000	750
1994	10,000	1,500
1995	5,000	750

   Assume that Carter's tax rate for all 4 years was a flat 15 percent; that is, each dollar of taxable income was taxed at 15 percent. In 1996, Carter incurred a loss of $17,000. Using corporate loss carry-back, what is Carter's adjusted tax payment for 1995?

   a. $850   **b.** $750   **c.** $610   **d.** $550   **e.** $450

5. A firm can undertake a new project which will generate a before-tax return of 20 percent or it can invest the same funds in the preferred stock of another company which yields 13 percent before taxes. If the only consideration is which alternative provides the highest relevant (after-tax) return and the applicable tax rate is 35 percent, should the firm invest in the project or the preferred stock?

   a. Preferred stock; its relevant return is 12 percent.
   b. Project; its relevant return is 1.36 percentage points higher.
   c. Preferred stock; its relevant return is 0.22 percentage points higher.
   d. Project; its before-tax return is 20 percent.
   e. Either alternative can be chosen; they have the same relevant return.

6. Cooley Corporation has $20,000 which it plans to invest in marketable securities. It is choosing between MCI bonds which yield 10 percent, state of Colorado municipal bonds which yield 7 percent, and MCI preferred stock with a dividend yield of 8 percent. Cooley's corporate tax rate is 25 percent, and 70 percent of its dividends received are tax exempt. What is the after-tax rate of return on the highest yielding security?

   a. 7.4%   b. 7.0%   c. 7.5%   d. 6.5%   e. 6.0%

ANSWERS TO SELF-TEST QUESTIONS

1. annual
2. earnings per share
3. balance sheet
4. liquidity
5. Net; common stockholders'
6. common stock; retained earnings
7. Retained earnings
8. operating assets
9. Statement of Cash Flows
10. operating; long-term investing; financing
11. common stock; paid-in capital
12. statement of retained earnings
13. cash flow

14. operating cash flows
15. cash flow cycle
16. progressive
17. bracket creep
18. 35; 39.6
19. municipal; high
20. 12
21. short-term
22. ordinary; 30
23. tax deductible
24. 3; 15
25. improper accumulation
26. consolidated
27. double; S

28. b. Debt financing is encouraged by the fact that interest payments are **tax deductible while** dividend payments are not.

29. d. The S corporation limits the liability of the individual, but permits losses to be deducted against personal income.

30. b. Statement a is incorrect. To avoid double taxation, stockholders would prefer that corporations retain more of its earnings because long-term capital gains are taxed at a maximum tax rate of 28 percent. Statement c is incorrect. Debt financing has been encouraged by the fact that interest on debt is tax deductible. Statement d is incorrect. Currently, interest on debt is fully tax deductible; allowing 50 percent of interest to be tax deductible would discourage debt financing.

SOLUTIONS TO SELF-TEST PROBLEMS

1. b. The first step is to determine taxable income:

Income from operations	$385,000
Interest income (fully taxable)	15,000
Interest expense (fully deductible)	(20,000)
Dividend income (30% taxable)	3,000
Taxable income	$383,000

(Note that dividends are paid from after-tax income and do not affect taxable income.)

Based on the current corporate tax table, the tax calculation is as follows:

Tax = $113,900 + 0.34($383,000 - $335,000) = $113,900 + $16,320 = $130,220.

2. c. The after-tax yield (or dollar return) equals the before-tax yield (or dollar return) multiplied by one minus the effective tax rate, or AT = BT(1 - Effective T). Therefore, AT = 16%(1 - 0.35) = 16%(0.65) = 10.40%.

3. e. Since the dividends are received by a corporation, only 30 percent are taxable, and the Effective T = Tax rate × 30%:

$$AT = BT(1 - \text{Effective T})$$
$$= 16\%[1 - 0.35(0.30)]$$
$$= 16\%(1 - 0.105)$$
$$= 16\%(0.895)$$
$$= 14.32\%.$$

4. e.

Year	Taxable Income	Tax Payment	Adjusted Taxable Income	Adjusted Tax Payment
1992	$10,000	$1,500	$10,000	$1,500
1993	5,000	750	0	0
1994	10,000	1,500	0	0
1995	5,000	750	3,000	450

The carry-back can only go back 3 years. Thus, there was no adjustment made in 1992. After a $5,000 adjustment in 1993 and $10,000 in 1994, there was a $2,000 loss remaining to apply to 1995. The 1995 adjusted tax payment is $3,000(0.15) = $450. Thus, Carter received a total of $2,550 in tax refunds after the adjustment.

5. b. The project is fully taxable; thus its after-tax return is as follows:

$$AT = 20\%(1 - 0.35) = 20\%(0.65) = 13\%.$$

But only 30 percent of the preferred stock dividends are taxable; thus its after-tax yield is AT = 13%[1 − 0.35(0.30)] = 13%(1 − 0.105) = 13%(0.895) = 11.64%. Therefore, the new project should be chosen since its after-tax return is 1.36 percentage points higher.

6. c. AT yield on Colorado bond = 7%.

AT yield on MCI bond = 10% − Taxes = 10% − 10%(0.25) = 7.5%.

Check: Invest $20,000 at 10% = $2,000 interest.

Pay 25% tax, so AT income = $2,000(1 − T) = $2,000(0.75) = $1,500.

AT rate of return = $1,500/$20,000 = 7.5%.

AT yield on MCI preferred stock = 8% − Taxes = 8% − 0.3(8%)(0.25) = 8% − 0.6% = 7.4%.

Therefore, invest in MCI bonds.

CHAPTER 3
ANALYSIS OF FINANCIAL STATEMENTS

OVERVIEW

Financial analysis is designed to determine the relative strengths and weaknesses of a company. Investors need this information to estimate both future cash flows from the firm and the riskiness of those cash flows. Financial managers need the information provided by analysis both to evaluate the firm's past performance and to map future plans. Financial analysis concentrates on *financial statement analysis*, which highlights the key aspects of a firm's operations.

Financial statement analysis involves a study of the relationships between income statement and balance sheet accounts, how these relationships change over time (*trend analysis*), and how a particular firm compares with other firms in its industry (*comparative ratio analysis*). Although financial analysis has limitations, when used with care and judgment, it can provide some very useful insights into a company's operations.

OUTLINE

Financial statements are used to help predict the firm's future earnings and dividends. From an investor's standpoint, predicting the future is what financial statement analysis is all about. From management's standpoint, financial statement analysis is useful both to help anticipate future conditions and, more importantly, as a starting point for planning actions that will influence the future course of events. Financial ratios are designed to show relationships between financial statement accounts.

Liquidity ratios are used to measure a firm's ability to meet its current obligations as they come due.

■ The *current ratio* measures the extent to which the claims of short-term creditors are covered by short-term assets. It is determined by dividing current assets by current liabilities.

The *quick*, or *acid test, ratio* is calculated by deducting inventory from current assets and then dividing the remainder by current liabilities. Inventory is excluded because it may be difficult to liquidate it at full book value.

Asset management ratios measure how effectively a firm is managing its assets and whether or not the level of those assets is properly related to the level of operations as measured by sales.

The *inventory turnover ratio* is defined as sales divided by inventory. It is often necessary to use the average inventory figure rather than the year-end figure, especially if a firm's business is highly seasonal.

The *days sales outstanding (DSO)* is used to appraise accounts receivable, and it is calculated by dividing average daily sales into accounts receivable to find the number of days' sales tied up in receivables. Thus, the DSO represents the average length of time that the firm must wait after making a sale before receiving cash.

The *fixed assets turnover ratio* is the ratio of sales to net fixed assets. It measures how effectively the firm uses its plant and equipment.

The *total assets turnover ratio* is calculated by dividing sales by total assets. It measures the utilization of all the firm's assets.

Debt management ratios measure the extent to which a firm is using debt financing, or financial leverage, and the degree of safety afforded to creditors.

The *debt ratio*, or ratio of total debt to total assets, measures the proportion of funds provided by creditors. The lower the ratio, the greater the protection afforded creditors in the event of liquidation.

The *times-interest-earned (TIE) ratio* is determined by dividing earnings before interest and taxes (EBIT) by the interest charges. The TIE measures the extent to which operating income can decline before the firm is unable to meet its annual interest costs.

The *fixed charge coverage ratio* is similar to the TIE ratio, but it is more inclusive because it recognizes that many firms lease assets and incur long-term obligations under lease contracts and sinking funds.

Profitability ratios show the combined effects of liquidity, asset management, and debt management on operating results.

- The *profit margin on sales* is calculated by dividing net income by sales.

- The *basic earning power (BEP) ratio* is calculated by dividing earnings before interest and taxes (EBIT) by total assets. It shows the raw earning power of the firm's assets, before the influence of taxes and leverage.

- The *return on total assets (ROA)* is the ratio of net income to total assets; it measures the return on all the firm's assets after interest and taxes.

- The *return on common equity (ROE)* measures the rate of return on the stockholders' investment. It is equal to net income divided by common equity.

Market value ratios relate the firm's stock price to its earnings and book value per share, and thus give management an indication of what investors think of the company's past performance and future prospects.

- The *price/earnings (P/E) ratio*, or price per share divided by earnings per share, shows how much investors are willing to pay per dollar of reported profits. P/E ratios are higher for firms with high growth prospects, other things held constant, but they are lower for riskier firms.

- The *market/book (M/B) ratio*, defined as market price per share divided by book value per share, gives another indication of how investors regard the company. Higher M/B ratios are generally associated with firms that have a high rate of return on common equity.

It is important to analyze trends in ratios as well as their absolute levels. Trend analysis can provide clues as to whether the firm's financial situation is improving or deteriorating in relation to past performance.

A modified Du Pont chart shows the relationships between return on investment, assets turnover, and profit margin.

- The profit margin times the total assets turnover is called the *Du Pont equation*. This equation gives the rate of return on assets (ROA):

$$ROA = \text{Profit margin} \times \text{Total assets turnover.}$$

- The ROA times the *equity multiplier* (total assets divided by common equity) yields the return on equity (ROE). This equation is referred to as the *extended Du Pont equation:*

$$ROE = \text{Profit margin} \times \text{Total assets turnover} \times \text{Equity multiplier.}$$

Comparative ratio analysis is useful in comparing a firm's ratios with those of other firms in the same industry. Sources for such ratios include Dun & Bradstreet, Robert Morris Associates, and the U.S. Commerce Department. Benchmarking is the process of comparing the ratios of a particular company with those of a smaller group of "benchmark" companies, rather than with the entire industry.

There are some inherent problems and limitations to ratio analysis that necessitate care and judgment.

■ Ratios are often not useful for analyzing the operations of large firms which operate in many different industries because comparative ratios are not meaningful.

■ The use of industry averages may not provide a very challenging target for high-level performance.

■ Inflation affects depreciation charges, inventory costs, and therefore the value of both balance sheet items and net income. For this reason, the analysis of a firm over time, or a comparative analysis of firms of different ages, can be misleading.

■ Ratios may be distorted by seasonal factors, or manipulated by management to give the impression of a sound financial condition (*window dressing techniques*).

■ Different operating policies and accounting practices, such as the decision to lease rather than to buy equipment, can distort comparisons.

■ Many ratios can be interpreted in different ways, and whether a particular ratio is good or bad should be based upon a complete financial analysis rather than the level of a single ratio at a single point in time.

SELF-TEST QUESTIONS

Definitional

1. The current ratio and acid-test ratio are examples of _liquidity_ ratios. They measure a firm's ability to meet its _short_ - _term_ obligations.

2. The days sales outstanding (DSO) ratio is found by dividing average sales per day into accounts _receivable_. The DSO is the length of time that a firm must wait after making a sale before it receives _cash_.

3. Debt management ratios are used to evaluate a firm's use of financial *leverage* .

4. The debt ratio, which is the ratio of *total debt* to *total assets*, measures the proportion of funds supplied by creditors.

5. The *times* - *interest* - *earned* ratio is calculated by dividing earnings before interest and taxes by the amount of interest charges.

6. The combined effects of liquidity, asset management, and debt management are measured by *profitability* ratios.

7. Dividing net income by sales gives the *profit margin* on sales.

8. The *price* / *earnings* ratio measures how much investors are willing to pay for each dollar of a firm's current income.

9. Firms with higher rates of return on stockholders' equity tend to sell at relatively high ratios of *market* price to *book* value.

10. Individual ratios are of little value in analyzing a company's financial condition. More important are the *analysis/trend* of a ratio over time and the comparison of the company's ratios to *industry* average ratios.

11. A(n) *Dupont* chart shows the relationships among return on investment, total assets turnover, and profit margin and how they combine to produce return on equity.

12. Return on assets is a function of two variables, the profit *margin* and *total* *asset* turnover.

13. Analyzing a particular ratio over time for an individual firm is known as *trend* analysis.

14. The process of comparing a particular company with a smaller set of companies in the same industry is called *benchmarking*.

Conceptual

15. The equity multiplier can be expressed as 1 − (Debt/Assets).

 a. True   b. False

16. A high quick ratio is *always* a good indication of a well-managed liquidity position.

    a. True   b. False

17. International Appliances Inc. has a current ratio of 0.5. Which of the following actions would improve (increase) this ratio?

    a. Use cash to pay off current liabilities.
    b. Collect some of the current accounts receivable.
    c. Use cash to pay off some long-term debt.
    d. Purchase additional inventory on credit (accounts payable).
    e. Sell some of the existing inventory at cost.

18. Refer back to Self-Test Question 17. Assume that International Appliances has a current ratio of 1.2. Now, which of the following actions would improve (increase) this ratio?

    a. Use cash to pay off current liabilities.
    b. Collect some of the current accounts receivable.
    c. Use cash to pay off some long-term debt.
    d. Purchase additional inventory on credit (accounts payable).
    e. Use cash to pay for some fixed assets.

19. Examining the ratios of a particular firm against the same measures for a group of firms from the same industry, at a point in time, is an example of

    a. Trend analysis.
    b. Comparative ratio analysis.
    c. Du Pont analysis.
    d. Simple ratio analysis.
    e. Industry analysis.

20. Which of the following statements is most *correct*?

    a. Having a high current ratio and a high quick ratio is always a good indication that a firm is managing its liquidity position well.
    b. A decline in the inventory turnover ratio suggests that the firm's liquidity position is improving.
    c. If a firm's times-interest-earned ratio is relatively high, then this is one indication that the firm should be able to meet its debt obligations.
    d. Since ROA measures the firm's effective utilization of assets (without considering how these assets are financed), two firms with the same EBIT must have the same ROA.

e. If, through specific managerial actions, a firm has been able to increase its ROA, then, because of the fixed mathematical relationship between ROA and ROE, it must also have increased its ROE.

21. Which of the following statements is most *correct*?

a. Suppose two firms with the same amount of assets pay the same interest rate on their debt and earn the same rate of return on their assets and that ROA is positive. However, one firm has a higher debt ratio. Under these conditions, the firm with the higher debt ratio will also have a higher rate of return on common equity.

b. One of the problems of ratio analysis is that the relationships are subject to manipulation. For example, we know that if we use some cash to pay off some of our current liabilities, the current ratio will always increase, especially if the current ratio is weak initially, for example, below 1.0.

c. Generally, firms with high profit margins have high asset turnover ratios and firms with low profit margins have low turnover ratios; this result is exactly as predicted by the extended Du Pont equation.

d. Firms A and B have identical earnings and identical dividend payout ratios. If Firm A's growth rate is higher than Firm B's, then Firm A's P/E ratio must be greater than Firm B's P/E ratio.

e. Each of the above statements is false.

SELF-TEST PROBLEMS

(The following financial statements apply to the next six problems.)

Roberts Manufacturing Balance Sheet
December 31, 1995
(Dollars in Thousands)

Cash	$ 200	Accounts payable	$ 205
Receivables	245	Notes payable	425
Inventory	625	Other current liabilities	115
Total current assets	$1,070	Total current liabilities	$ 745
Net fixed assets	1,200	Long-term debt	420
		Common equity	1,105
Total assets	$2,270	Total liabilities and equity	$2,270

Roberts Manufacturing Income Statement
for Year Ended December 31, 1995
(Dollars in Thousands)

Sales		$2,400
Cost of goods sold:		
Materials	$1,000	
Labor	600	
Heat, light, and power	89	
Indirect labor	65	
Depreciation	80	1,834
Gross profit		$ 566
Selling expenses		175
General and administrative expenses		216
Earnings before interest and taxes (EBIT)		$ 175
Less interest expense		35
Earnings before taxes (EBT)		$ 140
Less taxes (40%)		56
Net income (NI)		$ 84

1. Calculate the liquidity ratios, that is, the current ratio and the quick ratio.

    a. 1.20; 0.60   **b.** 1.20; 0.80   **c.** 1.44; 0.60   **d.** 1.44; 0.80   **e.** 1.60; 0.60

2. Calculate the asset management ratios, that is, the inventory turnover ratio, fixed assets turnover, total assets turnover, and days sales outstanding.

    a. 3.84; 2.00; 1.06; 36.75 days   **d.** 3.84; 2.00; 1.24; 34.10 days
    b. 3.84; 2.00; 1.06; 35.25 days   **e.** 3.84; 2.20; 1.48; 34.10 days
    c. 3.84; 2.00; 1.06; 34.10 days

3. Calculate the debt management ratios, that is, the debt and times-interest-earned ratios.

    a. 0.39; 3.16   **b.** 0.39; 5.00   **c.** 0.51; 3.16   **d.** 0.51; 5.00   **e.** 0.73; 3.16

4. Calculate the profitability ratios, that is, the profit margin on sales, return on total assets, return on common equity, and basic earning power of assets.

    a. 3.50%; 4.25%; 7.60%; 8.00%   **d.** 3.70%; 3.50%; 8.00%; 8.00%
    b. 3.50%; 3.70%; 7.60%; 7.71%   **e.** 4.25%; 3.70%; 7.60%; 8.00%
    c. 3.70%; 3.50%; 7.60%; 7.71%

5. Calculate the market value ratios, that is, the price/earnings ratio and the market/book value ratio. Roberts had an average of 10,000 shares outstanding during 1995, and the stock price on December 31, 1995, was $40.00.

   a. 4.21; 0.36   b. 3.20; 1.54   c. 3.20; 0.36   d. 4.76; 1.54   e. 4.76; 0.36

6. Use the extended Du Pont equation to determine Roberts' return on equity.

   a. 6.90%   b. 7.24%   c. 7.47%   d. 7.60%   e. 8.41%

7. Lewis Inc. has sales of $2 million per year, all of which are credit sales. Its days sales outstanding is 42 days. What is its average accounts receivable balance?

   a. $233,333   b. $266,667   c. $333,333   d. $350,000   e. $366,667

8. Southeast Jewelers Inc. sells only on credit. Its days sales outstanding is 60 days, and its average accounts receivable balance is $500,000. What are its sales for the year?

   a. $1,500,000   b. $3,000,000   c. $2,000,000   d. $2,750,000   e. $3,225,000

9. A firm has total interest charges of $20,000 per year, sales of $2 million, a tax rate of 40 percent, and a profit margin of 6 percent. What is the firm's times-interest-earned ratio?

   a. 10   b. 11   c. 12   d. 13   e. 14

10. Refer to Self-Test Problem 9. What is the firm's TIE, if its profit margin decreases to 3 percent and its interest charges double to $40,000 per year?

    a. 3.0   b. 2.5   c. 3.5   d. 4.2   e. 3.7

11. A fire has destroyed many of the financial records at Anderson Associates. You are assigned to piece together information to prepare a financial report. You have found that the firm's return on equity is 12 percent and its debt ratio is 0.40. What is its return on assets?

    a. 4.90%   b. 5.35%   c. 6.60%   d. 7.20%   e. 8.40%

12. Refer to Self-Test Problem 11. What is the firm's debt ratio if its ROE is 15 percent and its ROA is 10 percent?

    a. 67%   b. 50%   c. 25%   d. 33%   e. 45%

13. Rowe and Company has a debt ratio of 0.50, a total assets turnover of 0.25, and a profit margin of 10 percent. The president is unhappy with the current return on equity, and he thinks it could be doubled. This could be accomplished (1) by increasing the profit margin to 14 percent and (2) by increasing debt utilization. Total assets turnover will not change. What new debt ratio, along with the 14 percent profit margin, is required to double the return on equity?

    a. 0.55   **b.** 0.60   **c.** 0.65   **d.** 0.70   **e.** 0.75

14. Altman Corporation has $1,000,000 of debt outstanding, and it pays an interest rate of 12 percent annually. Altman's annual sales are $4 million, its federal-plus-state tax rate is 40 percent, and its net profit margin on sales is 10 percent. If the company does not maintain a TIE ratio of at least 5 times, its bank will refuse to renew the loan, and bankruptcy will result. What is Altman's TIE ratio?

    a. 9.33   **b.** 4.44   **c.** 2.50   **d.** 4.00   **e.** 6.56

15. Refer to Self-Test Problem 14. What is the maximum amount Altman's EBIT could decrease and its bank still renew its loan?

    a. $186,667   **b.** $45,432   **c.** $66,767   **d.** $47,898   **e.** $143,925

16. Pinkerton Packaging's ROE last year was 2.5 percent, but its management has developed a new operating plan designed to improve things. The new plan calls for a total debt ratio of 50 percent, which will result in interest charges of $240 per year. Management projects an EBIT of $800 on sales of $8,000, and it expects to have a total assets turnover ratio of 1.6. Under these conditions, the federal-plus-state tax rate will be 40 percent. If the changes are made, what return on equity will Pinkerton earn?

    a. 12.50%   **b.** 13.44%   **c.** 13.00%   **d.** 14.02%   **e.** 14.57%

(The following financial statements apply to the next three problems.)

Baker Corporation Balance Sheet
December 31, 1995

Cash and marketable securities	$ 50	Accounts payable	$ 250
Accounts receivable	200	Accruals	250
Inventory	250	Notes payable	500
Total current assets	$ 500	Total current liabilities	$1,000
Net fixed assets	1,500	Long-term debt	250
		Common stock	400
		Retained earnings	350
Total assets	$2,000	Total liabilities and equity	$2,000

17. What is Baker Corporation's current ratio as of December 31, 1995?

    a. 0.35   **b.** 0.65   **c.** 0.50   **d.** 0.25   **e.** 0.75

18. If Baker uses $50 of cash to pay off $50 of its accounts payable, what is its new current ratio after this action?

    a. 0.47   **b.** 0.44   **c.** 0.54   **d.** 0.33   **e.** 0.62

19. If Baker uses its $50 cash balance to pay off $50 of its long-term debt, what will be its new current ratio?

    a. 0.35   **b.** 0.50   **c.** 0.55   **d.** 0.60   **e.** 0.45

(The following financial statements apply to the next problem.)

Whitney Inc. Balance Sheet
December 31, 1995

		Total current liabilities	$100
		Long-term debt	250
		Common stockholders' equity	400
Total assets	$750	Total liabilities and equity	$750

Whitney Inc. Income Statement
for Year Ended December 31, 1995

Sales		$1,000
Cost of goods sold (excluding depreciation)	$550	
Other operating expenses	100	
Depreciation	50	
Total operating costs		700
Earnings before interest and taxes (EBIT)		$ 300
Less interest expense		25
Earnings before taxes (EBT)		$ 275
Less taxes (40%)		110
Net income		$ 165

20. What are Whitney Inc.'s basic earning power and ROA ratios?

a. 30%; 22%   **b.** 40%; 30% **c.** 50%; 22%   **d.** 40%; 22%   **e.** 40%; 40%

(The following financial statements apply to the next problem.)

Cotner Enterprises Balance Sheet
December 31, 1995

		Total current liabilities	$ 300
		Long-term debt	500
		Common stockholders' equity	450
Total assets	$1,250	Total liabilities and equity	$1,250

Cotner Enterprises Income Statement
for Year Ended December 31, 1995

Sales		$1,700
Cost of goods sold (excluding depreciation)	$1,190	
Other operating expenses	135	
Depreciation	75	
Total operating costs		1,400
Earnings before interest and taxes (EBIT)		$ 300
Less interest expense		54
Earnings before taxes (EBT)		$ 246
Less taxes (35%)		86
Net income		$ 160

21. What are Cotner Enterprise's basic earning power and ROA ratios?

    a. 20%; 12.80%   **d.** 17.5%; 12.80%
    b. 24%; 12.80%   **e.** 24%; 10.5%
    c. 24%; 15.75%

22. Dauten Enterprises is just being formed. It will need $2 million of assets, and it expects to have an EBIT of $400,000. Dauten will own no securities, so all of its income will be operating income. If it chooses to, Dauten can finance up to 50 percent of its assets with debt which will have a 9 percent interest rate. Dauten has no other liabilities. Assuming a 40 percent federal-plus-state tax rate on all taxable income, what is the difference between the expected ROE if Dauten finances with 50 percent debt versus the expected ROE if it finances entirely with common stock?

    a. 7.2%   **b.** 6.6%   **c.** 6.0%   **d.** 5.8%   **e.** 9.0%

ANSWERS TO SELF-TEST QUESTIONS

1. liquidity; short-term (or current)
2. receivable; cash
3. leverage
4. total debt; total assets
5. times-interest-earned
6. profitability
7. profit margin

8. price/earnings
9. market; book
10. trend; industry
11. Du Pont
12. margin; total assets
13. trend
14. benchmarking

15. b. 1 − (Debt/Assets) = Equity/Assets. The equity multiplier is equal to Assets/Equity.

16. b. Excess cash resulting from poor management could produce a high quick ratio. Similarly, if accounts receivable are not collected promptly, this could also lead to a high quick ratio.

17. d. This question is best analyzed using numbers. For example, assume current assets equal $50 and current liabilities equal $100; thus, the current ratio equals 0.5. For answer a, assume $5 in cash is used to pay off $5 in current liabilities. The new current ratio would be $45/$95 = 0.47. For answer d, assume a $10 purchase of inventory on credit (accounts payable). The new current ratio would be $60/$110 = 0.55, which is an increase over the old current ratio of 0.5. (Self-Test Problems 17 through 19 were set up to help visualize this question.)

18. a. Again, this question is best analyzed using numbers. For example, assume current assets equal $120 and current liabilities equal $100; thus, the current ratio equals 1.2. For answer a, assume $5 in cash is used to pay off $5 in current liabilities. The new current ratio would be $115/$95 = 1.21, which is an increase over the old current ratio of 1.2. For answer d, assume a $10 purchase of inventory on credit (accounts payable). The new current ratio would be $130/$110 = 1.18, which is a decrease over the old current ratio of 1.2.

19. b. The correct answer is comparative ratio analysis. A trend analysis compares the firm's ratios over time, while a Du Pont analysis shows the relationships among return on investment, assets turnover, profit margin, and leverage.

20. c. Excess cash resulting from poor management could produce high current and quick ratios; thus statement a is false. A decline in the inventory turnover ratio suggests that either sales have decreased or inventory has increased—which suggests that the firm's liquidity position is *not* improving; thus statement b is false. ROA = Net income/Total assets, and EBIT does not equal net income. Two firms with the same EBIT could have different financing and different taxes resulting in different net incomes. Also, two firms with the same EBIT do not necessarily have the same total assets; thus statement d is false. ROE = ROA × Assets/Equity. If ROA increases because total assets decrease, then the equity multiplier decreases, and depending on which effect is greater, ROE may or may not increase; thus statement e is false. Statement c is correct; the TIE ratio is used to measure whether the firm can meet its debt obligation, and a high TIE ratio would indicate this is so. (Self-Test Problems 20 and 21 were set up to help visualize statement d of this question.)

21. a. Ratio analysis is subject to manipulation; however, if the current ratio is less than 1.0 and we use cash to pay off some current liabilities, the current ratio will decrease, *not* increase; thus statement b is false. Statement c is just the reverse of what actually occurs. Firms with high profit margins have low turnover ratios and vice versa. Statement d is false; it does not necessarily follow that if a firm's growth rate is higher that its stock price will be higher. Statement a is correct. From the information given in statement a, one can determine that the two firms' net incomes are equal; thus, the firm with the higher debt ratio (lower equity ratio) will indeed have a higher ROE.

SOLUTIONS TO SELF-TEST PROBLEMS

1. c. $\text{Current ratio} = \dfrac{\text{Current assets}}{\text{Current liabilities}} = \dfrac{\$1,070}{\$745} = 1.44.$

$\text{Quick ratio} = \dfrac{\text{Current assets} - \text{Inventory}}{\text{Current liabilities}} = \dfrac{\$1,070 - \$625}{\$745} = 0.60.$

2. a. $\text{Inventory turnover} = \dfrac{\text{Sales}}{\text{Inventory}} = \dfrac{\$2,400}{\$625} = 3.84.$

$\text{Fixed assets turnover} = \dfrac{\text{Sales}}{\text{Net fixed assets}} = \dfrac{\$2,400}{\$1,200} = 2.00.$

$\text{Total assets turnover} = \dfrac{\text{Sales}}{\text{Total assets}} = \dfrac{\$2,400}{\$2,270} = 1.06.$

$\text{DSO} = \dfrac{\text{Accounts receivable}}{\text{Sales/360}} = \dfrac{\$245}{\$2,400/360} = 36.75 \text{ days.}$

3. d. Debt ratio = Total debt/Total assets = $\$1,165/\$2,270 = 0.51.$

TIE ratio = EBIT/Interest = $\$175/\$35 = 5.00.$

4. b. $\text{Profit margin} = \dfrac{\text{Net income}}{\text{Sales}} = \dfrac{\$84}{\$2,400} = 0.0350 = 3.50\%.$

$\text{ROA} = \dfrac{\text{Net income}}{\text{Total assets}} = \dfrac{\$84}{\$2,270} = 0.0370 = 3.70\%.$

$\text{ROE} = \dfrac{\text{Net income}}{\text{Common equity}} = \dfrac{\$84}{\$1,105} = 0.0760 = 7.60\%.$

$\text{BEP} = \dfrac{\text{EBIT}}{\text{Total assets}} = \dfrac{\$175}{\$2,270} = 0.0771 = 7.71\%.$

5. e.
$$EPS = \frac{Net\ income}{Number\ of\ shares\ outstanding} = \frac{\$84,000}{10,000} = \$8.40.$$

$$P/E\ ratio = \frac{Price}{EPS} = \frac{\$40.00}{\$8.40} = 4.76.$$

$$Market/book\ value = \frac{Market\ price}{Book\ value} = \frac{\$40(10,000)}{\$1,105,000} = 0.36.$$

6. d. ROE = Profit margin × Total assets turnover × Equity multiplier

$$= \frac{\$84}{\$2,400} \times \frac{\$2,400}{\$2,270} \times \frac{\$2,270}{\$1,105} = 0.035 \times 1.057 \times 2.054 = 0.0760 = 7.60\%.$$

7. a.
$$DSO = \frac{Accounts\ receivable}{Sales/360}$$

$$42\ days = \frac{AR}{\$2,000,000/360}$$

$$AR = \$233,333.$$

8. b.
DSO = Accounts receivable/(Sales/360)

60 days = $500,000/(Sales/360)

60(Sales/360) = $500,000

Sales = $3,000,000.

9. b. Net income = $2,000,000(0.06) = $120,000.

Earnings before taxes = $120,000/(1 − 0.4) = $200,000.

EBIT = $200,000 + $20,000 = $220,000.

TIE = EBIT/Interest = $220,000/$20,000 = 11.

10. c. Net income = $2,000,000(0.03) = $60,000.

Earnings before taxes = $60,000/(1 − 0.4) = $100,000.

EBIT = $100,000 + $40,000 = $140,000.

TIE = EBIT/Interest = $140,000/$40,000 = 3.5.

11. d. If Total debt/Total assets = 0.40, then Total equity/Total assets = 0.60, and the equity multiplier (Assets/Equity) = 1/0.60 = 1.667.

$$\frac{NI}{E} = \frac{NI}{A} \times \frac{A}{E}$$

$$ROE = ROA \times EM$$
$$12\% = ROA \times 1.667$$
$$ROA = 7.20\%.$$

12. d.   ROE = ROA × Equity multiplier
       15% = 10% × TA/Equity
        1.5 = TA/Equity
    Equity/TA = 0.67.
  Debt/TA = 1 − Equity/TA = 1 − 0.67 = 0.33 = 33%.

13. c. If Total debt/Total assets = 0.50, then Total equity/Total assets = 0.50 and the equity multiplier (Assets/Equity) = 1/0.50 = 2.0.

ROE = PM × Total assets turnover × EM.

Before: ROE = 10% × 0.25 × 2.00 = 5.00%.

After: 10.00% = 14% × 0.25 × EM; thus EM = 2.8571.

$$Equity\ multiplier = \frac{Assets}{Equity}$$

$$2.8571 = \frac{1}{Equity}$$

$$0.35 = Equity.$$

Debt = Assets - Equity = 100% - 35% = 65%.

14. e. TIE = EBIT/Interest, so find EBIT and Interest.

Interest = $1,000,000(0.12) = $120,000.

Net income = $4,000,000(0.10) = $400,000.

Pre-tax income = $400,000/(1 − T) = $400,000/0.6 = $666,667.

EBIT = $666,667 + $120,000 = $786,667.

TIE = $786,667/$120,000 = 6.56×.

15. a.   TIE = EBIT/INT

$$5 = EBIT/\$120,000$$

EBIT = \$600,000.

From Self-Test Problem 14, EBIT = \$786,667, so EBIT could decrease by \$786,667 − \$600,000 = \$186,667.

16. b. ROE =   Profit margin × Total assets turnover × Equity multiplier

  =   NI/Sales × Sales/TA × TA/Equity.

Now we need to determine the inputs for the equation from the data that were given. On the left we set up an income statement, and we put numbers in it on the right:

Sales (given)	\$8,000
− Cost	NA
EBIT (given)	\$ 800
− Interest (given)	240
EBT	\$ 560
− Taxes (40%)	224
Net income	\$ 336

Now we can use some ratios to get some more data:

Total assets turnover = S/TA = 1.6 (given).
D/A = 50%, so E/A = 50%, and therefore TA/E = 1/(E/A) = 1/0.5 = 2.00.

Now we can complete the extended Du Pont equation to determine ROE:
ROE = \$336/\$8,000 × 1.6 × 2.0 = 13.44%.

17. c. Baker Corporation's current ratio equals Current assets/Current liabilities = \$500/\$1,000 = 0.50.

18. a. Baker Corporation's new current ratio equals (\$500 − \$50)/(\$1,000 − \$50) = \$450/\$950 = 0.47.

19. e. Only the current asset balance is affected by this action. Baker's new current ratio = (\$500 − \$50)/\$1,000 = \$450/\$1,000 = 0.45.

20. d. Whitney's BEP ratio equals EBIT/Total assets = \$300/\$750 = 40%.
Whitney's ROA equals Net income/Total assets = \$165/\$750 = 22%.

21. b. Cotner's BEP ratio equals EBIT/Total assets = $300/$1,250 = 24%.
Cotner's ROA equals Net income/Total assets = $160/$1,250 = 12.80%.

22. b. Known data: Total assets = $2,000,000, EBIT = $400,000, k_d = 9%, T = 40%.

D/A = 0.5 = 50%, so Equity = 0.5($2,000,000) = $1,000,000.

	D/A = 0%	D/A = 50%
EBIT	$400,000	$400,000
Interest	0	90,000 *
Taxable income	$400,000	$310,000
Taxes (40%)	160,000	124,000
Net income (NI)	$240,000	$186,000

For D/A = 0%, ROE = NI/Equity = $240,000/$2,000,000 = 12%. For D/A = 50%, ROE = $186,000/$1,000,000 = 18.6%. Difference = 18.6% − 12.0% = 6.6%.

*If D/A = 50%, then half of assets are financed by debt, so Debt = 0.5($2,000,000) = $1,000,000. At a 9 percent interest rate, INT = 0.09($1,000,000) = $90,000.

OVERVIEW

It is critical that financial managers understand the environment and markets within which they operate. In this chapter, we examine the markets where capital is raised, securities are traded, and stock prices are established. We examine the institutions that operate in these markets and hence through which securities transactions are conducted. In the process, we shall see how money costs are determined, and we shall explore the principal factors that determine both the general level of interest rates in the economy and the interest rate on a particular debt security.

OUTLINE

Financial markets bring together people and organizations wanting to borrow money with those having surplus funds.

■ There are many different financial markets in a developed economy, each dealing with a different type of instrument, serving a different set of customers, or operating in a different part of the country.

■ The major types of financial markets include the following:
  □ *Money markets* are the markets for short-term debt securities, those securities that mature in less than one year.
  □ *Capital markets* are the markets for long-term debt and corporate stocks.
  □ *Primary markets* are the markets in which corporations sell newly issued securities to raise capital.
  □ *Secondary markets* are the markets in which existing, outstanding securities are bought and sold.

■ Wall Street firms have been busy developing new financial products. One such type of product are *derivatives*, the new name of a broad class of transactions to which futures and options contracts belong. A derivative is any security whose value is *derived* from the price of some other "underlying" asset. The market for derivatives has grown faster than any other market in recent years, providing corporations with additional opportunities but also exposing them to additional risks.

Transfer of capital between savers and borrowers takes place in three different ways.

■ *Direct transfers* of money and securities occur when a business sells its stock or bonds directly to savers, without going through any type of financial institution.

■ Transfers through an *investment banking house* occur when a brokerage firm, such as Merrill Lynch, serves as a middleman. These middlemen help corporations design securities that will be attractive to investors, buy these securities from the corporations, and then resell them to savers in the primary markets.

■ Transfers through a *financial intermediary* occur when a bank or mutual fund obtains funds from savers, issues its own securities in exchange, and then uses these funds to purchase other securities.
   ☐ Some major classes of intermediaries include commercial banks, savings and loan (S&L) associations, mutual savings banks, credit unions, pension funds, life insurance companies, and mutual funds.
   ☐ Ongoing regulatory changes have resulted in a blurring of distinctions between the different types of financial institutions. As a result, in the United States the trend has been toward huge *financial service corporations*, which own any number of financial intermediaries with national and even global operations.

The stock market is one of the most important markets to financial managers because it is here that the price of each stock, and hence the value of all publicly-owned firms, is established. There are two basic types of stock markets.

■ The *organized security exchanges*, typified by the New York Stock Exchange (NYSE) and the American Stock Exchange (AMEX), are tangible, physical entities.

■ The *over-the-counter (OTC) market* is, basically, all the dealers, brokers, and communications facilities that provide for security transactions not conducted on the organized exchanges.
   ☐ Brokers and dealers who make up the over-the-counter market are members of a self-regulating body known as the *National Association of Securities Dealers (NASD)*, which licenses brokers and oversees trading practices.

Capital in a free economy is allocated through the price system. The interest rate is the price paid to borrow debt capital.

■ The level of *interest rates* is determined by the supply of, and demand for, investment capital.
  □ The demand for investment capital is determined by *production opportunities* available, and the rates of return producers can expect to earn on invested capital.
  □ The supply of investment capital depends on *consumers' time preferences* for current versus future consumption.

Two additional factors affecting the level of interest rates are risk and inflation. The higher the perceived risk, the higher the required rate of return, and the higher the expected rate of inflation, the higher the required return.

The quoted (or nominal) interest rate on a debt security, k, is composed of a real risk-free rate of interest, k*, plus several premiums that reflect inflation, the riskiness of the security, and the security's marketability: $k = k^* + IP + DRP + LP + MRP$.

The *real risk-free rate of interest (k*)* is the interest rate that would exist on a riskless security if no inflation were expected, and it may be thought of as the rate of interest that would exist on short-term U.S. Treasury securities in an inflation-free world.

The *quoted, or nominal, risk-free rate of interest (k_{RF})* is the real risk-free rate plus a premium for expected inflation: $k_{RF} = k^* + IP$. The actual rate of interest on short-term Treasury bills is normally used to measure k_{RF}, although the rate on long-term Treasury bonds is also used.

The *inflation premium (IP)*, which is the average inflation rate expected over the life of the security, compensates investors for the expected loss of purchasing power.

The *default risk premium (DRP)* compensates investors for the risk that a borrower will default and hence not pay the interest or principal on a loan.

A security which can be sold and quickly converted into cash at a fair market value is said to be *liquid*. A *liquidity premium (LP)* is also added to the real rate for securities that are not liquid.

Long-term securities are more price sensitive to interest rate changes than are short-term securities. Therefore, a *maturity risk premium (MRP)* is added to longer-term securities to compensate investors for interest rate risk.

The term structure of interest rates is the relationship between yield to maturity and time to maturity for bonds of a given default risk class.

■ When plotted, this relationship produces a *yield curve*.

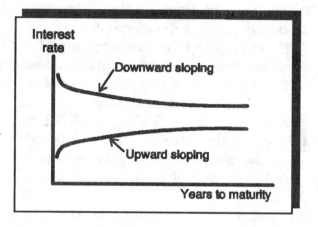

■ Yield curves have different shapes depending on expected inflation rates and supply and demand conditions.

  □ The "normal" yield curve is *upward sloping* because investors charge higher rates on longer term bonds, even when inflation is expected to remain constant.

  □ An inverted, or *downward sloping*, yield curve signifies that investors expect inflation to decrease.

Three theories have been proposed to explain the shape of the yield curve, or the term structure of interest rates.

■ The *expectations theory* states that the yield curve depends on expectations about future inflation rates. If the rate of inflation is expected to decline, the curve will be downward sloping, and if the rate of inflation is expected to increase, the curve will be upward sloping. According to the pure expectations theory, the maturity risk premium is equal to zero.

■ The *liquidity preference theory* states that the yield curve tends to be upward sloping because investors prefer short-term to long-term securities due to the interest rate risk associated with long-term securities.

■ The *market segmentation theory* states that the slope of the yield curve depends on supply and demand conditions in the long-term and short-term markets. Under this theory, the curve could, at any time, be either upward or downward sloping.

■ All three theories have merit; that is, actual yield curves are influenced by all three sets of factors.

There are other factors that influence both the general level of interest rates and the shape of the yield curve.

■ Expansionary monetary policy (growth in monetary supply) by the Federal Reserve initially lowers the interest rate but inflationary pressures could cause a rise in the interest rate in the long term. Contractionary monetary policy has the opposite effect.

■ Federal budget deficits drive interest rates up due to increased demand for loanable funds, while surpluses drive rates down due to increased supply of loanable funds.

■ Foreign trade deficits push interest rates up because deficits must be financed from abroad and rates must be high enough relative to world interest rates to draw foreign investors.

■ In relation to the business cycle, there is a general tendency for interest rates to decline during a recession.

The level of interest rates also has a significant effect on stock prices.

■ Since interest is a cost to companies, interest rates have a direct effect on corporate profits.

■ Stocks and bonds compete in the marketplace for investors' capital. Therefore, a rise in interest rates will increase the rate of return on bonds, causing investors to transfer funds from the stock market to the bond market. The resultant selling of stocks lowers stock prices.

Interest rate movements have a significant impact on business decisions.

■ Wrong decisions, such as using short-term debt to finance long-term projects just before interest rates rise, can be very costly.

■ It is extremely difficult, if not impossible, to predict future interest rate levels.

■ Sound financial policy calls for using a mix of long-term and short-term debt, and equity, so that the firm can survive in almost any interest rate environment.

SELF-TEST QUESTIONS

Definitional

1. Markets for short-term debt securities are called _money_ markets, while markets for long-term debt and equity are called _capital_ markets.

2. Firms raise capital by selling newly issued securities in the _primary_ markets, while existing, outstanding securities are traded in the _secondary_ markets.

3. An institution which issues its own securities in exchange for funds and then uses these funds to purchase other securities is called a financial *intermediary* .

4. A(n) *investment banking* firm facilitates the transfer of capital between savers and borrowers by acting as a middleman.

5. The two basic types of stock markets are the *organized security exchange* , such as the NYSE, and the *over -the- county* market.

6. The risk that a borrower will not pay the interest or principal on a loan is *default* risk.

7. *U S Treasury* bonds have zero default risk.

8. A(n) *inflation* premium is added to the real risk-free rate to protect investors against loss of purchasing power.

9. The nominal rate of interest is determined by adding a(n) *inflation* premium plus a(n) *default* risk premium plus a(n) *liquidity* premium plus a(n) *maturity* risk premium to the real risk-free rate of return.

10. The relationship between yield to maturity and time to maturity for bonds in a given default risk class is called the *term structure* of interest rates, while the resulting plotted curve is the *yield* curve.

11. The "normal" yield curve has a(n) *upward positive* slope.

12. Three theories have been proposed to explain the term structure of interest rates. They are the market *expectations* theory, the *liquidity* preference theory, and the *expectations* theory. *inflation*

13. Because interest rates fluctuate, a sound financial policy calls for using a mix of *short -term* and *long -term* debt and *equity* .

Conceptual

14. If management is sure that the economy is at the peak of a boom and is about to enter a recession, a firm which needs to borrow money should probably use short-term rather than long-term debt.

   a. True   **b.** False

15. Long-term interest rates reflect expectations about future inflation. Inflation has varied greatly from year to year over the last 10 years, and, as a result, long-term rates have fluctuated more than short-term rates.

    a. True   **b.** False

16. Suppose the Fed takes actions which lower expectations for inflation this year by 1 percentage point, but these same actions raise expectations for inflation in Years 2 and thereafter by 2 percentage points. Other things held constant, the yield curve becomes steeper.

    a. True   **b.** False

17. Assume interest rates on 30-year government and corporate bonds were as follows: T-bond = 7.72%; AAA = 8.72%; A = 9.64%; BBB = 10.18%. The differences in rates among these issues are caused primarily by:

    a. Tax effects.   **c.** Maturity risk differences.   **e.** Both b and d.
    b. Default risk differences.   **d.** Inflation differences.

18. Which of the following statements is most *correct*?

    a. The introduction of a new technology, such as computers, might be expected to improve labor productivity, making businesses more able and willing to pay a higher price for capital. This would put upward pressure on interest rates. However, the productivity improvements might give rise to lower inflationary expectations, which would put downward pressure on interest rates. Thus, the net effect of the new technology on interest rates might be uncertain.
    b. If future inflation were expected to remain constant at 6 percent for all future years, then for all bonds (government and corporate combined) we could measure the maturity risk premium as the difference between the yields on 30-year and 1-year bonds.
    c. If investors expect the inflation rate to *decrease* over time, e.g., the expected inflation rate in Year t exceeds the expected rate in Year t+1 for all values of t, then we can be *certain* that the yield curve for U.S. Treasury securities will be downward sloping.
    d. Each of the above statements is correct.
    e. Statements a and c are both correct.

19. Which of the following statements is most *correct*?

    a. Suppose financial institutions, such as savings and loans, were required by law to make long-term, fixed interest rate mortgages, but, at the same time, they were largely restricted, in terms of their capital sources, to taking deposits that could be withdrawn on demand. Under these conditions, these financial institutions should prefer a "normal" yield curve to an inverted curve.

b. You are considering establishing a new firm, the University Assistance Company (UAC). UAC would obtain funds in the short-term money market and write long-term mortgage loans to students so that they might buy condominiums rather than rent. A downward sloping yield curve, if it persisted over time, would be best for UAC.

c. The yield curve is upward sloping, or normal, if short-term rates are higher than long-term rates.

d. All of the above statements are correct.

e. Only statements a and b are correct.

20. Which of the following statements is most *correct*?

a. One of the major benefits of well-developed stock markets such as the New York Stock Exchange is that they increase liquidity, which makes it easier for firms to raise capital.

b. In the United States, we have a number of specialized financial institutions, but, according to the text, the trend is toward larger, more diversified institutions which offer broad arrays of financial services.

c. If the expected rate of inflation rose by 2 percentage points, from 5 to 7 percent, then the *real* risk-free rate (k*) would also rise by 2 percentage points.

d. Statements a, b, and c are all true.

e. Only statements a and b are true.

SELF-TEST PROBLEMS

1. You have determined the following data for a given bond: Real risk-free rate (k*) = 3%; inflation premium = 8%; default risk premium = 2%; liquidity premium = 2%; and maturity risk premium = 1%. What is the nominal risk-free rate, k_{RF}?

   a. 10%   b. 11%   c. 12%   d. 13%   e. 14%

2. Refer to Self-Test Problem 1. What is the interest rate on long-term Treasury securities, or T-bonds, of the relevant maturity?

   a. 10%   b. 11%   c. 12%   d. 13%   e. 14%

3. Assume that a 3-year Treasury note has no maturity risk nor liquidity risk and that the real risk-free rate of interest falls to 2 percent. A 3-year T-note carries a yield to maturity of 12

percent. If the expected inflation rate is 12 percent for the coming year and 10 percent the year after, what is the implied expected inflation rate for the third year?

   a. 8%   **b.** 9%   **c.** 10%   **d.** 11%   **e.** 12%

4. Assume that the real risk-free rate is 2 percent, that the expected inflation rate during Year 2 is 3 percent, and that 2-year T-bonds yield 5.5 percent. If the maturity risk premium is zero, what is the inflation rate during Year 1?

   a. 3.0%   **b.** 5.0%   **c.** 3.5%   **d.** 4.0%   **e.** 2.5%

5. Refer to Self-Test Problem 4. Given the same information, what is the rate of return on 1-year T-bonds?

   a. 5.5%   **b.** 6.0%   **c.** 5.0%   **d.** 6.5%   **e.** 4.5%

6. Assume that the real risk-free rate, k*, is 4 percent and that inflation is expected to be 7 percent in Year 1, 4 percent in Year 2, and 3 percent thereafter. Assume also that all Treasury bonds are highly liquid and free of default risk. If 2-year and 5-year Treasury bonds both yield 11 percent, what is the difference in the maturity risk premiums (MRPs) on the two bonds; that is, what is $MRP_5 - MRP_2$?

   a. 0.5%   **b.** 1.0%   **c.** 2.25%   **d.** 1.5%   **e.** 1.25%

7. Due to the recession, the rate of inflation expected for the coming year is only 3.5 percent. However, the rate of inflation in Year 2 and thereafter is expected to be constant at some level above 3.5 percent. Assume that the real risk-free rate is k* = 2% for all maturities and that the expectations theory fully explains the yield curve, so there are no maturity premiums. If 3-year Treasury bonds yield 3 percentage points (0.03) more than 1-year bonds, what rate of inflation is expected after Year 1?

   a. 4%   **b.** 5%   **c.** 7%   **d.** 6%   **e.** 8%

ANSWERS TO SELF-TEST QUESTIONS

1. money; capital
2. primary; secondary
3. intermediary
4. investment banking

5. organized security exchanges; over-the-counter (OTC)
6. default
7. U.S. Treasury

8. inflation
9. inflation; default; liquidity; maturity
10. term structure; yield

11. upward
12. segmentation; liquidity; expectations
13. short-term; long-term; equity

14. a. The firm should borrow short-term until interest rates drop due to the recession, then go long-term. Predicting interest rates is extremely difficult, for managers can rarely be sure about what is going to happen to the economy.

15. b. Fluctuations in long-term rates are smaller because the long-term inflation premium is an average of inflation expectations over many years, and hence the IP on long-term bonds is quite stable relative to the IP on short-term bonds. Also, short-term rates fluctuate as a result of Federal Reserve policy (the Fed intervenes in the short-term rather than the long-term market).

16. a. The yield curve becomes steeper. Although interest rates in Year 1 decrease by 1 percent, interest rates in the following years increase by 2 percent, making the yield curve steeper.

17. b. $k = k^* + IP + DRP + LP + MRP$. Since each of these bonds has a 30-year maturity, the MRP and IP would all be equal. Thus, the differences in the interest rates among these issues are the default risk and liquidity premiums.

18. a. Statement b is false because $k = k^* + IP + DRP + LP + MRP$. $k^* + IP$ would be the same for the two bonds; however, the default risk premium and liquidity premium would not be the same for the two bonds. Thus, you could not simply subtract the two yields to determine the MRP. Statement c is false because the expectations theory is not the only theory proposed to explain the shape of the yield curve. The market segmentation theory states that the slope depends on supply/demand conditions, and the liquidity preference theory states that under normal conditions a positive maturity risk premium exists. So, we cannot be certain that the yield curve would be downward sloping.

19. a. Statement b is incorrect. If a downward-sloping yield curve existed, long-term interest rates would be lower than short-term rates. This would be very serious for UAC: UAC receives as income the interest it charges on its long-term mortgage loans, but it has to pay out interest for obtaining funds in the short-term money market. Therefore, UAC would be receiving low interest income, but it would be paying out even higher interest. Statement c is incorrect. An upward-sloping yield curve would indicate higher interest rates for long-term securities than for short-term securities.

20. e. Statement c is incorrect because the nominal rate ($k_{RF} = k^* + IP$) would increase (not the real rate, k^*) if inflation increased by 2 percentage points.

SOLUTIONS TO SELF-TEST PROBLEMS

1. b. $k_{RF} = k^* + IP = 3\% + 8\% = 11\%$.

2. c. There is virtually no risk of default on a U.S. Treasury security, and they trade in active markets, which provide liquidity, so

$$k = k^* + IP + DRP + LP + MRP$$
$$= 3\% + 8\% + 0\% + 0\% + 1\%$$
$$= 12\%.$$

3. a. $k = k^* + IP + DRP + LP + MRP$
   $12\% = 2\% + IP + 0\% + 0\% + 0\%$
   $IP = 10\%$.

   Thus, the average expected inflation rate over the next 3 years (IP) is 10 percent. Given that the average expected inflation rate over the next three years is 10%, we can find the implied expected inflation rate for the third year by solving the equation that sets the two known plus the one unknown expected inflation rates equal to 10%:

$$\frac{12\% + 10\% + I_3}{3} = 10\%$$
$$I_3 = 8\%.$$

4. d.

Year	k^*	Inflation	Average Inflation	k_t
1	2%	?	$I_1/1 = ?$	?
2	2%	3	$(I_1 + 3\%)/2$	5.5%

   $k_2 = 2\% + (I_1 + 3\%)/2 = 5.5\%$. Solving for I_1, we find I_1 = Year 1 inflation = 4%.

5. b. $I_1 = IP = 4\%$. $k_1 = k^* + IP = 2\% + 4\% = 6\%$.

6. d. First, note that we will use the equation $k_t = 4\% + IP_t + MRP_t$. We have the data needed to find the IPs:

   $IP_5 = (7\% + 4\% + 3\% + 3\% + 3\%)/5 = 20\%/5 = 4\%$.

   $IP_2 = (7\% + 4\%)/2 = 5.5\%$.

Now we can substitute into the equation:

$k_2 = 4\% + 5.5\% + MRP_2 = 11\%$.

$k_5 = 4\% + 4\% + MRP_5 = 11\%$.

Now we can solve for the MRPs, and find the difference:

$MRP_5 = 11\% - 8\% = 3\%$.

$MRP_2 = 11\% - 9.5\% = 1.5\%$.

Difference $= 3\% - 1.5\% = 1.5\%$.

7. e. Basic relevant equations:

$k_t = k^* + IP_t + DRP_t + MRP_t + LP_t$. But $DRP_t = MRP_t = LP_t = 0$, so

$k_t = k^* + IP_t$

$$IP_t = \frac{\text{Average}}{\text{inflation}} = \frac{I_1 + I_2 + \cdots}{N}.$$

We know that $I_1 = IP_1 = 3.5\%$, and $k^* = 2\%$. Therefore,

$k_1 = 2\% + 3.5\% = 5.5\%$.

$k_3 = k_1 + 3\% = 5.5\% + 3\% = 8.5\%$.

But $k_3 = k^* + IP_3 = 2\% + IP_3 = 8.5\%$, so

$IP_3 = 8.5\% - 2\% = 6.5\%$.

We also know that $I_t = $ Constant after $t = 1$.

Avg. $I = IP_3 = (3.5\% + 2I)/3 = 6.5\%$; $2I = 16\%$, so $I = 8\%$.

We can set up this table:

Year	k^*	I_t	Avg. $I = IP_t$	$k = k^* + IP_t$
1	2%	3.5%	3.5%/1 = 3.5%	5.5%
2	2%	I	(3.5% + I)/2 = IP_2	
3	2%	I	(3.5% + I + I)/3 = IP_3	8.5%, so IP_3 = 8.5% - 2% = 6.5%.

CHAPTER 5
RISK AND RATES OF RETURN

OVERVIEW

Risk is an important concept in financial analysis, especially in terms of how it affects security prices and rates of return. Investment risk is associated with the probability of low or negative future returns.

The riskiness of an asset can be considered in two ways: (1) on a *stand-alone basis,* where the asset's cash flows are analyzed all by themselves, or (2) in a *portfolio context,* where the cash flows from a number of assets are combined, and then the consolidated cash flows are analyzed.

In a portfolio context, an asset's risk can be divided into two components: (1) a *diversifiable risk component,* which can be diversified away and hence is of little concern to diversified investors, and (2) a *market risk component,* which reflects broad market movements and which cannot be eliminated by diversification, and therefore, is of concern to investors. Only market risk is *relevant;* diversifiable risk is irrelevant because it can be eliminated.

An attempt has been made to quantify market risk with a measure called *beta.* Beta is a measurement of how a particular firm's stock returns move relative to overall movements of stock market returns. The *Capital Asset Pricing Model (CAPM),* using the concept of beta and investors' aversion to risk, specifies the relationship between market risk and the required rate of return. This relationship can be visualized graphically with the Security Market Line (SML). The slope of the SML can change, or the line can shift upward or downward, in response to changes in risk or required rates of return.

OUTLINE

Risk refers to the chance that some unfavorable event will occur. Investment risk is related to the probability of actually earning less than the expected return; thus, the greater the chance of low or negative returns, the riskier the investment.

■ An asset's risk can be analyzed in two ways: (1) on a *stand-alone basis*, where the asset is considered in isolation, and (2) on a *portfolio basis*, where the asset is held as one of a number of assets in a portfolio.

■ The *probability distribution* for an event is the listing of all the possible outcomes for the event, with mathematical probabilities assigned to each.

■ The sum of the probabilities for a particular event must equal 1.0.

■ The *expected rate of return* ($\hat{k}$) is the sum of the products of each possible outcome times its associated probability—it is a weighted average of the various possible outcomes, with the weights being their probabilities of occurrence:

$$\text{Expected rate of return} = \hat{k} = \sum_{i=1}^{n} P_i k_i.$$

□ Where the number of possible outcomes is virtually unlimited, *continuous probability distributions* are used in determining the expected rate of return of the event.
□ The tighter, or more peaked, a distribution, the more likely it is that the actual outcome will be closer to the expected value, and thus, the smaller is the risk.

■ One measure for determining the tightness of a distribution is the *standard deviation*, σ.

$$\text{Standard deviation} = \sigma = \sqrt{\sum_{i=1}^{n} (k_i - \hat{k})^2 P_i}.$$

□ Thus, the standard deviation is a probability-weighted average deviation from the expected value, and it gives you an idea of how far above or below the expected value the actual value is likely to be. The standard deviation is a measure of dispersion around the mean.

■ Another useful measure of risk is the *coefficient of variation (CV)*, which is the standard deviation divided by the expected return. It shows the risk per unit of return and provides a more meaningful basis for comparison when the expected returns on two alternatives are not the same:

$$\text{Coefficient of variation (CV)} = \frac{\sigma}{\hat{k}}.$$

■ Most investors are *risk averse*. This means that for two alternatives with the same expected rate of return, investors will choose the one with the lower risk. Therefore, in market equilibrium, riskier securities must have higher expected returns than less risky ones.

An asset held as part of a portfolio is less risky than the same asset held in isolation. This is important, because most financial assets are not held in isolation; rather, they are held as parts of portfolios. From the investor's standpoint, what is important is the return on his or her portfolio, and the portfolio's risk——not the fact that a particular stock goes up or down. Thus, the risk and return of an individual security should be analyzed in terms of how it affects the risk and return of the portfolio in which it is held.

■ The expected return on a portfolio, $\hat{k}_p$, is the weighted average expected return of the individual stocks in the portfolio, with the weights being the fraction of the total portfolio invested in each stock:

$$\hat{k}_p = \sum_{i=1}^{n} w_i \hat{k}_i.$$

■ The riskiness of a portfolio, σ_p, is generally *not* a weighted average of the standard deviations of the individual securities in the portfolio. The riskiness of a portfolio depends not only on the standard deviations of the individual stocks, but also on the *correlation between the stocks*.
   □ The correlation coefficient, r, measures the tendency of two variables to move together. With stocks, these variables are the individual stock returns.
   □ Diversification does nothing to reduce risk if the portfolio consists of perfectly positively correlated stocks.
   □ As a rule, the riskiness of a portfolio will be reduced as the number of stocks in the portfolio increases.
   □ However, in the typical case, where the correlation among the individual stocks are positive, but less than +1.0, some, but not all, risk can be eliminated.

■ While very large portfolios end up with a substantial amount of risk, it is not as much risk as if all the money were invested in only one stock. Almost half of the riskiness inherent in an average individual stock can be eliminated if the stock is held in a reasonably well-diversified portfolio, which is one containing 40 or more stocks.
   □ Diversifiable risk is that part of the risk of a stock which can be eliminated. It is caused by events particular to the firm.
   □ Market risk is that part of the risk which cannot be eliminated, and it stems from factors which systematically affect all firms, such as war, inflation, recessions, and high interest rates. It can be measured by the degree to which a given stock tends to move up and down with the market. Thus, market risk is the *relevant* risk, which reflects a security's contribution to the portfolio's risk.

☐ The Capital Asset Pricing Model is an important tool for analyzing the relationship between risk and rates of return. The model is based on the proposition that a stock's required rate of return is equal to the risk-free rate of return plus a risk premium, where risk reflects diversification.

The tendency of a stock to move with the market is reflected in its beta coefficient, b, which is a measure of the stock's volatility relative to that of an average stock.

■ An average-risk stock is defined as one that tends to move up and down in step with the general market. By definition it has a beta of 1.0.

■ A stock that is twice as volatile as the market will have a beta of 2.0, while a stock that is half as volatile as the market will have a beta coefficient of 0.5.

■ The beta coefficient of a portfolio of securities is the weighted average of the individual securities' betas:

$$b_p = \sum_{i=1}^{n} w_i b_i.$$

■ Since a stock's beta measures its contribution to the riskiness of a portfolio, beta is the appropriate measure of the stock's relevant risk.

The Capital Asset Pricing Model (CAPM) employs the concept of beta, which measures risk as the relationship between a particular stock's movements and the movements of the overall stock market. The CAPM uses a stock's beta, in conjunction with the average investor's degree of risk aversion, to calculate the return that investors require, k_s, on that particular stock.

■ The *Security Market Line (SML)* shows the relationship between risk as measured by beta and the required rate of return for individual securities. The SML equation can be used to find the required rate of return on Stock i:

SML: $k_i = k_{RF} + (k_M - k_{RF})b_i.$

Here k_{RF} is the rate of interest on risk-free securities, b_i is the *i*th stock's beta, and k_M is the return on the market or, alternatively, on an average stock.

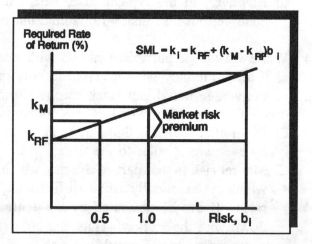

- ☐ The term $k_M - k_{RF}$ is the *market risk premium, RP_M*. This is a measure of the additional return over the risk-free rate needed to compensate investors for assuming an average amount of risk.
- ☐ In the CAPM the market risk premium, $k_M - k_{RF}$, is multiplied by the stock's beta to determine the additional premium over the risk-free rate that is required to compensate investors for the risk inherent in a particular stock.
- ☐ This premium may be larger or smaller than the premium required on an average stock, depending on the riskiness of that stock in relation to the overall market as measured by the stock's beta.
- ☐ The risk premium calculated by $(k_M - k_{RF})b_i$ is added to the risk-free rate, k_{RF} (the rate on Treasury securities), to determine the total rate of return required by investors on a particular stock, k_s.

- ■ The risk-free (also known as the nominal, or quoted) rate of interest consists of two elements: (1) a real inflation-free rate of return, k^*, and (2) an inflation premium, IP, equal to the anticipated rate of inflation.
  - ☐ The real risk-free rate on long-term Treasury bonds has historically ranged from 2 to 4 percent.
  - ☐ As the expected rate of inflation increases, a higher premium must be added to the real risk-free rate of return to compensate for the loss of purchasing power.

- ■ As risk aversion increases, so does the risk premium and, thus, the slope of the SML.

- ■ Many factors can affect a company's beta. When such changes occur, the required rate of return also changes.

A word of caution is in order regarding betas and the Capital Asset Pricing Model. The entire theory is based on ex ante, or expected, conditions, yet we have available only ex post, or past, data. Thus, the betas we calculate show how volatile a stock has been in the past, but conditions may change, and its future volatility, which is the item of real concern to investors, might be quite different from its past volatility.

Because returns on foreign investments are not perfectly positively correlated with returns on U.S. assets, it has been argued that multinational corporations are less risky than companies which operate strictly within the boundaries of any one country.

Appendix 5A presents a discussion on the calculation of beta coefficients. The discussion concentrates on graphic and least squares regression techniques.

SELF-TEST QUESTIONS

Definitional

1. Investment risk is associated with the _____ of low or negative returns; the greater the chance of loss, the riskier the investment.

2. A listing of all possible _____, with a probability assigned to each, is known as a probability _____.

3. Weighting each possible outcome of a distribution by its _____ of occurrence and summing the results give the expected _____ of the distribution.

4. One measure of the tightness of a probability distribution is the _____ _____.

5. Investors who prefer outcomes with a high degree of certainty to those that are less certain are described as being _____ _____.

6. Owning a portfolio of securities enables investors to benefit from _____.

7. Diversification of a portfolio can result in lower _____ for the same level of return.

8. Diversification of a portfolio is achieved by selecting securities that are not perfectly _____ correlated with each other.

9. That part of a stock's risk that can be eliminated is known as _____ risk, while the portion that cannot be eliminated is called _____ risk.

10. The _____ coefficient measures a stock's relative volatility as compared with a stock market index.

11. A stock that is twice as volatile as the market would have a beta coefficient of ____, while a stock with a beta of 0.5 would be only _____ as volatile as the market.

12. The beta coefficient of a portfolio is the _____ _____ of the betas of the individual stocks.

13. The minimum expected return that will induce investors to buy a particular security is the _____ rate of return.

14. The security used to measure the _____ - _____ rate is the return available on U.S. Treasury securities.

15. The risk premium for a particular stock may be calculated by multiplying the market risk premium times the stock's _____ _____.

16. A stock's required rate of return is equal to the _____ - _____ rate plus the stock's _____ _____.

17. The risk-free rate on a short-term Treasury security is made up of two parts: the _____ _____ - _____ rate of return plus a(n) _____ premium.

18. Changes in investors' risk aversion alter the _____ of the Security Market Line.

Conceptual

19. The Y-axis intercept of the Security Market Line (SML) indicates the required rate of return on an individual stock with a beta of 1.0.

    a. True   b. False

20. If a stock has a beta of zero, it will be riskless when held in isolation.

    a. True   b. False

21. A group of 200 stocks each has a beta of 1.0. We can be certain that each of the stocks was positively correlated with the market.

    a. True   b. False

22. Refer to Self-Test Question 21. If we combined these same 200 stocks into a portfolio, market risk would be reduced below the average market risk of the stocks in the portfolio.

    a. True   b. False

23. Refer to Self-Test Question 22. The standard deviation of the portfolio of these 200 stocks would be lower than the standard deviations of the individual stocks.

    a. True   b. False

24. Suppose $k_{RF} = 7\%$ and $k_M = 12\%$. If investors became more risk averse, k_M would be likely to decrease.

    a. True   **b.** False

25. Refer to Self-Test Question 24. The required rate of return for a stock with $b = 0.5$ would increase more than for a stock with $b = 2.0$.

    a. True   **b.** False

26. Refer to Self-Test Questions 24 and 25. If the expected rate of inflation increased, the required rate of return on a $b = 2.0$ stock would rise by more than that of a $b = 0.5$ stock.

    a. True   **b.** False

27. Which is the best measure of risk for an asset held in a well-diversified portfolio?

    a. Variance   **c.** Beta   **e.** Expected value
    b. Standard deviation   **d.** Semi-variance

28. In a portfolio of three different stocks, which of the following could *not* be true?

    a. The riskiness of the portfolio is less than the riskiness of each stock held in isolation.
    b. The riskiness of the portfolio is greater than the riskiness of one or two of the stocks.
    c. The beta of the portfolio is less than the beta of each of the individual stocks.
    d. The beta of the portfolio is greater than the beta of one or two of the individual stocks.
    e. The beta of the portfolio is equal to the beta of one of the individual stocks.

29. If investors expected inflation to increase in the future, and they also became more risk averse, what could be said about the change in the Security Market Line (SML)?

    a. The SML would shift up and the slope would increase.
    b. The SML would shift up and the slope would decrease.
    c. The SML would shift down and the slope would increase.
    d. The SML would shift down and the slope would decrease.
    e. The SML would remain unchanged.

30. Which of the following statements is most *correct*?

    a. The SML relates required returns to firms' market risk. The slope and intercept of this line *cannot* be controlled by the financial manager.

b. The slope of the SML is determined by the value of beta.

c. If you plotted the returns of a given stock against those of the market, and if you found that the slope of the regression line was negative, then the CAPM would indicate that the required rate of return on the stock should be less than the risk-free rate for a well-diversified investor, assuming that the observed relationship is expected to continue on into the future.

d. If investors become less risk averse, the slope of the Security Market Line will increase.

e. Statements a and c are both true.

31. Which of the following statements is most *correct*?

a. Normally, the Security Market Line has an upward slope. However, at one of those unusual times when the yield curve on bonds is downward sloping, the SML will also have a downward slope.

b. The market risk premium, as it is used in the CAPM theory, is equal to the required rate of return on an average stock minus the required rate of return on an average company's bonds.

c. If the marginal investor's aversion to risk decreases, then the slope of the yield curve would, other things held constant, tend to increase. If expectations for inflation also increased at the same time risk aversion was decreasing——say the expected inflation rate rose from 5 percent to 8 percent——the net effect could possibly result in a parallel upward shift in the SML.

d. According to the text, it is theoretically possible to combine two stocks, each of which would be quite risky if held as your only asset, and to form a 2-stock portfolio that is riskless. However, the stocks would have to have a correlation coefficient of expected future returns of -1.0, and it is hard to find such stocks in the real world.

e. Each of the above statements is false.

32. Which of the following statements is most *correct*?

a. The expected future rate of return, $\hat{k}$, is always *above* the past realized rate of return, $\bar{k}$, except for highly risk-averse investors.

b. The expected future rate of return, $\hat{k}$, is always *below* the past realized rate of return, $\bar{k}$, except for highly risk-averse investors.

c. The expected future rate of return, $\hat{k}$, is always *below* the required rate of return, k, except for highly risk-averse investors.

d. There is no logical reason to think that any relationship exists between the expected future rate of return, $\hat{k}$, on a security and the security's required rate of return, k.

e. Each of the above statements is false.

33. Which of the following statements is most *correct*?

   a. Someone who is highly averse to risk should invest in stocks with high betas (above +1.0), other things held constant.
   b. The returns on a stock might be highly uncertain in the sense that they could actually turn out to be much higher or much lower than the expected rate of return (that is, the stock has a high standard deviation of returns), yet the stock might still be regarded by most investors as being less risky than some other stock whose returns are less variable.
   c. The standard deviation is a better measure of risk when comparing securities than the coefficient of variation. This is true because the standard deviation "standardizes" risk by dividing each security's variance by its expected rate of return.
   d. Market risk can be reduced by holding a large portfolio of stocks, and if a portfolio consists of all traded stocks, market risk will be completely eliminated.
   e. The market risk in a portfolio declines as more stocks are added to the portfolio, and the risk decline is linear, that is, each additional stock reduces the portfolio's risk by the same amount.

SELF-TEST PROBLEMS

1. Stock A has the following probability distribution of expected returns:

Probability	Rate of Return
0.1	-15%
0.2	0
0.4	5
0.2	10
0.1	25

   What is Stock A's expected rate of return and standard deviation?

   a. 8.0%; 9.5%   b. 8.0%; 6.5%   c. 5.0%; 3.5%   d. 5.0%; 6.5%   e. 5.0%; 9.5%

2. If $k_{RF} = 5\%$, $k_M = 11\%$, and $b = 1.3$ for Stock X, what is k_X, the required rate of return for Stock X?

   a. 18.7%   b. 16.7%   c. 14.8%   d. 12.8%   e. 11.9%

3. Refer to Self-Test Problem 2. What would k_X be if investors expected the inflation rate to increase by 2 percentage points?

    a. 18.7%   **b.** 16.7%   **c.** 14.8%   **d.** 12.8%   **e.** 11.9%

4. Refer to Self-Test Problem 2. What would k_X be if an increase in investors' risk aversion caused the market risk premium to increase by 3 percentage points? k_{RF} remains at 5 percent.

    a. 18.7%   **b.** 16.7%   **c.** 14.8%   **d.** 12.8%   **e.** 11.9%

5. Refer to Self-Test Problem 2. What would k_X be if investors expected the inflation rate to increase by 2 percentage points *and* their risk aversion increased by 3 percentage points?

    a. 18.7%   **b.** 16.7%   **c.** 14.8%   **d.** 12.8%   **e.** 11.9%

6. Jan Middleton owns a 3-stock portfolio with a total investment value equal to $300,000.

Stock	Investment	Beta
A	$100,000	0.5
B	100,000	1.0
C	100,000	1.5
Total	$300,000	

What is the weighted average beta of Jan's 3-stock portfolio?

    a. 0.9   **b.** 1.3   **c.** 1.0   **d.** 0.4   **e.** 1.2

7. The Apple Investment Fund has a total investment of $450 million in five stocks.

Stock	Investment (Millions)	Beta
1	$130	0.4
2	110	1.5
3	70	3.0
4	90	2.0
5	50	1.0
Total	$450	

What is the fund's overall, or weighted average, beta?

    a. 1.14   **b.** 1.22   **c.** 1.35   **d.** 1.46   **e.** 1.53

8. Refer to Self-Test Problem 7. If the risk-free rate is 12 percent and the market risk premium is 6 percent, what is the required rate of return on the Apple Fund?

a. 20.76%   **b.** 19.92%   **c.** 18.81%   **d.** 17.62%   **e.** 15.77%

9. Stock A has a beta of 1.2, Stock B has a beta of 0.6, the expected rate of return on an average stock is 12 percent, and the risk-free rate of return is 7 percent. By how much does the required return on the riskier stock exceed the required return on the less risky stock?

a. 4.00%   **b.** 3.25%   **c.** 3.00%   **d.** 2.50%   **e.** 3.75%

10. You are managing a portfolio of 10 stocks which are held in equal dollar amounts. The current beta of the portfolio is 1.8, and the beta of Stock A is 2.0. If Stock A is sold and the proceeds are used to purchase a replacement stock, what does the beta of the replacement stock have to be to lower the portfolio beta to 1.7?

a. 1.4   **b.** 1.3   **c.** 1.2   **d.** 1.1   **e.** 1.0

11. Consider the following information for the Alachua Retirement Fund, with a total investment of $4 million.

Stock	Investment	Beta
A	$ 400,000	1.2
B	600,000	-0.4
C	1,000,000	1.5
D	2,000,000	0.8
Total	$4,000,000	

The market required rate of return is 12 percent, and the risk-free rate is 6 percent. What is its required rate of return?

a. 9.98%   **b.** 10.45%   **c.** 11.01%   **d.** 11.50%   **e.** 12.56%

12. You are given the following distribution of returns:

Probability	Return
0.4	$30
0.5	25
0.1	-20

What is the coefficient of variation of the expected dollar returns?

a. 206.2500   **b.** 0.6383   **c.** 14.3614   **d.** 0.7500   **e.** 1.2500

13. If the risk-free rate is 8 percent, the expected return on the market is 13 percent, and the expected return on Security J is 15 percent, then what is the beta of Security J?

a. 1.40   **b.** 0.90   **c.** 1.20   **d.** 1.50   **e.** 0.75

Appendix 5A

A-1. Given the information below, calculate the betas for Stocks A and B.

Year	Stock A	Stock B	Market
1	-5%	10%	-10%
2	10	20	10
3	25	30	30

(Hint: Think rise over run.)

a. 1.0; 0.5   **b.** 0.75; 0.5   **c.** 0.75; 1.0   **d.** 0.5; 0.5   **e.** 0.75; 0.25

(The following data apply to the next two Self-Test Problems.)

You are given the following information:

Year	Stock N	Market
1	-5%	10%
2	-8	15
3	7	-10

The risk-free rate is equal to 7 percent, and the market required return is equal to 10 percent.

A-2. What is Stock N's beta coefficient?

a. 1.00   **b.** -0.50   **c.** 0.60   **d.** -0.75   **e.** -0.60

A-3. What is Stock N's required rate of return?

    a. 6.40%   **b.** 5.20%   **c.** 8.80%   **d.** 5.90%   **e.** 7.00%

A-4. Stock Y and the Market had the following rates of return during the last 4 years. What is Stock Y's beta? (Hint: You will need a financial calculator to calculate the beta coefficient.)

	Y	Market
1992	10.0%	10.0%
1993	16.0	13.5
1994	-7.5	-4.0
1995	0.0	5.5

    a. 1.25   **b.** 0.75   **c.** 1.00   **d.** 1.34   **e.** 1.57

A-5. Stock Y, Stock Z, and the Market had the following rates of return during the last 4 years:

	Y	Z	Market
1992	10.0%	10.0%	10.0%
1993	16.0	11.5	13.5
1994	-7.5	1.0	-4.0
1995	0.0	6.0	5.5

The expected future return on the market is 15 percent, the real risk-free rate is 3.75 percent, and the expected inflation rate is a constant 5 percent. If the market risk premium rises by 3 percentage points, what will be the change in the required rate of return of the riskier stock?

    a. 4.01%   **b.** 3.67%   **c.** 4.88%   **d.** 3.23%   **e.** 4.66%

ANSWERS TO SELF-TEST QUESTIONS

1. probability
2. outcomes; distribution
3. probability; return
4. standard deviation
5. risk averse
6. diversification
7. risk
8. positively
9. diversifiable; market
10. beta
11. 2.0; half
12. weighted average

13. required

14. risk-free

15. beta coefficient

16. risk-free; risk premium

17. real risk-free; inflation

18. slope

19. b. The Y-axis intercept of the SML is k_{RF}, which is the required rate of return of a security with a beta of zero.

20. b. A zero beta stock could be made riskless if it were combined with enough other zero beta stocks, but it would still have company-specific risk and be risky when held in isolation.

21. a. By definition, if a stock has a beta of 1.0 it moves exactly with the market. In other words, if the market moves up by 7 percent, the stock will also move up by 7 percent, while if the market falls by 7 percent, the stock will fall by 7 percent.

22. b. Market risk is measured by the beta coefficient. The beta for the portfolio would be a weighted average of the betas of the stocks, so b_p would also be 1.0. Thus, the market risk for the portfolio would be the same as the market risk of the stocks in the portfolio.

23. a. Note that with a 200-stock portfolio, the actual returns would all be on or close to the regression line. However, when the portfolio (and the market) returns are quite high, some individual stocks would have higher returns than the portfolio, and some would have much lower returns. Thus, the range of returns, and the standard deviation, would be higher for the individual stocks.

24. b. RP_M, which is equal to $k_M - k_{RF}$, would rise, leading to an increase in k_M.

25. b. The required rate of return for a stock with b = 0.5 would increase less than for a stock with b = 2.0.

26. b. If the expected rate of inflation increased, the SML would shift parallel due to an increase in k_{RF}. Thus, the effect on the required rates of return for both the b = 0.5 and b = 2.0 stocks would be the same.

27. c. The best measure of risk is the beta coefficient, which is a measure of the extent to which the returns on a given stock move with the stock market.

28. c. The beta of the portfolio is a weighted average of the individual securities' betas, so it could not be less than the betas of all of the stocks. (See Self-Test Problem 6.)

29. a. The increase in inflation would cause the SML to shift up, and investors becoming more risk averse would cause the slope to increase. (This can be demonstrated by graphing the SML lines on the same graph in Self-Test Problems 2 through 5.)

30. e. Statement b is false because the slope of the SML is $k_M - k_{RF}$. Statement d is false because as investors become less risk averse the slope of the SML decreases. Statement a is correct because the financial manager has no control over k_M or k_{RF}. ($k_M - k_{RF}$ = slope and k_{RF} = intercept of the SML.) Statement c is correct because the slope of the regression line is beta and beta would be negative; thus, the required return would be less than the risk-free rate. (See Self-Test Problems A-2 and A-3.)

31. d. Statement a is false. The yield curve determines the value of k_{RF}; however, SML = k_{RF} + ($k_M - k_{RF}$)b. The average return on the market will always be greater than the risk-free rate; thus, the SML will always be upward sloping. Statement b is false because RP_M is equal to $k_M - k_{RF}$. k_{RF} is equal to the risk-free rate, not the rate on an average company's bonds. Statement c is false. A decrease in an investor's aversion to risk would indicate a downward sloping yield curve. A decrease in risk aversion and an increase in inflation would cause the SML slope to decrease and to shift upward simultaneously.

32. e. All the statements are false. For equilibrium to exist, the expected return must equal the required return.

33. b. Statement b is correct because the stock with the higher standard deviation might not be highly correlated with most other stocks, hence have a relatively low beta, and thus not be very risky if held in a well-diversified portfolio. The other statements are simply false.

ANSWERS TO SELF-TEST PROBLEMS

1. e. $\hat{k}_A$ = 0.1(-15%) + 0.2(0%) + 0.4(5%) + 0.2(10%) + 0.1(25%) = 5.0%.

   Variance = 0.1(-0.15 − 0.05)² + 0.2(0.0 − 0.05)² + 0.4(0.05 − 0.05)²
   + 0.2(0.10 − 0.05)² + 0.1(0.25 − 0.05)²
   = 0.009.

   Standard deviation = $\sqrt{0.009}$ = 0.0949 ≈ 9.5%.

2. d. $k_X = k_{RF} + (k_M - k_{RF})b_X$ = 5% + (11% − 5%)1.3 = 12.8%.

3. c. $k_X = k_{RF} + (k_M - k_{RF})b_X = 7\% + (13\% - 7\%)1.3 = 14.8\%$.

   A change in the inflation premium does *not* change the market risk premium $(k_M - k_{RF})$ since both k_M and k_{RF} are affected.

4. b. $k_X = k_{RF} + (k_M - k_{RF})b_X = 5\% + (14\% - 5\%)1.3 = 16.7\%$.

5. a. $k_X = k_{RF} + (k_M - k_{RF})b_X = 7\% + (16\% - 7\%)1.3 = 18.7\%$.

6. c. The calculation of the portfolio's beta is as follows: $b_p = (1/3)(0.5) + (1/3)(1.0) + (1/3)(1.5) = 1.0$.

7. d. $b_p = \sum_{i=1}^{5} w_i b_i$

   $= \dfrac{\$130}{\$450}(0.4) + \dfrac{\$110}{\$450}(1.5) + \dfrac{\$70}{\$450}(3.0) + \dfrac{\$90}{\$450}(2.0) + \dfrac{\$50}{\$450}(1.0) = 1.46$.

8. a. $k_p = k_{RF} + (k_M - k_{RF})b_p = 12\% + (6\%)1.46 = 20.76\%$.

9. c. We know $b_A = 1.20$, $b_B = 0.60$; $k_M = 12\%$, and $k_{RF} = 7\%$.

   $k_i = k_{RF} + (k_M - k_{RF})b_i = 7\% + (12\% - 7\%)b_i$.

   $k_A = 7\% + 5\%(1.20) = 13.0\%$.

   $k_B = 7\% + 5\%(0.60) = 10.0\%$.

   $k_A - k_B = 13\% - 10\% = 3\%$.

10. e. First find the beta of the remaining 9 stocks:

   $1.8 = 0.9(b_R) + 0.1(b_A)$
   $1.8 = 0.9(b_R) + 0.1(2.0)$
   $1.8 = 0.9(b_R) + 0.2$
   $1.6 = 0.9(b_R)$
   $b_R = 1.78$.

Now find the beta of the new stock that produces $b_p = 1.7$.

$1.7 = 0.9(1.78) + 0.1(b_N)$
$1.7 = 1.6 + 0.1(b_N)$
$0.1 = 0.1(b_N)$
$b_N = 1.0$.

11. c. Determine the weight each stock represents in the portfolio:

Stock	Investment	w_i	Beta	$w_i \times$ Beta
A	$ 400,000	0.10	1.2	0.1200
B	600,000	0.15	-0.4	-0.0600
C	1,000,000	0.25	1.5	0.3750
D	2,000,000	0.50	0.8	0.4000

$$b_p = \underline{0.8350} = \text{Portfolio beta}$$

Write out the SML equation, and substitute known values including the portfolio beta. Solve for the required portfolio return.

$$k_p = k_{RF} + (k_M - k_{RF})b_p = 6\% + (12\% - 6\%)0.8350$$

$$= 6\% + 5.01\% = 11.01\%.$$

12. b. Use the given probability distribution of returns to calculate the expected value, variance, standard deviation, and coefficient of variation.

P_i	k_i		P_ik_i	k_i	$\hat{k}$		$(k_i - \hat{k})$	$(k_i - \hat{k})^2$	$P(k_i - \hat{k})^2$
0.4 ×	$30	=	$12.0	$30	- $22.5	=	$ 7.5	$ 56.25	$ 22.500
0.5 ×	25	=	12.5	25	- 22.5	=	2.5	6.25	3.125
0.1 ×	-20	=	-2.0	-20	- 22.5	=	-42.5	1,806.25	180.625
			$\hat{k} = \underline{\$22.5}$				$\sigma^2 = $ Variance $= \underline{\$206.250}$		

The standard deviation (σ) of $\hat{k}$ is $\sqrt{\$206.25}$ = $14.3614.

Use the standard deviation and the expected return to calculate the coefficient of variation: $14.3614/$22.5 = 0.6383.

13. a. Use the SML equation, substitute in the known values, and solve for beta.

$$k_{RF} = 8\%; \quad k_M = 13\%; \quad k_j = 15\%.$$

$$k_j = k_{RF} + (k_M - k_{RF})b_j$$
$$15\% = 8\% + (13\% - 8\%)b_j$$
$$7\% = (5\%)b_j$$
$$b_j = 1.4.$$

Appendix 5A

A-1. b. Stock A: $b_A = \dfrac{\text{Rise}}{\text{Run}} = \dfrac{10 - (-5)}{10 - (-10)} = \dfrac{15}{20} = 0.75.$

Stock B: $b_B = \dfrac{\text{Rise}}{\text{Run}} = \dfrac{20 - 10}{10 - (-10)} = \dfrac{10}{20} = 0.50.$

This problem can also be worked using most financial calculators having statistical functions.

A-2. e. $b_N = \text{Rise/Run} = [-8 - (-5)]/(15 - 10) = -3/5 = -0.60.$

Again, this problem can also be worked using most financial calculators having statistical functions.

A-3. b. $k_N = 7\% + (10\% - 7\%)(-0.60) = 7\% + (-1.80\%) = 5.20\%.$

A-4. d. Use the regression feature of the calculator. Enter data for the market and Stock Y, and then find $\text{Beta}_Y = 1.3374$ rounded to 1.34.

A-5. a. We know $k_M = 15\%$; $k^* = 3.75\%$; $IP = 5\%$.

Original $RP_M = k_M - k_{RF} = 15\% - (3.75\% + 5\%) = 6.25\%.$

RP_M increases by 3%, to 9.25%.

Find the change in $k = \Delta k$ for the riskier stock.

First, find the betas for the two stocks. Enter data in the regression register, then find $b_Y = 1.3374$ and $b_Z = 0.6161$.

Y is the riskier stock. Originally, its required return was $k_Y = 8.75\% + 6.25\%(1.3374)$ = 17.11%. When RP_M increases by 3 percent, $k_Y = 8.75\% + (6.25\% + 3\%)(1.3374)$ = 21.12%. Difference = 21.12% - 17.11% = 4.01%.

CHAPTER 6
TIME VALUE OF MONEY

OVERVIEW

A dollar in the hand today is worth more than a dollar to be received in the future because, if you had it now, you could invest that dollar and earn interest. Of all the techniques used in finance, none is more important than the concept of *time value of money,* or *discounted cash flow (DCF) analysis.* Future value and present value techniques can be applied to a single cash flow (lump sum), ordinary annuities, annuities due, and uneven cash flow streams. Future and present values can be calculated using interest factor tables, a regular calculator, or a calculator with financial functions. When compounding occurs more frequently than once a year, the effective rate of interest is greater than the quoted rate.

OUTLINE

The time line is one of the most important tools in time value of money calculations. Time lines help to visualize what is happening in a particular problem. Cash flows are placed directly below the tick marks, and interest rates are shown directly above the time line; unknown cash flows are indicated by question marks. Thus, to find the future value of $100 after 5 years at 5 percent interest, the following time line can be set up:

Time:	0		1	2	3	4	5
		5%					
Cash flows:	-100						FV_5=?

Finding the future value (FV), or compounding, is the process of going from today's values (or present values) to future amounts (or future values). It can be calculated as

$$FV_n = PV(1 + i)^n,$$

where PV = present value, or beginning amount; i = interest rate per year; and n = number of periods involved in the analysis. This equation can be solved in one of three ways: numerically, with interest tables, or with a financial calculator. For calculations, assume the following data that were presented in the time line above: present value (PV) = $100, interest rate (i) = 5%, and number of years (n) = 5.

■ To solve numerically, use a regular calculator to find 1 + i = 1.05 raised to the fifth power, which equals 1.2763. Multiply this figure by PV = $100 to get the final answer of FV_5 = $127.63.

■ To solve with interest tables, look at Table A-3 at the end of your textbook for future value interest factors. Look down the first column to Period 5, then look across that row to the 5% column for the number 1.2763. Multiplying by PV = $100 results in FV_5 = $127.63.

■ With a financial calculator, the future value can be found by using the time value of money input keys, where N = number of periods, I = interest rate per period, PV = present value, PMT = payment, and FV = future value. By entering N = 5, I = 5, PV = -100, and PMT = 0, and then pressing the FV key, the answer 127.63 is displayed.
   □ Some financial calculators require that all cash flows be designated as either inflows or outflows, thus an outflow must be entered as a negative number (for example, PV = -100 instead of PV = 100).
   □ Some calculators require you to press a "Compute" key before pressing the FV key.

■ Note that small rounding differences will often occur among the various solution methods.

■ A graph of the compounding process shows how any sum grows over time at various interest rates. The greater the rate of interest, the faster is the rate of growth.

Finding present values is called discounting, and it is simply the reverse of compounding. In general, the present value of a cash flow due n years in the future is the amount which, if it were on hand today, would grow to equal the future amount. By solving for PV in the future value equation, the present value, or discounting, equation can be developed and written in several forms:

$$PV = \frac{FV_n}{(1 + i)^n} = FV_n \left(\frac{1}{1 + i} \right)^n = FV_n (PVIF_{i,n}).$$

■ To solve for the present value of $127.63 discounted back 5·years at a 5% opportunity cost rate, one can utilize any of the three solution methods:
   □ Numerical solution: Divide $127.63 by 1.05 five times to get PV = $100.

- □ Tabular solution: Refer to Table A-1 in Appendix A of the text for the present value interest factors ($PVIF_{i,n}$). The value of $PVIF_{i,n}$ for i = 5% and n = 5 is 0.7835. Multiply this number by $127.63 to get PV = $100.
- □ Financial calculator solution: Enter N = 5, I = 5, PMT = 0, and FV = 127.63, and then press the PV key to get PV = -100.

■ A graph of the discounting process shows how the present value of any sum to be received in the future diminishes as the years to receipt increases. At relatively high interest rates, funds due in the future are worth very little today, and even at a relatively low discount rate, the present value of a sum due in the very distant future is quite small.

There are four variables in the time value of money compounding and discounting equations: PV, FV, i, and n. If three of the four variables are known, you can find the value of the fourth.

■ If we are given PV, FV, and n, we can determine i by substituting the known values into either the present value or future value equations, and then solving for i. Thus, if you can buy a security at a price of $78.35 which will pay you $100 after 5 years, what is the interest rate earned on the investment?
- □ Numerical solution: Use a trial and error process to reach the 5% value for i. This is a tedious and inefficient process.
- □ Tabular solution: Find the interest rate in Table A-3 of the text that corresponds to the future value interest factor of 1.2763 (calculated by dividing $100 by $78.35).
- □ Financial calculator solution: Enter N = 5, PV = -78.35, PMT = 0, and FV = 100, then press the I key, and I = 5 is displayed.

■ Likewise, if we are given PV, FV, and i, we can determine n by substituting the known values into either the present value or future value equations, and then solving for n. Thus, if you can buy a security with a 5 percent interest rate at a price of $78.35 today, how long will it take for your investment to return $100?
- □ Numerical solution: Use a trial and error process to reach the value of 5 for n. This is a tedious and inefficient process.
- □ Tabular solution: Find the value of n in Table A-3 of the text that corresponds to the future value interest factor of 1.2763 (found by dividing $100 by $78.35).
- □ Financial calculator solution: Enter I = 5, PV = -78.35, PMT = 0, and FV = 100, then press the N key, and N = 5 is displayed.

An annuity is a series of equal payments at fixed intervals for a specified number of periods. If the payments occur at the end of each period, as they typically do, the annuity is an ordinary (or deferred) annuity. If the payments occur at the beginning of each period, it is called an annuity due.

■ The future value of an annuity is the total amount one would have at the end of the annuity period if each payment were invested at a given interest rate and held to the end of the annuity period.

☐ Defining FVA_n as the compound sum of an ordinary annuity of n years, and PMT as the periodic payment, we can write

$$FVA_n = PMT \sum_{t=1}^{n} (1 + i)^{n-t} = PMT(FVIFA_{i,n}).$$

☐ $FVIFA_{i,n}$ is the future value interest factor for an ordinary annuity. FVIFAs may be found in Table A-4 of the text.

☐ For example, the future value of a 3-year, 5 percent ordinary annuity of $100 per year would be $100(3.1525) = $315.25.

☐ The same calculation can be made using the financial function keys of a calculator. Enter N = 3, I = 5, PV = 0, and PMT = -100. Then press the FV key, and 315.25 is displayed.

☐ For an annuity due, each payment is compounded for one additional period, so the future value of the entire annuity is equal to the future value of an ordinary annuity compounded for one additional period. Thus:

$$FVA_n \text{ (Annuity due)} = PMT(FVIFA_{i,n})(1 + i).$$

☐ For example, the future value of a 3-year, 5 percent annuity due of $100 per year is $100(3.1525)(1.05) = $331.01.

☐ Most financial calculators have a switch, or key, marked "DUE" or "BEG" that permits you to switch from end-of-period payments (an ordinary annuity) to beginning-of-period payments (an annuity due). Switch your calculator to "BEG" mode, and calculate as for an ordinary annuity. Do not forget to switch your calculator back to "END" mode when you are finished.

■ The present value of an annuity is the single (lump sum) payment today that would be equivalent to the annuity payments spread over the annuity period. It is the amount today that would permit withdrawals of an equal amount (PMT) at the end (or beginning for an annuity due) of each period for n periods.

☐ Defining PVA_n as the present value of an ordinary annuity of n years and PMT as the periodic payment, we can write

$$PVA_n = PMT \sum_{t=1}^{n} \left(\frac{1}{1 + i} \right)^{t} = PMT(PVIFA_{i,n}).$$

☐ $PVIFA_{i,n}$ is the present value interest factor for an ordinary annuity. PVIFAs may be found in Table A-2 at the back of the text.

- ☐ For example, an annuity of $100 per year for 3 years at 5 percent would have a present value of $100(2.7232) = $272.32.
- ☐ Using a financial calculator, enter N = 3, I = 5, PMT = -100, and FV = 0, and then press the PV key, for an answer of $272.32.
- ☐ The present value for an annuity due is

$$PVA_n \text{ (Annuity due)} = PMT(PVIFA_{i,n})(1 + i).$$

- ☐ For example, the present value of a 3-year, 5 percent annuity due of $100 is $100(2.7232)(1.05) = $285.94.
- ☐ Using a financial calculator, switch to the "BEG" mode, and then enter N = 3, I = 5, PMT = -100, and FV = 0, and then press PV to get the answer, $285.94. Again, do not forget to switch your calculator back to "END" mode when you are finished.

An annuity that goes on indefinitely is called a perpetuity. The payments of a perpetuity constitute an infinite series.

- ■ The present value of a perpetuity is:

$$PV \text{ (Perpetuity)} = Payment/Interest \ rate = PMT/i.$$

- ■ For example, if the interest rate were 12 percent, a perpetuity of $1,000 a year would have a present value of $1,000/0.12 = $8,333.33.

Many financial decisions require the analysis of uneven, or nonconstant, cash flows rather than a stream of fixed payments such as an annuity.

- ■ The present value of an uneven stream of income is the sum of the PVs of the individual cash flow components. Similarly, the future value of an uneven stream of income is the sum of the FVs of the individual cash flow components.
  - ☐ With a financial calculator, enter each cash flow (beginning with the t=0 cash flow) into the cash flow register, CF_j, enter the appropriate interest rate, and then press the NPV key to obtain the PV of the cash flow stream.
  - ☐ Some calculators have a net future value (NFV) key which allows you to obtain the FV of an uneven cash flow stream.

- ■ If one knows the relevant cash flows, the effective interest rate can be calculated efficiently with a financial calculator. Enter each cash flow (beginning with the t=0 cash flow) into the cash flow register, CF_j, and then press the IRR key to obtain the interest rate of an uneven cash flow stream.

Semiannual, quarterly, and other compounding periods more frequent than on an annual basis are often used in financial transactions. Compounding on a nonannual basis requires an adjustment to both the compounding and discounting procedures discussed previously.

■ The *effective annual rate* (EAR or EFF%) is the rate that would have produced the final compound value under annual compounding. The effective annual percentage rate is given by the following formula:

$$\text{Effective annual rate (EAR)} = \text{EFF\%} = (1 + i_{Nom}/m)^m - 1.0,$$

where i_{Nom} is the nominal, or quoted, annual rate and m is the number of compounding periods per year. The EAR is useful in comparing securities with different compounding periods.

■ For example, to find the effective annual rate if the nominal rate is 6 percent and semiannual compounding is used, we have:

$$\text{EAR} = (1 + 0.06/2)^2 - 1.0 = 6.09\%.$$

■ For annual compounding use the formula to find the future value of a single payment (lump sum):

$$FV_n = PV(1 + i)^n.$$

When compounding occurs more frequently than once a year, use this formula:

$$FV_n = PV(1 + i_{Nom}/m)^{mn}.$$

Here m is the number of times per year compounding occurs, and n is the number of years.

■ The amount to which $1,000 will grow after 5 years if quarterly compounding is applied to a nominal 8 percent interest rate is found as follows:

$$FV_n = \$1,000(1 + 0.08/4)^{(4 \times 5)} = \$1,000(1.02)^{20} = \$1,485.95.$$

☐ Tabular solution: Divide the interest rate by 4, so i = 8%/4 = 2%, and multiply the number of years by 4, so n = 5 × 4 = 20. Look down the first column of Table A-3 to Period 20 and then across to the 2% column to find $FVIF_{2\%,20} = 1.4859$. FV = 1.4859 × $1,000 = $1,485.90.

☐ Financial calculator solution: Enter N = 20, I = 2, PV = -1000, and PMT = 0, and then press the FV key to find FV = $1,485.95.

■ The present value of a 5-year future investment equal to $1,485.95, with an 8 percent nominal interest rate, compounded quarterly, is found as follows:

$$\$1,485.95 = PV(1 + 0.08/4)^{(4)(5)}$$

$$PV = \frac{\$1,485.95}{(1.02)^{20}} = \$1,000.$$

☐ Tabular solution: Use Table A-1, look down to Period 20 and then across to the 2% column to find $PVIF_{2\%,20} = 0.6730$. PV = $1,485.95 × 0.6730 = $1,000.04.
☐ Financial calculator solution: Enter N = 20, I = 2, PMT = 0, and FV = 1485.95, and then press the PV key to find PV = -$1,000.00.

The nominal rate is the rate that is quoted by borrowers and lenders. Nominal rates can only be compared with one another if the instruments being compared use the same number of compounding periods per year. Note also that the nominal rate is never shown on a time line, or used as an input in a financial calculator, unless compounding occurs only once a year. In general, nonannual compounding can be handled one of two ways.

■ State everything on a periodic rather than on an annual basis. Thus, n = 6 periods rather than n = 3 years and i = 3% instead of i = 6% with semiannual compounding.

■ Find the effective annual rate (EAR) with the equation below and then use the EAR as the rate over the given number of years.

$$EAR = \left(1 + \frac{i_{Nom}}{m}\right)^m - 1.0.$$

Fractional time periods are used when payments occur within periods, instead of at either the beginning or the end of periods. Solving these problems requires using the fraction of the time period for n, number of periods, and then solving either numerically or with a financial calculator. (Some older calculators will produce incorrect answers because of their internal "solution" programs.)

An important application of compound interest involves amortized loans, which are paid off in equal installments over time.

■ The amount of each payment, PMT, is found as follows: PV of the annuity = $PMT(PVIFA_{i,n})$, so PMT = PV of the annuity$/PVIFA_{i,n}$.

■ With a financial calculator, enter N (number of years), I (interest rate), PV (amount borrowed), and FV = 0, and then press the PMT key to find the periodic payment.

■ Each payment consists partly of interest and partly of the repayment of principal. This breakdown is often developed in a loan amortization schedule.
  ☐ The interest component is largest in the first period, and it declines over the life of the loan.
  ☐ The repayment of principal is smallest in the first period, and it increases thereafter.

Appendix 6A discusses the formulas necessary for continuous compounding and discounting. The equation for continuous compounding is $FV_n = PV(e^{in})$ where e is the approximate value 2.7183; the equation for continuous discounting is $PV = FV_n(e^{-in})$.

SELF-TEST QUESTIONS

Definitional

1. The beginning value of an account or investment in a project is known as its _____ _____.

2. Using a savings account as an example, the difference between the account's present value and its future value at the end of the period is due to _____ earned during the period.

3. The equation $FV_n = PV(1 + i)^n$ determines the future value of a sum at the end of n periods. The factor $(1 + i)^n$ is known as the _____ _____ _____ _____.

4. The process of finding present values is often referred to as _____ and is the reverse of the _____ process.

5. The $PVIF_{i,n}$ for a 5-year, 5 percent investment is 0.7835. This value is the _____ of the $FVIF_{i,n}$ for 5 years at 5 percent.

6. For a given number of time periods, the $PVIF_{i,n}$ will decline as the _____ _____ increases.

7. A series of payments of a constant amount for a specified number of periods is a(n) _____. If the payments occur at the end of each period it is a(n) _____ annuity, while if the payments occur at the beginning of each period it is an annuity _____.

8. The present value of an uneven stream of future payments is the ____ of the PVs of the individual payments.

9. Since different types of investments use different compounding periods, it is important to distinguish between the quoted, or _____, rate and the _____ annual interest rate.

10. To use the interest factor tables when compounding occurs more than once a year, divide the _____ _____ by the number of times compounding occurs and multiply the years by the number of _____ _____ per year.

Conceptual

11. If a bank uses quarterly compounding for savings accounts, the nominal rate will be greater than the effective annual rate (EAR).

   a. True   b. False

12. If money has time value (that is, i > 0), the future value of some amount of money will always be more than the amount invested. The present value of some amount to be received in the future is always less than the amount to be received.

   a. True   b. False

13. You have determined the profitability of a planned project by finding the present value of all the cash flows from that project. Which of the following would cause the project to look less appealing, that is, have a lower present value?

   a. The discount rate decreases.
   b. The cash flows are extended over a longer period of time.
   c. The discount rate increases.
   d. Statements b and c are both correct.
   e. Statements a and b are both correct.

14. As the discount rate increases without limit, the present value of a future cash inflow

   a. Gets larger without limit.
   b. Stays unchanged.
   c. Approaches zero.
   d. Gets smaller without limit; that is, approaches minus infinity.
   e. Goes to e^{in}.

15. Which of the following statements is most *correct?*

    a.   For all positive values of i and n, $FVIF_{i,n} \geq 1.0$ and $PVIFA_{i,n} \geq n$.
    b.   You may use the PVIF tables to find the present value of an uneven series of payments. However, the PVIFA tables can never be of use, even if some of the payments constitute an annuity (for example, $100 each year for Years 3, 4, 5, and 6), because the entire series does not constitute an annuity.
    c.   If a bank uses quarterly compounding for savings accounts, the nominal rate will be greater than the effective annual rate.
    d.   The present value of a future sum decreases as either the nominal interest rate or the number of discounting periods per year increases.
    e.   All of the above statements are false.

16. Which of the following statements is most *correct?*

    a.   Except in situations where compounding occurs annually, the periodic interest rate exceeds the nominal interest rate.
    b.   The effective annual rate always exceeds the nominal rate, no matter how few or many compounding periods occur each year.
    c.   If compounding occurs more frequently than once a year, and if payments are made at times other than at the end of compounding periods, it is impossible to determine present or future values, even with a financial calculator. The reason is that under these conditions, the basic assumptions of discounted cash flow analysis are not met.
    d.   Assume that compounding occurs quarterly, that the nominal interest rate is 8 percent, and that you need to find the present value of $1,000 due 6 months from today. You could get the correct answer by discounting the $1,000 at 2 percent for 2 periods.
    e.   Statements a, b, c, and d are all false.

SELF-TEST PROBLEMS

(Note: In working these problems, you may get an answer which differs from ours by a few cents due to differences in rounding. This should not concern you; just pick the closest answer.)

1. Assume that you purchase a 6-year, 8 percent savings certificate for $1,000. If interest is compounded annually, what will be the value of the certificate when it matures?

   a. $630.17   b. $1,469.33   c. $1,677.10   d. $1,586.90   e. $1,766.33

2. A savings certificate similar to the one in the previous problem is available with the exception that interest is compounded semiannually. What is the difference between the ending value of the savings certificate compounded semiannually and the one compounded annually?

   a. The semiannual is worth $14.10 more than the annual.
   b. The semiannual is worth $14.10 less than the annual.
   c. The semiannual is worth $21.54 more than the annual.
   d. The semiannual is worth $21.54 less than the annual.
   e. The semiannual is worth the same as the annual.

3. A friend promises to pay you $600 two years from now if you loan him $500 today. What annual interest rate is your friend offering?

   a. 7.5%   b. 8.5%   c. 9.5%   d. 10.5%   e. 11.5%

4. At an inflation rate of 9 percent, the purchasing power of $1 would be cut in half in just over 8 years (some calculators round to 9 years). How long, to the nearest year, would it take for the purchasing power of $1 to be cut in half if the inflation rate were only 4 percent?

   a. 12 years   b. 15 years   c. 18 years   d. 20 years   e. 23 years

5. You are offered an investment opportunity with the "guarantee" that your investment will double in 5 years. Assuming annual compounding, what annual rate of return would this investment provide?

   a. 40.00%   b. 100.00%   c. 14.87%   d. 20.00%   e. 18.74%

6. You decide to begin saving toward the purchase of a new car in 5 years. If you put $1,000 at the end of each of the next 5 years in a savings account paying 6 percent compounded annually, how much will you accumulate after 5 years?

   a. $6,691.13   b. $5,637.10   c. $1,338.23   d. $5,975.33   e. $5,732.00

7. Refer to Self-Test Problem 6. What would be the ending amount if the payments were made at the beginning of each year?

   a. $6,691.13   b. $5,637.10   c. $1,338.23   d. $5,975.33   e. $5,732.00

8. Refer to Self-Test Problem 6. What would be the ending amount if $500 payments were made at the end of each 6-month period for 5 years and the account paid 6 percent compounded semiannually?

   a. $6,691.13   **b.** $5,637.10   **c.** $1,338.23   **d.** $5,975.33   **e.** $5,732.00

9. Calculate the present value of $1,000 to be received at the end of 8 years. Assume an interest rate of 7 percent.

   a. $582.00   **b.** $1,718.19   **c.** $531.82   **d.** $5,971.30   **e.** $649.37

10. How much would you be willing to pay today for an investment that would return $800 each year at the end of each of the next 6 years? Assume a discount rate of 5 percent.

    a. $5,441.53   **b.** $4,800.00   **c.** $3,369.89   **d.** $4,060.56   **e.** $4,632.37

11. You have applied for a mortgage of $60,000 to finance the purchase of a new home. The bank will require you to make annual payments of $7,047.55 at the end of each of the next 20 years. Determine the interest rate in effect on this mortgage.

    a. 8.0%   **b.** 9.8%   **c.** 10.0%   **d.** 51.0%   **e.** 11.2%

12. If you would like to accumulate $7,500 over the next 5 years, how much must you deposit each six months, starting six months from now, given a 6 percent interest rate and semiannual compounding?

    a. $1,330.47   **b.** $879.23   **c.** $654.22   **d.** $569.00   **e.** $732.67

13. A company is offering bonds which pay $100 per year indefinitely. If you require a 12 percent return on these bonds—that is, the discount rate is 12 percent—what is the value of each bond?

    a. $1,000.00   **b.** $962.00   **c.** $904.67   **d.** $866.67   **e.** $833.33

14. What is the present value (t = 0) of the following cash flows if the discount rate is 12 percent?

0	12% 1	2	3	4	5
0	2,000	2,000	2,000	3,000	-4,000

    a. $4,782.43   **b.** $4,440.50   **c.** $4,221.79   **d.** $4,041.23   **e.** $3,997.98

15. What is the effective annual percentage rate (EAR) of 12 percent compounded monthly?

   a. 12.00%   b. 12.55%   c. 12.68%   d. 12.75%   e. 13.00%

16. Martha Mills, manager of Plaza Gold Emporium, wants to sell on credit, giving customers 4 months in which to pay. However, Martha will have to borrow from her bank to carry the accounts payable. The bank will charge a nominal 18 percent, but with monthly compounding. Martha wants to quote a nominal rate to her customers (all of whom are expected to pay on time at the end of 4 months) *which will exactly cover her financing costs*. What nominal annual rate should she quote to her credit customers? (Note: Interest factor tables cannot be used to solve this problem.)

   a. 15.44%   b. 19.56%   c. 17.11%   d. 18.41%   e. 16.88%

17. Self-Test Problem 11 refers to a 20-year mortgage of $60,000. This is an amortized loan. How much principal will be repaid in the second year?

   a. $1,152.30   b. $1,725.70   c. $5,895.25   d. $7,047.55   e. $1,047.55

18. You have $1,000 invested in an account which pays 16 percent compounded annually. A commission agent (called a "finder") can locate for you an equally safe deposit which will pay 16 percent, compounded quarterly, for 2 years. What is the maximum amount you should be willing to pay him now as a fee for locating the new account?

   a. $10.92   b. $13.78   c. $16.14   d. $16.81   e. $21.13

19. The present value (t = 0) of the following cash flow stream is $11,958.20 when discounted at 12 percent annually. What is the value of the missing t = 2 cash flow?

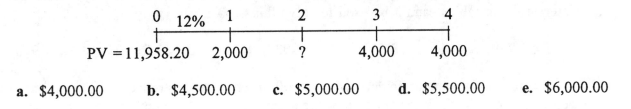

   a. $4,000.00   b. $4,500.00   c. $5,000.00   d. $5,500.00   e. $6,000.00

20. Today is your birthday, and you decide to start saving for your college education. You will begin college on your 18th birthday and will need $4,000 per year at the *end* of each of the following 4 years. You will make a deposit 1 year from today in an account paying 12 percent annually and continue to make an identical deposit each year up to and including the year you begin college. If a deposit amount of $2,542.05 will allow you to reach your goal, what birthday are you celebrating today?

   a. 13   b. 14   c. 15   d. 16   e. 17

21. Assume that your aunt sold her house on December 31 and that she took a mortgage in the amount of $50,000 as part of the payment. The mortgage has a stated (or nominal) interest rate of 8 percent, but it calls for payments every 6 months, beginning on June 30, and the mortgage is to be amortized over 20 years. Now, one year later, your aunt must file Schedule B of her tax return with the IRS informing them of the interest that was included in the two payments made during the year. (This interest will be income to your aunt and a deduction to the buyer of the house.) What is the total amount of interest that was paid during the first year?

   a. $1,978.95   b. $526.17   c. $3,978.95   d. $2,000.00   e. $750.02

22. Assume that you inherited some money. A friend of yours is working as an unpaid intern at a local brokerage firm, and her boss is selling some securities which call for five payments, $75 at the end of each of the next 4 years, plus a payment of $1,075 at the end of Year 5. Your friend says she can get you some of these securities at a cost of $960 each. Your money is now invested in a bank that pays an 8 percent nominal (quoted) interest rate, but with quarterly compounding. You regard the securities as being just as safe, and as liquid, as your bank deposit, so your required effective annual rate of return on the securities is the same as that on your bank deposit. You must calculate the value of the securities to decide whether they are a good investment. What is their present value to you? (Note: Interest factor tables cannot be used to solve this problem.)

   a. $957.75   b. $888.66   c. $923.44   d. $1,015.25   e. $970.51

23. Your company is planning to borrow $500,000 on a 5-year, 7 percent, annual payment, fully amortized term loan. What fraction of the payment made at the end of the second year will represent repayment of principal?

   a. 76.29%   b. 42.82%   c. 50.28%   d. 49.72%   e. 60.27%

24. Your firm can borrow from its bank for one month. The loan will have to be "rolled over" at the end of the month, but you are sure the rollover will be allowed. The nominal interest

rate is 14 percent, but interest will have to be paid at the end of each month, so the bank interest rate is 14 percent, monthly compounding. Alternatively, your firm can borrow from an insurance company at a nominal rate which would involve quarterly compounding. What nominal quarterly rate would be equivalent to the rate charged by the bank? (Note: Interest factor tables cannot be used to solve this problem.)

    a. 12.44%   **b.** 14.16%   **c.** 13.55%   **d.** 13.12%   **e.** 12.88%

25. Assume that you have $15,000 in a bank account that pays 5 percent annual interest. You plan to go back to school for a combination MBA/law degree 5 years from today. It will take you an additional 5 years to complete your graduate studies. You figure you will need a fixed income of $25,000 in today's dollars; that is, you will need $25,000 of today's dollars during your first year and each subsequent year. (*Thus, your real income will decline while you are in school.*) You will withdraw funds for your annual expenses at the beginning of each year. Inflation is expected to occur at the rate of 3 percent per year. How much must you save during each of the next 5 years in order to achieve your goal? The first increment of savings will be deposited one year from today.

    a. $20,241.66   **b.** $19,224.55   **c.** $18,792.11   **d.** $19,559.42   **e.** $20,378.82

26. You plan to buy a new HDTV. The dealer offers to sell the set to you on credit. You will have 3 months in which to pay, but the dealer says you will be charged a 15 percent interest rate; that is, the nominal rate is 15 percent, quarterly compounding. As an alternative to buying on credit, you can borrow the funds from your bank, but the bank will make you pay interest each month. At what nominal bank interest rate should you be indifferent between the two types of credit?

    a. 13.7643%   **b.** 14.2107%   **c.** 14.8163%   **d.** 15.5397%   **e.** 15.3984%

27. Assume that your father is now 40 years old, that he plans to retire in 20 years, and that he expects to live for 25 years after he retires, that is, until he is 85. He wants a fixed retirement income that has the same purchasing power at the time he retires as $75,000 has today (he realizes that the real value of his retirement income will decline year-by-year after he retires). His retirement income will begin the day he retires, 20 years from today, and he will then get 24 additional annual payments. Inflation is expected to be 4 percent per year from today forward; he currently has $200,000 saved up; and he expects to earn a return on his savings of 7 percent per year, annual compounding. To the nearest dollar, how much must he save during each of the next 20 years (with deposits being made at the end of each year) to meet his retirement goal?

    a. $31,105.90   **b.** $35,709.25   **c.** $54,332.88   **d.** $41,987.33   **e.** $62,191.25

Appendix 6A

A-1. If you receive $30,000 today and can invest it at a 4 percent annual rate compounded continuously, then what will its future value be in 10 years?

   a. $31,224.32   **b.** $38,327   **c.** $40,765   **d.** $44,754.74   **e.** $42,121

A-2. What is the present value of $125,000 due in 15 years, if the appropriate continuous discount rate is 6 percent?

   a. $44,754.74   **b.** $50,821.21   **c.** $38,327   **d.** $42,121   **e.** $40,765

ANSWERS TO SELF-TEST QUESTIONS

1. present value
2. interest
3. future value interest factor
4. discounting; compounding
5. reciprocal

6. interest rate
7. annuity; ordinary; due
8. sum
9. nominal; effective
10. nominal rate; compounding periods

11. b. The EAR is always greater than or equal to the nominal rate.

12. a. Both these statements are correct.

13. d. The slower the cash flows come in and the higher the interest rate, the lower the present value.

14. c. As the discount rate increases, the present value of a future sum decreases and eventually approaches zero.

15. d. As a future sum is discounted over more and more periods, the present value will get smaller and smaller. Likewise, as the discount rate increases, the present value of a future sum decreases and eventually approaches zero.

16. d. Statement a is false because the periodic interest rate is equal to the nominal rate divided by the number of compounding periods, so it will be equal to or smaller than the nominal rate. Statement b is false because the EAR will equal the nominal rate if there is one compounding period per year (annual compounding). Statement c is false because we can determine present or future values under the stated conditions. Statement d is

correct; using a financial calculator, enter N = 2, I = 2, PMT = 0, and FV = 1000 to find PV = -961.1688.

SOLUTIONS TO SELF-TEST PROBLEMS

1. d.

```
      0  8% 1    2    3    4    5    6
      +--+--+----+----+----+----+----+
    -1,000                         FV₆=?
```

$FV_n = PV(FVIF_{i,n}) = \$1,000(FVIF_{8\%,6}) = \$1,000(1.5869) = \$1,586.90$.

With a financial calculator, input N = 6, I = 8, PV = -1000, PMT = 0, and solve for FV = $1,586.87.

2. a.

```
    0         1         2         3         4         5         6     Years
    0  4% 1   2   3    4    5    6    7    8    9   10   11   12     Periods
    +--+--+---+---+----+----+----+----+----+----+----+----+----+
 -1,000                                                     FV=?
```

$FVIF_{i,n} = FVIF_{4\%,12} = 1.6010$.

Thus, $FV_n = \$1,000(1.6010) = \$1,601.00$. The difference, \$1,601.00 - \$1,586.90 = \$14.10, is the additional interest.

With a financial calculator, input N = 12, I = 4, PV = -1000, and PMT = 0, and then solve for FV = $1,601.03. The difference, $1,601.03 - $1,586.87 = $14.16.

3. c.

```
    0      i=?      1                   2
    +---------------+-------------------+
  -500                               600
```

$$FV_2 = PV(FVIF_{i,2})$$
$$\$600 = \$500(FVIF_{i,2})$$
$$FVIF_{i,2} = 1.2000.$$

Looking across the Period 2 row in Table A-3, we see $FVIF_{9\%,2} = 1.1881$ and $FVIF_{10\%,2} = 1.2100$. Therefore, the annual interest rate is between 9% and 10%.

With a financial calculator, input N = 2, PV = -500, PMT = 0, FV = 600, and solve for I = 9.54%.

4. c.

```
 0              N=?
      4%
 |-----------|
1.00        0.50
```

With a financial calculator, input I = 4, PV = -1.00, PMT = 0, and FV = 0.50. Solve for N = 17.67 ≈ 18 years.

5. c.

```
 0    1    2    3    4    5
   i=?
 |----|----|----|----|----|
-1                        2
```

Assume any value for the present value and double it:

$$FV_5 = PV(FVIF_{i,5})$$
$$\$2 = \$1(FVIF_{i,5})$$
$$FVIF_{i,5} = 2.0000.$$

Looking across the Period 5 row in Table A-3, we see that 2.0000 occurs between 14% and 15%.

With a financial calculator, input N = 5, PV = -1, PMT = 0, FV = 2, and solve for I = 14.87%.

6. b.

```
 0    1      2      3      4      5
   6%
 |----|------|------|------|------|
   -1,000 -1,000 -1,000 -1,000 -1,000
                              FVA_5=?
```

$$FVA_5 = PMT(FVIFA_{6\%,5}) = \$1,000(5.6371) = \$5,637.10.$$

With a financial calculator, input N = 5, I = 6, PV = 0, PMT = -1000, and solve for FV = $5,637.09.

7. d.

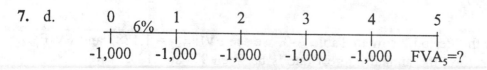

$$FVA_5(\text{Annuity due}) = PMT(FVIFA_{6\%,5})(1 + i) = \$1,000(5.6371)(1.06) = \$5,975.33.$$

With a financial calculator, switch to "BEG" mode, then input N = 5, I = 6, PV = 0, PMT = -1000, and solve for FV = $5,975.32. Be sure to switch back to "END" mode.

8. e.

$$FVA_{10} = PMT(FVIFA_{3\%,10}) = \$500(11.464) = \$5,732.00.$$

With a financial calculator, input N = 10, I = 3, PV = 0, PMT = -500, and solve for FV = $5,731.94.

(Note: In order to use the annuity tables, the compounding period and payment period *must be the same*; in this case, both are semiannual. If this is not the case, each cash flow must be treated individually.)

9. a.

$$PV = FV_8(PVIF_{7\%,8}) = \$1,000(0.5820) = \$582.00.$$

With a financial calculator, input N = 8, I = 7, PMT = 0, FV = 1000, and solve for PV = -$582.01.

(Note: Annual compounding is assumed if not otherwise specified.)

10. d.

$$PVA_6 = PMT(PVIFA_{5\%,6}) = \$800(5.0757) = \$4,060.56.$$

With a financial calculator, input N = 6, I = 5, PMT = 800, FV = 0, and solve for PV = -$4,060.55.

11. c.

The amount of the mortgage ($60,000) is the present value of a 20-year ordinary annuity with payments of $7,047.55. Therefore,

$$PVA_{20} = PMT(PVIFA_{i,20})$$
$$\$60,000 = \$7,047.55(PVIFA_{i,20})$$
$$PVIFA_{i,20} = 8.5136$$
$$i = 10.00\% \text{ exactly.}$$

With a financial calculator, input N = 20, PV = 60000, PMT = -7047.55, FV = 0, and solve for I = 10.00%.

12. c.

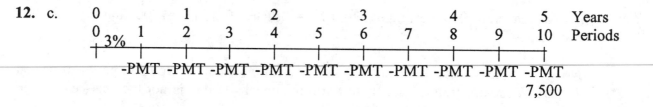

$$FVA_{10} = PMT(FVIFA_{3\%,10})$$
$$\$7,500 = PMT(11.464)$$
$$PMT = \$654.22.$$

With a financial calculator, input N = 10, I = 3, PV = 0, FV = 7500, and solve for PMT = -$654.23.

13. e. PV = PMT/i = $100/0.12 = $833.33.

14. b. PV $= \$2,000(PVIFA_{12\%,3}) + \$3,000(PVIF_{12\%,4}) - \$4,000(PVIF_{12\%,5})$
$\qquad = \$2,000(2.4018) + \$3,000(0.6355) - \$4,000(0.5674)$
$\qquad = \$4,440.50.$

With a financial calculator, using the cash flow register, CF_j, input 0; 2000; 2000; 2000; 3000; and -4000. Enter I = 12 and solve for NPV = $4,440.51.

15. c. EAR $= (1 + i_{Nom}/m)^m - 1.0$
$\qquad = (1 + 0.12/12)^{12} - 1.0$
$\qquad = (1.01)^{12} - 1.0$
$\qquad = 1.1268 - 1.0$
$\qquad = 0.1268 = 12.68\%.$

With a financial calculator, enter P/YR = 12 and NOM% = 12, and then solve for EFF% = 12.68%.

16. d. Here we want to have the same effective annual rate on the credit extended as on the bank loan that will be used to finance the credit extension.

First, we must find the EAR = EFF% on the bank loan. With a financial calculator, enter P/YR = 12, NOM% = 18, and press EFF% to get EAR = 19.56%.

Because 4 months of credit is being given there are 3 credit periods in a year, so enter P/YR = 3, EFF% = EAR = 19.56, and press NOM% to find the nominal rate of 18.41%. Therefore, if Martha charges an 18.41% nominal rate and gives credit for 4 months, she will cover the cost of her bank loan.

Alternative solution: First, we need to find the effective annual rate charged by the bank:

$$\begin{aligned} EAR &= (1 + k_{Nom}/m)^m - 1 \\ &= (1 + 0.18/12)^{12} - 1 \\ &= (1.0150)^{12} - 1 = 19.56\%. \end{aligned}$$

Now, we can find the nominal rate Martha must quote her customers so that her financing costs are exactly covered:

$$\begin{aligned} 19.56\% &= (1 + k_{Nom}/3)^3 - 1 \\ 1.1956 &= (1 + k_{Nom}/3)^3 \\ 1.0614 &= 1 + k_{Nom}/3 \\ 0.0614 &= k_{Nom}/3 \\ k_{Nom} &= 18.41\%. \end{aligned}$$

17. a.

Year	Payment	Interest	Repayment on Principal	Remaining Principal Balance
1	$7,047.55	$6,000.00	$1,047.55	$58,952.45
2	7,047.55	5,895.25	1,152.30	57,800.15

18. d. Currently: $FV_n = \$1,000(FVIF_{16\%,2}) = \$1,000(1.3456) = \$1,345.60.$

With a financial calculator, input N = 2, I = 16, PV = -1000, PMT = 0, and solve for FV = $1,345.60.

New account: $FV_n = \$1,000(1 + i_{Nom}/m)^{mn} = \$1,000(1.3686) = \$1,368.60.$

With a financial calculator, input N = 8, I = 4, PV = -1000, PMT = 0, and solve for FV = $1,368.57.

Thus, the new account will be worth $1,368.60 − $1,345.60 = $23.00 more after 2 years. With a financial calculator, the new account will be worth $22.97 more after 2 years.

PV of difference = $23(PVIF$_{4\%,8}$) = $23(0.7307) = $16.81. With a financial calculator, input N = 8, I = 4, PMT = 0, FV = 22.97, and solve for PV = -$16.78.

Therefore, the most you should be willing to pay the finder for locating the new account is $16.81.

19. e. $11,958.20 = $2,000(PVIF$_{12\%,1}$) + CF$_2$(PVIF$_{12\%,2}$)
     $\qquad$ + $4,000(PVIF$_{12\%,3}$) + $4,000(PVIF$_{12\%,4}$)
    $11,958.20 = $2,000(0.8929) + CF$_2$(0.7972) + $4,000(0.7118) + $4,000(0.6355)
    $11,958.20 = $7,175.00 + 0.7972CF$_2$
    $\quad$ 0.7972CF$_2$ = $4,783.20
    $\qquad$ CF$_2$ = $6,000.00.

With a financial calculator, input cash flows into the cash flow register, using -11,958.20 as the cash flow for time 0 (CF$_0$), and using 0 as the value for the unknown cash flow, input I = 12, and then press the NPV key to solve for the present value of the unknown cash flow, $4,783.29. This value should be compounded by (1.12)^2, so that $4,783.29(1.2544) = $6,000.16.

20. b. First, how much must you accumulate on your 18th birthday?

PVA$_n$ = $4,000(PVIFA$_{12\%,4}$) = $4,000(3.0373) = $12,149.20.
Present birthday = ?

			18		19	20	21	22
12%				12%				
2,542.05	2,542.05		2,542.05		4,000	4,000	4,000	4,000

3,571.43
3,188.78
2,847.12
2,542.07
Total FV needed = $12,149.40

Using a financial calculator (with the calculator set for an ordinary annuity), enter N = 4, I = 12, PMT = 4000, FV = 0, and solve for PV = -$12,149.40. This is the amount (or lump sum) that must be present in your bank account on your 18th birthday in order for you to be able to withdraw $4,000 at the end of each year for the next 4 years.

Now, how many payments must you make to accumulate $12,149.20?

$$FVA_n = \$12,149.20 = \$2,542.05(FVIFA_{12\%,n}).$$
$$FVIFA_{12\%,n} = 4.7793$$
$$n = 4, \text{ from Table A-4 in text.}$$

Using a financial calculator, enter I = 12, PV = 0, PMT = -2542.05, FV = 12149.40, and solve for N = 4. Therefore, if you make payments at 18, 17, 16, and 15, you are now 14.

21. c. This can be done with a calculator by specifying an interest rate of 4 percent per period for 40 periods.

N = 20 × 2 = 40.
I = 8/2 = 4.
PV = -50000.
FV = 0.
PMT = $2,526.17.

Set up an amortization table:

Period	Beginning Balance	Payment	Interest	Payment of Principal	Ending Balance
1	$50,000.00	$2,526.17	$2,000.00	$526.17	$49,473.83
2	49,473.83	2,526.17	1,978.95		
			$3,978.95		

You can really just work the problem with a financial calculator using the amortization function. Find the interest in each 6-month period, sum them, and you have the answer. Even simpler, with some calculators such as the HP 17B, just input 2 for periods and press INT to get the interest during the first year, $3,978.95.

22. e.

Input the cash flows in the cash flow register, input I = 2, and solve for NPV = $970.51.

23. a. Input N = 5, I = 7, PV = -500000, and FV = 0 to solve for PMT = $121,945.35.

Year	Beginning Balance	Payment	Interest	Payment of Principal	Ending Balance
1	$500,000.00	$121,945.35	$35,000.00	$86,945.35	$413,054.65
2	413,054.65	121,945.35	28,913.83	93,031.52	320,023.13

The fraction that is principal is $93,031.52/$121,945.35 = 76.29%.

24. b. Start with a time line to picture the situation:

Bank: 14% nominal EAR = 14.93%.

```
0  1  2  3  4  5  6  7  8  9  10 11 12
+--+--+--+--+--+--+--+--+--+--+--+--+
```

Insurance company: EAR = 14.93%; Nominal = 14.16%.

```
0          1          2          3          4
+----------+----------+----------+----------+
```

Here we must find the EAR on the bank loan and then find the quarterly nominal rate for that EAR. The bank loan amounts to a nominal 14 percent, monthly compounding.

Using the interest conversion feature of the calculator, or the EAR formula, we must find the EAR on the bank loan. Enter P/YR = 12 and NOM% = 14, and then press the EFF% key to find EAR bank loan = 14.93%.

Now, we can find the nominal rate with quarterly compounding that also has an EAR of 14.93 percent. Enter P/YR = 4 and EFF% = 14.93, and then press the NOM% key to get 14.16%. If the insurance company quotes a nominal rate of 14.16%, with quarterly compounding, then the bank and insurance company loans would be equivalent in the sense that they both have the same effective annual rate, 14.93%.

Alternative solution:

$$EAR = (1 + k_{Nom}/12)^{12} - 1$$
$$= (1 + 0.14/12)^{12} - 1$$
$$= 14.93\%.$$
$$14.93\% = (1 + k_{Nom}/4)^4 - 1$$
$$1.1493 = (1 + k_{Nom}/4)^4$$
$$1.0354 = 1 + k_{Nom}/4$$
$$0.0354 = k_{Nom}/4$$
$$k_{Nom} = 14.16\%.$$

25. e. Inflation = 3%.

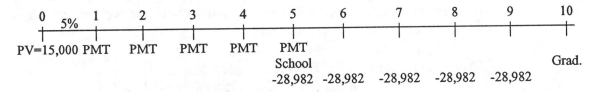

Fixed income = $25,000(1.03)^5 = \$28,981.85.$

1. Find the FV of $25,000 compounded for 5 years at 3 percent; that FV, $28,981.85, is the amount you will need each year while you are in school. (Note: Your real income will decline.)

2. You must have enough in 5 years to make the $28,981.85 payments to yourself. These payments will begin as soon as you start school, so we are dealing with a 5-year, 5 percent interest rate *annuity due*. Set the calculator to "BEG" mode, because we are dealing with an annuity due, and then enter N = 5, I = 5, PMT = -28981.85, and FV = 0. Then press the PV key to find the PV, $131,750.06. This is the amount you must have in your account 5 years from today. (Do not forget to switch the calculator back to "END" mode.)

3. You now have $15,000. It will grow at 5 percent to $19,144.22 after 5 years. Enter N = 5, I = 5, PV = -15000, and PMT = 0. You can subtract this amount to determine the FV of the amount you must save: $131,750.06 − $19,144.22 = $112,605.84.

4. Therefore, you must accumulate an additional $112,605.84 by saving PMT per year for 5 years, with the first PMT being deposited at the end of this year and earning a 5 percent interest rate. Now we have an ordinary annuity, so be sure you returned

your calculator to "END" mode. Enter N = 5, I = 5, PV = 0, FV = 112605.84, and then press PMT to find the required payments, -$20,378.82.

Alternative Solution (using interest factor tables)

1. Find the FV of $25,000 compounded for 5 years at 3 percent:

$$FV_5 = \$25,000(FVIF_{3\%,5}) = \$25,000(1.1593) = \$28,982.50.$$

This is the amount you will need each year while you're in school. (Note: Your real income will decline.)

2. You must have enough in 5 years to make the $28,982.50 payments to yourself. These payments will begin as soon as you start school, so we are dealing with a 5-year, 5 percent interest rate *annuity due*.

$$
\begin{aligned}
PVA_5 \text{ (Annuity due)} &= PMT(PVIFA_{5\%,5})(1.05) \\
&= \$28,982.50(4.3295)(1.05) = \$131,753.72.
\end{aligned}
$$

This is the amount you must have in your account 5 years from today.

3. You now have $15,000. It will grow at 5 percent for 5 years.

$$FV_5 = \$15,000(FVIF_{5\%,5}) = \$15,000(1.2763) = \$19,144.50.$$

You can subtract this amount to determine the FV of the amount you must save: $131,753.72 - $19,144.50 = $112,609.22.

4. Therefore, you must accumulate an additional $112,609.22 by saving PMT per year for 5 years, with the first PMT being deposited at the end of this year and earning a 5 percent interest rate. Now we have an ordinary annuity:

$$
\begin{aligned}
FVA_5 &= PMT(FVIFA_{5\%,5}) \\
\$112,609.22 &= PMT(5.5256) \\
PMT &= \$20,379.55.
\end{aligned}
$$

26. c. Find the EAR on the TV dealer's credit. Use the interest conversion feature of your calculator. First, though, note that if you are charged a 15 percent nominal rate, you will have to pay interest of 15%/4 = 3.75% after 3 months. The dealer then has the use of the interest, so he can earn 3.75 percent on it for the next three months, and so forth.

Thus, we are dealing with quarterly compounding. The nominal rate is 15 percent, quarterly compounding.

Enter NOM% = 15, P/YR = 4, and then press EFF% to get EAR = 15.8650%.

You should be indifferent between the dealer credit and the bank loan if the bank loan has an EAR of 15.8650 percent. The bank is using monthly compounding, or 12 periods per year. To find the nominal rate at which you should be indifferent, enter P/YR = 12, EFF% = 15.8650, and then press NOM% to get NOM% = 14.8163%.

Conclusion: A loan that has a 14.8163 percent nominal rate with monthly compounding is equivalent to a 15 percent nominal rate loan with quarterly compounding. Both have an EAR of 15.8650 percent.

<u>Alternative Solution</u>

$$EAR = (1 + k_{Nom}/4)^4 - 1 = (1 + 0.15/4)^4 - 1 = (1.0375)^4 - 1 = 15.8650\%.$$
$$15.8650\% = (1 + k_{Nom}/12)^{12} - 1$$
$$1.15865 = (1 + k_{Nom}/12)^{12}$$
$$1.012347 = 1 + k_{Nom}/12$$
$$k_{Nom} = 14.8163\%.$$

27. a. Information given:

1. Will save for 20 years, then receive payments for 25 years.

2. Wants payments of $75,000 per year in today's dollars for first payment only. Real income will decline. Inflation will be 4 percent. Therefore, to find the inflated fixed payments, we have this time line:

Enter N = 20, I = 4, PV = -75000, PMT = 0, and press FV to get FV = $164,334.24.

3. He now has $200,000 in an account which pays 7 percent, annual compounding. We need to find the FV of $200,000 after 20 years. Enter N = 20, I = 7, PV = -200000, PMT = 0, and press FV to get FV = $773,936.89.

4. He wants to withdraw, or have payments of, $164,334.24 per year for 25 years, with the first payment made at the beginning of the first retirement year. So, we have a 25-year annuity due with PMT = $164,334.24, at an interest rate of 7 percent. (The interest rate is 7 percent annually, so no adjustment is required.) Set the calculator to "BEG" mode, then enter N = 25, I = 7, PMT = -164334.24, FV = 0, and press PV to get PV = $2,049,138.53. This amount must be on hand to make the 25 payments.

5. Since the original $200,000, which grows to $773,936.89, will be available, he must save enough to accumulate $2,049,138.53 − $773,936.89 = $1,275,201.64.

6. The $1,275,201.64 is the FV of a 20-year ordinary annuity. The payments will be deposited in the bank and earn 7 percent interest. Therefore, set the calculator to "END" mode and enter N = 20, I = 7, PV = 0, FV = 1275201.64, and press PMT to find PMT = $31,105.90.

Alternative Solution (using interest factor tables)

Information given:

1. Will save for 20 years, then receive payments for 25 years.

2. Wants payments of $75,000 per year in today's dollars for *first payment only*. Real income will decline. Inflation will be 4 percent. Therefore, to find the inflated fixed payment use the following equation:

$$FV_{20} = PV(FVIF_{4\%,20}) = \$75,000(2.1911) = \$164,332.50.$$

3. He now has $200,000 in an account which pays 7 percent, annual compounding. We need to find the FV of the $200,000 after 20 years:

$$FV_{20} = PV(FVIF_{7\%,20}) = \$200,000(3.8697) = \$773,940.$$

4. He wants to withdraw, or have payments of, $164,332.50 per year for 25 years, with the first payment made at the beginning of the first retirement year. So, we have a 25-year *annuity due* with payments of $164,332.50, at an interest rate of 7 percent annually.

$$
\begin{aligned}
PVA_{25} \text{ (Annuity due)} &= \$164,332.50(PVIFA_{7\%,25})(1.07) \\
&= \$164,332.50(11.6536)(1.07) \\
&= \$2,049,119.79.
\end{aligned}
$$

This amount must be on hand to make the 25 payments.

5. Since the original $200,000, which grows to $773,940, will be available, he must save enough to accumulate $2,049,119.79 − $773,940.00 = $1,275,179.79.

6. The $1,275,179.79 is the FV of a 20-year ordinary annuity. The payments will be deposited in the bank and earn 7 percent interest. Therefore, use the following equation to calculate the yearly payments:

$$FVA_{20} = PMT(FVIFA_{7\%,20})$$
$$\$1,275,179.79 = PMT(40.995)$$
$$PMT = \$31,105.74.$$

Appendix 6A

A-1. d. $FV_n = PV\ e^{in}$
$FV_{10} = \$30,000\ e^{0.04(10)}$
$\quad\quad = \$30,000\ e^{0.4}$
$\quad\quad = \$44,754.74.$

A-2. b. $PV = FV_n\ e^{-in} = \$125,000\ e^{-0.90} = \$50,821.21.$

OVERVIEW

This chapter presents a discussion of the key characteristics of bonds, and then uses time value of money concepts to determine bond values. Bonds are one of the most important types of securities to investors, a major source of financing for corporations and governments.

The value of any financial asset is the present value of the cash flows expected from that asset. Therefore, once the cash flows have been estimated, and a discount rate determined, the value of the financial asset can be calculated.

A bond is valued as the present value of the stream of interest payments (an annuity) plus the present value of the par value which is received by the investor on the bond's maturity date. Depending on the relationship between the current interest rate and the bond's coupon rate, a bond can sell at its par value, at a *discount*, or at a *premium*. The total rate of return on a bond is comprised of two components: *interest yield* and *capital gains yield*.

The bond valuation concepts developed earlier in the chapter are used to illustrate interest rate and reinvestment rate risk. In addition, default risk, various types of corporate bonds, bond ratings, and bond markets are discussed.

OUTLINE

A bond is a long-term contract under which a borrower agrees to make payments of interest and principal, on specific dates, to the holders of the bond. There are four main types of bonds: Treasury, corporate, municipal, and foreign. Each type differs with respect to level of return and degree of risk.

■ *Treasury bonds*, sometimes referred to as government bonds, are issued by the Federal government and are not exposed to default risk.

■ *Corporate bonds* are issued by corporations and are exposed to default risk. Different corporate bonds have different levels of default risk, depending on the issuing company's characteristics and on the terms of the specific bond.

■ *Municipal bonds* are issued by state and local governments. The interest earned on most municipal bonds is exempt from federal taxes.

■ *Foreign bonds* are issued by foreign governments or foreign corporations. These bonds are not only exposed to default risk, but are also exposed to an additional risk if the bonds are denominated in a currency other than that of the investor's home currency.

Differences in contractual provisions, and in the underlying strength of the companies backing these provisions, lead to major differences in bonds' risks, prices, and expected returns. It is important to understand both the key characteristics, which are common to all bonds, and how differences in these characteristics affect the values and risks of individual bonds.

The *par value* is the stated face value of a bond, usually $1,000. This is the amount of money that the firm borrows and promises to repay at some future date.

The *coupon interest payment* is the dollar amount that is paid yearly to a bondholder by the issuer for use of the $1,000 loan. This payment is a fixed amount, established at the time the bond is issued. The *coupon interest rate* is obtained by dividing the coupon payment by the par value of the bond.

☐ In some cases, a bond's coupon payment may vary over time. These bonds are called *floating rate bonds*. Floating rate debt is advantageous to investors because the market value of the debt is stabilized. It is advantageous to corporations because firms can issue long-term debt without committing themselves to paying a historically high rate of interest for the entire life of the loan.

☐ *Zero coupon bonds* pay no coupons at all, but are offered at a substantial discount below their par values and hence provide capital appreciation rather than interest income. Appendix 7A discusses zero coupon bonds and their valuation in more detail.

The *maturity date* is the date on which the par value must be repaid. Most bonds have original maturities of from 10 to 40 years.

Most bonds have a *call provision*, whereby the issuer may pay off the bonds prior to maturity. The call provision generally states that if the bonds are called, the company must pay the bondholders an amount greater than the par value, a *call premium*.

■ A *sinking fund provision* facilitates the orderly retirement of a bond issue. This can be achieved in one of two ways:
    ☐ The company can call in for redemption (at par value) a certain percentage of bonds each year.
    ☐ The company may buy the required amount of bonds on the open market.

■ *Convertible bonds* are securities that are convertible into shares of common stock, at a fixed price, at the option of the bondholder.

■ Bonds issued with *warrants* are similar to convertibles. Warrants are options which permit the holder to buy stock for a stated price, thereby providing a capital gain if the stock price rises.

■ *Income bonds* pay interest only if the interest is earned. These securities cannot bankrupt a company, but from an investor's standpoint they are riskier than "regular" bonds.

■ The interest rate of an *indexed, or purchasing power, bond* is based on an inflation index, so the interest paid rises automatically when the inflation rate rises, thus protecting the bondholders against inflation.

The value of any financial asset is simply the present value of the cash flows the asset is expected to produce. The cash flows from a specific bond depend on its contractual features.

■ A bond represents an annuity plus a lump sum, and its value is found as the present value of this payment stream:

$$
\begin{array}{ccccccc}
0 & k_d\% & 1 & 2 & 3 & & N \\
\vdash & & \vdash & \vdash & \vdash & & \vdash \\
\text{Value} & & \text{INT} & \text{INT} & \text{INT} & & \text{INT} \\
& & & & & & M
\end{array}
$$

$$
\text{Bond value} = V_B = \sum_{t=1}^{N} \frac{\text{INT}}{(1 + k_d)^t} + \frac{M}{(1 + k_d)^N}
$$

$$
= \text{INT}(\text{PVIFA}_{k_d,N}) + M(\text{PVIF}_{k_d,N}),
$$

where INT = dollars of interest paid each year, M = par, or maturity, value, which is typically \$1,000, k_d = rate of interest on the bond, and N = number of years until the bond matures.

■ For example, consider a 15-year, $1,000 bond paying $150 annually, when the appropriate interest rate, k_d, is 15 percent. Utilizing the PVIFA and PVIF tables in the text, we find:

$$
\begin{aligned}
V_B &= \$150(5.8474) + \$1,000(0.1229) \\
&= \$877.11 + \$122.90 \\
&= \$1,000.01 \approx \$1,000.
\end{aligned}
$$

Using a financial calculator, enter $N = 15$, $k_d = I = 15$, $PMT = 150$, and $FV = 1000$, and then press the PV key for an answer of -$1,000.

■ A *new issue* is the term applied to a bond that has just been issued. At the time of issue, the coupon payment is generally set at a level that will force the market price of the bond to equal its par value. Once the bond has been on the market for a while, it is classified as an outstanding bond, or a *seasoned issue*.

■ Bond prices and interest rates are *inversely* related; that is, they tend to move in the opposite direction from one another.
  □ A bond will sell at par when its coupon interest rate is equal to the going rate of interest, k_d.
  □ When the going rate of interest is above the coupon rate, the bond will sell at a "discount" below its par value.
  □ If current interest rates are below the coupon rate, the bond will sell at a "premium" above its par value.
  □ The discount is equal to the present value of the amount of interest payment one sacrifices to buy a low-coupon old bond rather than a high-coupon new bond. The premium is equal to the present value of the additional interest payment one receives by buying a high-coupon old bond rather than a low-coupon new bond. The exact amount can be obtained by using the formula:

$$
\text{Discount or premium} = \sum_{t=1}^{n} \frac{\text{Interest on old bond} - \text{Interest on new bond}}{(1 + k_d)^t}.
$$

The expected interest rate on a bond, also called its "yield," can be calculated in a variety of different ways.

■ The rate of interest earned on a bond if it is held until redeemed by the issuer is known as the *yield to maturity (YTM)*. The YTM for a bond that sells at par consists entirely of an interest yield, but if the bond sells at a price other than its par value, the YTM consists of the interest yield plus a positive or negative capital gains yield.
  □ The yield to maturity can also be viewed as the bond's promised rate of return.

☐ The yield to maturity equals the expected rate of return only if the probability of default is zero and the bond will not be called.

■ If current interest rates are well below an outstanding bond's coupon rate, then a *callable bond* is likely to be called, and investors should estimate the expected rate of return on the bond as the *yield to call (YTC)* rather than as the yield to maturity. To calculate the YTC, solve this equation for k_d:

$$\text{Price of bond} = \sum_{t=1}^{N} \frac{\text{INT}}{(1 + k_d)^t} + \frac{\text{Call price}}{(1 + k_d)^N}.$$

■ The *current yield* is the annual interest payment divided by the bond's current price. The current yield provides information regarding the amount of cash income that a bond will generate in a given year.

The bond valuation model must be adjusted when interest is paid semiannually:

$$V_B = \sum_{t=1}^{2N} \frac{\text{INT}/2}{(1 + k_d/2)^t} + \frac{M}{(1 + k_d/2)^{2N}}$$

$$= (\text{INT}/2)(\text{PVIFA}_{k_d/2,2N}) + M(\text{PVIF}_{k_d/2,2N}).$$

■ Interest rates fluctuate over time, and people or firms who invest in bonds are exposed to risk from changing interest rates, or *interest rate risk*. The longer the maturity of the bond, the greater the exposure to interest rate risk.

■ The shorter the maturity of the bond, the greater the risk of a decrease in interest rates. The risk of a decline in income due to a drop in interest rates is called *reinvestment rate risk*.

■ Interest rate risk relates to the *value* of the bonds in a portfolio, while reinvestment rate risk relates to the *income* the portfolio produces. No bond can be considered totally riskless. Bond portfolio managers try to balance these two risks, but some risk always exists in any security.

Another important risk associated with bonds is default risk. If the issuer defaults, investors receive less than the promised return on the bond.

■ The greater the default risk, the higher the bond's yield to maturity.

■ Corporations can influence the default risk of their bonds by changing the type of bonds they issue.

- ☐ Under a *mortgage bond*, the corporation pledges certain assets as security for the bond. All such bonds are written subject to an indenture, which is a legal document that spells out in detail the rights of both the bondholders and the corporation.
- ☐ A *debenture* is an unsecured bond, and as such, it provides no lien against specific property as security for the obligation. Debenture holders are, therefore, general creditors whose claims are protected by property not otherwise pledged.
- ☐ *Subordinated debentures* have claims on assets, in the event of bankruptcy, only after senior debt as named in the subordinated debt's indenture has been paid off. Subordinated debentures may be subordinated to designated notes payable or to all other debt.

- ■ Bond issues are normally assigned quality ratings by major rating agencies, such as Moody's Investors Service and Standard & Poor's Corporation. These ratings reflect the probability that a bond will go into default. Aaa (Moody's) and AAA (S&P) are the highest ratings.
  - ☐ Rating assignments are based on qualitative and quantitative factors including the firm's debt/assets ratio, current ratio, and coverage ratios.
  - ☐ Bond ratings are important both to firms and to investors.
  - ☐ Because a bond's rating is an indicator of its default risk, the rating has a direct, measurable influence on the bond's interest rate and the firm's cost of debt capital.
  - ☐ Most bonds are purchased by institutional investors rather than individuals, and many institutions are restricted to investment-grade securities.
  - ☐ Rating agencies review outstanding bonds on a periodic basis, occasionally upgrading or downgrading a bond as the issuer's circumstances change. Also, if a company issues more bonds, this will trigger a review by the rating agencies.

- ■ The *junk bond* is a high-risk, high-yield bond issued to finance a leveraged buyout, a merger, or a troubled company.
  - ☐ The emergence of junk bonds as an important type of debt is another example of how the investment banking industry adjusts to and facilitates new developments in capital markets.

- ■ In the event of bankruptcy, debtholders have a prior claim over the claims of both common and preferred stockholders to a firm's income and assets.
  - ☐ When a business becomes insolvent, it does not have enough cash to meet scheduled interest and principal payments. Thus, it must decide whether to dissolve the firm through liquidation or to permit it to reorganize and thus stay alive. These issues are discussed in Chapters 7 and 11 of the federal bankruptcy statutes.
  - ☐ In a reorganization, a plan may call for restructuring of the firm's debt, in which case the interest rate may be reduced, the term to maturity lengthened, or some of the debt may be exchanged for equity.
  - ☐ Liquidation occurs if the company is deemed to be too far gone to be saved. Upon liquidation, assets are distributed as specified in Chapter 7 of the Bankruptcy Act,

beginning with highest priority to secured creditors and ending with lowest priority to common stockholders (assuming anything is left).
☐ Appendix 7B discusses bankruptcy and reorganization in more detail.

Bonds are traded primarily in the over-the-counter market. Most bonds are owned by and traded among the large financial institutions, and it is relatively easy for the over-the-counter bond dealers to arrange the transfer of large blocks of bonds among the relatively few holders of the bonds.

■ Information on bond trades in the over-the-counter market is not published, but a representative group of bonds is listed and traded on the bond division of the NYSE.

SELF-TEST QUESTIONS

Definitional

1. A(n) _bond_ is a long-term promissory note issued by a business firm or governmental unit.

2. _Municipal_ bonds are issued by state and local governments, and the _interest_ earned on these bonds is exempt from federal taxes.

3. The stated face value of a bond is referred to as its _par_ value and is usually set at $_1,000_.

4. The "coupon interest rate" on a bond is determined by dividing the _coupon_ _payment_ by the _par value_ of the bond.

5. The date at which the par value of a bond is repaid to each bondholder is known as the _maturity date_.

6. A(n) _floating rate_ bond is one whose interest rate fluctuates with shifts in the general level of interest rates.

7. A(n) _zero coupon_ bond is one that pays no annual interest but is sold at a discount below par, thus providing compensation to investors in the form of capital appreciation.

8. The legal document setting forth the terms and conditions of a bond issue is known as the _indenture_.

9. In meeting its sinking fund requirements, a firm may _call_ the bonds or purchase them on the _open_ _market_ .

10. Except when the call is for sinking fund purposes, when a bond issue is called, the firm must pay a(n)_call premium_, or an amount in excess of the _par_ value of the bond.

11. A bond with annual coupon payments represents an annuity of INT dollars per year for N years, plus a lump sum of M dollars at the end of N years, and its value, V_B, is the _present_ _value_ of this payment stream.

12. At the time a bond is issued, the coupon interest rate is generally set at a level that will cause the _market_ _price_ and the _par_ _value_ of the bond to be approximately equal.

13. Market interest rates and bond prices move in _opposite_ directions from one another.

14. The rate of interest earned by purchasing a bond and holding it until maturity is known as the bond's _yield_ _to_ _maturity_ .

15. To adjust the bond valuation formula for semiannual coupon payments, the _coupon_ _payment_ and _interest_ _rate_ must be divided by 2, and the number of _years_ must be multiplied by 2.

16. A bond secured by real estate is known as a(n) _mortgage_ bond.

Conceptual

17. Changes in economic conditions cause interest rates and bond prices to vary over time.

    a. True   b. False

18. If the appropriate rate of interest on a bond is greater than its coupon rate, the market value of that bond will be above par value.

    a. True   b. False

19. A 20-year, annual coupon bond with one year left to maturity has the same interest rate risk as a 10-year, annual coupon bond with one year left to maturity. Both bonds are of equal risk, have the same coupon rate, and the prices of the two bonds are equal.

    a. True   b. False

20. There is a direct relationship between bond ratings and the required rate of return of bonds; that is, the higher the rating, the higher is the required rate of return.

    a. True   **b.** False

21. The "penalty" for having a low bond rating is less severe when the Security Market Line is relatively steep than when it is not so steep.

    a. True   **b.** False

22. Which of the following statements is *false*? In all of the statements, assume that "other things are held constant."

    a. Price sensitivity—that is, the change in price due to a given change in the required rate of return—increases as a bond's maturity increases.
    b. For a given bond of any maturity, a given percentage point increase in the going interest rate (k_d) causes a *larger* dollar capital loss than the capital gain stemming from an identical decrease in the interest rate.
    c. For any given maturity, a given percentage point increase in the interest rate causes a *smaller* dollar capital loss than the capital gain stemming from an identical decrease in the interest rate.
    d. From a borrower's point of view, interest paid on bonds is tax deductible.
    e. A 20-year zero-coupon bond has less reinvestment rate risk than a 20-year coupon bond.

23. Which of the following statements is most *correct*?

    a. Ignoring interest accrued between payment dates, if the required rate of return on a bond is less than its coupon interest rate, and k_d remains below the coupon rate until maturity, then the market value of that bond will be below its par value until the bond matures, at which time its market value will equal its par value.
    b. Assuming equal coupon rates, a 20-year original maturity bond with one year left to maturity has more interest rate risk than a 10-year original maturity bond with one year left to maturity.
    c. Regardless of the size of the coupon payment, the price of a bond moves in the same direction as interest rates; for example, if interest rates rise, bond prices also rise.
    d. For bonds, price sensitivity to a given change in interest rates generally increases as years remaining to maturity increases.
    e. Because short-term interest rates are much more volatile than long-term rates, you would, in the real world, be subject to more interest rate risk if you purchased a 30-*day* bond than if you bought a 30-*year* bond.

24. Which of the following statements is most *correct?*

   a. Bonds C and Z both have a $1,000 par value and 10 years to maturity. They have the same risk of default, and they both have an effective annual rate of EAR = 8%. If Bond C has a 15 percent annual coupon and Bond Z a zero coupon (paying just $1,000 at maturity), then Bond Z will be exposed to more *interest rate risk,* which is defined as the *percentage* loss of value in response to a given increase in the going interest rate.
   b. If the words "interest rate risk" were replaced by the words "reinvestment rate risk" in Statement a, then the statement would be true.
   c. The interest rate paid by the state of Florida on its debt would be lower, other things held constant, if interest on the debt was not exempt from federal income taxes.
   d. Given the conditions in Statement a, we can be sure that Bond Z would have the higher price.
   e. Statements a, b, c, and d are all false.

25. If a company's bonds are selling at a *discount*, then:

   a. The YTM is the return investors probably expect to earn.
   b. The YTC is probably the expected return.
   c. Either a or b could be correct, depending on the yield curve.
   d. The current yield will exceed the expected rate of return.
   e. The after-tax cost of debt to the company will have to be less than the coupon rate on the bonds.

SELF-TEST PROBLEMS

1. Delta Corporation has a bond issue outstanding with an annual coupon rate of 7 percent and 4 years remaining until maturity. The par value of the bond is $1,000. Determine the current value of the bond if present market conditions justify a 14 percent required rate of return. The bond pays interest annually.

   a. $1,126.42   b. $1,000.00   c. $796.06   d. $791.00   e. $536.42

2. Refer to Self-Test Problem 1. Suppose the bond had a semiannual coupon. Now what would be its current value?

   a. $1,126.42   b. $1,000.00   c. $796.06   d. $791.00   e. $536.42

3. Refer to Self-Test Problem 1. Assume an annual coupon but 20 years remaining to maturity. What is the current value under these conditions?

   a. $1,126.42   **b.** $1,000.00   **c.** $796.06   **d.** $791.00   **e.** $536.42

4. Acme Products has a bond issue outstanding with 8 years remaining to maturity, a coupon rate of 10 percent with interest paid annually, and a par value of $1,000. If the current market price of the bond issue is $814.45, what is the yield to maturity, k_d?

   a. 12%   **b.** 13%   **c.** 14%   **d.** 15%   **e.** 16%

5. You have just been offered a bond for $863.73. The coupon rate is 8 percent, payable annually, and interest rates on new issues with the same degree of risk are 10 percent. You want to know how many more interest payments you will receive, but the party selling the bond cannot remember. If the par value is $1,000, how many interest payments remain?

   a. 10   **b.** 11   **c.** 12   **d.** 13   **e.** 14

6. Bird Corporation's 12 percent coupon rate, semiannual payment, $1,000 par value bonds which mature in 20 years are callable at a price of $1,100 five years from now. The bonds sell at a price of $1,300, and the yield curve is flat. Assuming that interest rates in the economy are expected to remain at their current level, what is the best estimate of Bird's *nominal interest rate* on the new bonds? (Hint: You will need a financial calculator to work this problem.)

   a. 8.46%   **b.** 6.16%   **c.** 9.28%   **d.** 6.58%   **e.** 8.76%

7. The Graf Company needs to finance some new R&D programs, so it will sell new bonds for this purpose. Graf's currently outstanding bonds have a $1,000 par value, a 10 percent coupon rate, and pay interest semiannually. The outstanding bonds have 25 years remaining to maturity, are callable after 5 years at a price of $1,090, and currently sell at a price of $700. The yield curve is expected to remain flat. On the basis of these data, what is the best estimate of Graf's *nominal interest rate* on the new bonds it plans to sell? (Hint: You will need a financial calculator to work this problem.)

   a. 21.10%   **b.** 14.48%   **c.** 15.67%   **d.** 16.25%   **e.** 18.29%

8. Suppose Hadden Inc. is negotiating with an insurance company to sell a bond issue. Each bond has a par value of $1,000, it would pay 10 percent per year in quarterly payments of $25 per quarter for 10 years, and then it would pay 12 percent per year ($30 per quarter) for the next 10 years (Years 11-20). The $1,000 principal would be returned at the end of

20 years. The insurance company's alternative investment is in a 20-year mortgage which has a nominal rate of 14 percent and which provides monthly payments. If the mortgage and the bond issue are equally risky, how much should the insurance company be willing to pay Hadden for each bond? (Hint: You will need a financial calculator to work this problem.)

    a. $750.78   **b.** $781.50   **c.** $804.65   **d.** $710.49   **e.** $840.97

Appendix 7A

A-1. J.C. Nickel is planning a zero coupon bond issue. The bond has a par value of $1,000, matures in 10 years, and will be sold at an 80 percent discount, or for $200. The firm's marginal federal-plus-state tax rate is 40 percent. What is the annual after-tax cost of debt to Nickel on this issue? (Hint: You will need to use a financial calculator.)

    a. 10.48%   **b.** 10.00%   **c.** 11.62%   **d.** 14.79%   **e.** 17.46%

A-2. Assume that the city of Miami sold an issue of $1,000 maturity value, tax exempt (muni), zero coupon bonds 10 years ago. The bonds had a 30-year maturity when they were issued, and the interest rate built into the issue was a nominal 12 percent, but with semiannual compounding. The bonds are now callable at a premium of 12 percent over the accrued value. What effective annual rate of return would an investor who bought the bonds when they were issued and who still owns them earn if they are called today? (Hint: You will need to use a financial calculator.)

    a. 13.33%   **b.** 12.00%   **c.** 12.37%   **d.** 11.76%   **e.** 13.64%

Appendix 7B

B-1. The Stanton Marble Company has the following balance sheet:

Current assets	$15,120	Accounts payable	$ 3,240
		Notes payable (to bank)	1,620
		Accrued taxes	540
		Accrued wages	540
		Total current liabilities	$ 5,940
Fixed assets	8,100	First mortgage bonds	2,700
		Second mortgage bonds	2,700
		Total mortgage bonds	$ 5,400
		Subordinated debentures	3,240
		Total debt	$14,580
		Preferred stock	1,080
		Common stock	7,560
Total assets	$23,220	Total liabilities and equity	$23,220

The debentures are subordinated only to the notes payable. Suppose Stanton Marble goes bankrupt and is liquidated with $5,400 being received from the sale of the fixed assets, which were pledged as security for the first and second mortgage bonds, and $8,640 received from the sale of current assets. The trustee's costs total $1,440. How much will the holders of subordinated debentures receive?

    a. $2,052   **b.** $2,448   **c.** $3,240   **d.** $2,709   **e.** $3,056

ANSWERS TO SELF-TEST QUESTIONS

1. bond
2. Municipal; interest
3. par; 1,000
4. coupon payment; par value
5. maturity date
6. floating rate
7. zero coupon
8. indenture

9. call; open market
10. call premium; par
11. present value
12. market price; par value
13. opposite
14. yield to maturity
15. coupon payment; interest rate; years
16. mortgage

17. a. For example, if inflation increases, the interest rate (or required return) will increase, resulting in a decline in bond price.

18. b. It will sell at a discount.

19. a. Both bonds are valued as 1-year bonds regardless of their original issue dates, and since they are of equal risk and have the same coupon rate, their prices must be equal.

20. b. The relationship is inverse. The higher the rating, the lower is the default risk and hence the lower is the required rate of return. Aaa/AAA is the highest rating, and as we go down the alphabet, the ratings are lower.

21. b. A steeper SML implies a higher risk premium on risky securities and thus a greater "penalty" on lower-rated bonds.

22. b. Statements a, d, and e are all true. To determine which of the remaining statements is false, it is best to use an example. Assume you have a 10-year, 10 percent annual coupon bond which sold at par. If interest rates increase to 13 percent, the value of the bond decreases to $837.21, while if interest rates decrease to 7 percent, the value of the bond increases to $1,210.71. Thus, the capital gain is greater than the capital loss and statement b is false.

23. d. Statement a is false because the bond would have a premium and thus sell above par value. Statement b is false because both bonds would have the same interest rate risk because they both have one year left to maturity. Statement c is false because the price of a bond moves in the opposite direction as interest rates. Statement e is false because the 30-year bond would have more interest rate risk than the 30-day bond. Statement d is correct. As years to maturity increases for a bond, the number of discount periods used in finding the current bond value also increases. Therefore, bonds with longer maturities will have more price sensitivity to a given change in interest rates.

24. a. Statement a is correct. Bond C has a high coupon (hence its name), so bondholders get cash flows right away. Bond Z has a zero coupon, so its holders will get no cash flows until the bond matures. Since all of the cash flows on Z come at the end, a given increase in the interest rate will cause this bond's value to fall sharply relative to the decline in value of the zero coupon bond.

You could also use the data in the problem to find the value of the two bonds at two different interest rates, and then calculate the percentage change. For example, at $k_d = 15\%$, $V_C = \$1,000$ and $V_Z = \$247.18$. At $k_d = 20\%$, $V_C = \$790.38$ and $V_Z = \$161.51$. Therefore, Bond Z declines in value by 34.66%, while Bond C declines by only 20.96 percent. Note that Bond Z is exposed to *less* reinvestment rate risk than Bond C.

25. a. When bonds sell at a discount, the going interest rate (k_d) is above the coupon rate. If a company called the old discount bonds and replaced them with new bonds, the new coupon would be above the old coupon. This would increase a firm's interest cost, hence the company would not call the discount bonds. Therefore, the YTM would be the expected rate of return. The shape of the yield curve would have no effect in the situation described in this question, but if the bonds had been selling at a premium, making the YTC the relevant yield, then the yield curve in a sense would have an effect. The YTC would be below the cost if the company were to sell new long-term bonds, if the yield curve were steeply upward sloping. Statement d is false because the expected rate of return would include a current yield component and a capital gains component (because the bond's price will rise from its current discounted price to par as maturity approaches). Therefore, the current yield will *not* exceed the expected rate of return. The after-tax cost of debt is the expected rate adjusted for taxes, $k_d(1 - T)$. Because the bonds are selling at a discount, the coupon rate could be quite low, even zero, so we know that statement e is false. Therefore, statement a is correct.

SOLUTIONS TO SELF-TEST PROBLEMS

1. c. $V_B = INT(PVIFA_{k_d,N}) + M(PVIF_{k_d,N})$
       $= \$70(PVIFA_{14\%,4}) + \$1,000(PVIF_{14\%,4})$
       $= \$70(2.9137) + \$1,000(0.5921) = \$796.06.$

   Calculator solution: Input N = 4, I = 14, PMT = 70, FV = 1000, and solve for PV = -$796.04.

2. d. $V_B = (INT/2)(PVIFA_{k_d/2,2N}) + M(PVIF_{k_d/2,2N})$
       $= \$35(PVIFA_{7\%,8}) + \$1,000(PVIF_{7\%,8})$
       $= \$35(5.9713) + \$1,000(0.5820) = \$791.00.$

   Calculator solution: Input N = 8, I = 7, PMT = 35, FV = 1000, and solve for PV= -$791.00.

3. e. $V_B = INT(PVIFA_{k_d,N}) + M(PVIF_{k_d,N})$
       $= \$70(PVIFA_{14\%,20}) + \$1,000(PVIF_{14\%,20})$
       $= \$70(6.6231) + \$1,000(0.0728) = \$536.42.$

   Calculator solution: Input N = 20, I = 14, PMT = 70, FV = 1000, and solve for PV= -$536.38.

4. c. $$V_B = INT(PVIFA_{k_d,N}) + M(PVIF_{k_d,N})$$
    $$\$814.45 = \$100(PVIFA_{k_d,8}) + \$1,000(PVIF_{k_d,8}).$$

    Now use trial and error techniques. Try $I = k_d = 12\%$:
    $\$814.45 = \$100(4.9676) + \$1,000(0.4039) = \$900.66.$

    Since $\$814.45 \neq \$900.66$, the yield to maturity is not 12 percent. The calculated value is too large. Therefore, increase the value of I to 14 percent to lower the calculated value: $\$814.45 = \$100(4.6389) + \$1,000(0.3506) = \$814.49$. This is close enough to conclude that k_d = yield to maturity = 14%.

    Calculator solution: Input $N = 8$, $PV = -814.45$, $PMT = 100$, $FV = 1000$, and solve for $I = k_d = 14.00\%$.

5. c. $$V_B = INT(PVIFA_{k_d,N}) + M(PVIF_{k_d,N})$$
    $$\$863.73 = \$80(PVIFA_{10\%,N}) + \$1,000(PVIF_{10\%,N})$$

    Now use trial and error to find the value of N for which the equality holds. For $N = 12$, $\$80(6.8137) + \$1,000(0.3186) = \$863.70$. Or using a financial calculator, input $I = 10$, $PV = -863.73$, $PMT = 80$, $FV = 1000$, and solve for $N = 12$.

6. d. The bond is selling at a large premium, which means that its coupon rate is much higher than the going rate of interest. Therefore, the bond is likely to be called—it is more likely to be called than to remain outstanding until it matures. Thus, it will probably provide a return equal to the YTC rather than the YTM. So, there is no point in calculating the YTM; just calculate the YTC. Enter these values: $N = 10$, $PV = -1300$, $PMT = 60$, and $FV = 1100$. The periodic rate is 3.29 percent, so the nominal YTC is $2(3.29\%) = 6.58\%$. This would be close to the going rate, and it is about what Bird would have to pay on new bonds.

7. b. Investors would expect to earn either the YTM or the YTC, and the expected return on the old bonds is the cost Graf would have to pay in order to sell new bonds.

    YTM: Enter $N = 2(25) = 50$; $PV = -700$; $PMT = 100/2 = 50$; and $FV = 1000$. Press I to get $I = k_d/2 = 7.24\%$. Multiply $7.24\%(2) = 14.48\%$ to get the YTM.

    YTC: Enter $N = 2(5) = 10$, $PV = -700$, $PMT = 50$, $FV = 1090$, and then press I to get $I = 10.55\%$. Multiply by 2 to get YTC = 21.10%.

    Would investors expect the company to call the bonds? Graf currently pays 10 percent on its debt (the coupon rate). New debt would cost at least 14.48 percent. Because k_d

> 10% coupon rate, it would be stupid for the company to call, so investors would not expect a call. Therefore, they would expect to earn 14.48 percent on the bonds. This is k_d, so 14.48 percent is the rate Graf would probably have to pay on new bonds.

8. a. Time line:

```
                         10                         20  Years
        0   1   2        40   41   42               80  Quarters
        ├───┼───┼──...───┼────┼────┼──────...──────┤
           25   25       25   30   30                   30
                                                      1,000
                                                      1,030
```

1. You could enter the time line values into the cash flow register, but one element is missing: the interest rate. Once we have the interest rate, we could press the NPV key to get the value of the bond.

2. We need a *periodic* interest rate, and it needs to be a quarterly rate, found as the annual nominal rate divided by 4: $k_{PER} = k_{NOM}/4$. So, we need to find k_{NOM} so that we can find k_{PER}.

3. The insurance company will insist on earning at least the same effective annual rate on the bond issue as it can earn on the mortgage. The mortgage pays 14 percent monthly, which is equivalent to an EAR = 14.93%. Using a financial calculator, enter NOM% = 14, P/YR = 12, and press EFF% to obtain 14.93%. So, the bond issue will have to have a k_{NOM}, with quarterly payments, which translates into an EAR of 14.93 percent.

4. EAR = 14.93% is equivalent to a quarterly nominal rate of 14.16 percent; that is, a nominal rate of 14.16 percent with quarterly compounding has an EAR of 14.93 percent. You can find this by entering EFF% = 14.93, P/YR = 4, and pressing the NOM% key to get NOM% = 14.16%. If this nominal rate is set on the bond issue, the insurance company will earn the same effective rate as it can get on the mortgage.

5. The periodic rate for a 14.16 percent nominal rate, with quarterly compounding, is 14.16%/4 = 3.54%. This 3.54% is the rate to use in the time line calculations.

With an HP 10B calculator, enter the following data:
CF$_0$ = 0, CF$_j$ = 25; N$_j$ = 40; CF$_j$ = 30; N$_j$ = 39; CF$_j$ = 1030; I = 3.54.
Solve for NPV = $750.78 = Value of each bond.

With an HP 17B calculator, enter the following data:
Flow(0) = 0 Input; Flow(1) = 25 Input; # Times = 40 Input; Flow(2) = 30 Input; # Times = 39 Input; Flow(3) = 1030 Input; # Times = 1 Input;
Exit, Calc; I = 3.54; NPV = $750.78 = Value of each bond.

If each bond is priced at $750.78, the insurance company will earn the same effective rate of return as on the mortgage.

Appendix 7A

A-1. a. Maturity = N = 10; Issue price = PV = 200; PMT = 0; Maturity value = FV = 1000; Corporate tax rate = 40%.

Enter into a financial calculator: N = 10, PV = -200, PMT = 0, and FV = 1000, and then solve for k_d = I = 17.46%. However, this is a before-tax cost of debt. $k_d(1 - T)$ = 17.46%(1 − 0.4) = 10.48%.

Alternatively, set the analysis up on a time line:

	0	1	2	3	4	5	6	7	8	9	10
Year-end accrued value[1]	200	234.92	275.94	324.12	380.71	447.18	525.25	616.96	724.69	851.22	1,000.00
Interest deduction[2]		34.92	41.02	48.18	56.59	66.47	78.07	91.71	107.73	126.53	148.78
Tax savings (40%)[3]		13.97	16.41	19.27	22.64	26.59	31.23	36.68	43.09	50.61	59.51
Cash flow[4]	200	13.97	16.41	19.27	22.64	26.59	31.23	36.68	43.09	50.61	-940.49

After-tax cost of debt: 10.48%.

Notes:

[1]Year-end accrued value = Issue price × $(1 + k_d)^n$.
[2]Interest in Year n = Accrued value$_n$ − Accrued value$_{n-1}$.
[3]Tax savings = (Interest deduction)(T).
[4]Cash flow in Year 10 = Tax savings − Maturity value.

A-2. e.

```
        0                          20              60
        |----6%------------------+--------------+
      -30.3143

                    × (1.06)²⁰ =   97.2222
                                  ×  1.12
                                  108.8889

                  IRR=6.6024
      -30.3143 ————————————————————|
```

Periodic rate = 6.6024%.

EAR $= (1.066024)^2 - 1 = 0.1364 = 13.64\%$.

The solution to this problem requires three steps:

(1) Solve for the PV of the original issue. Using a financial calculator, enter N = 60, I = 6, PMT = 0, and FV = 1000, and then solve for PV = $30.3143.

(2) Determine the accrued value at the end of 20 periods, and multiply by the call premium.

$$\$30.3143 \times (1.06)^{20} \times 1.12 = \$108.8889.$$

(3) Solve for the EAR to an investor if the bonds are called today. Using a financial calculator, enter N = 20, PV = -30.3143, PMT = 0, and FV = 108.8889, and then solve for $k_d/2 = I = 6.6024$.

$$EAR = (1.066024)^2 - 1 = 0.1364 = 13.64\%.$$

Appendix 7B

B-1.   a.

Claimant	Claim Amount (1)	Priority Distribution and General Creditor (2)	Subordinate Adjustment (3)	Percent of Claim (4)
Accounts payable	$ 3,240	$ 2,448	$ 2,448	75.56%
Notes payable	1,620	1,224	1,620	100.00
Accrued taxes	540	540	540	100.00
Accrued wages	540	540	540	100.00
1st mortgage bonds	2,700	2,700	2,700	100.00
2nd mortgage bonds	2,700	2,700	2,700	100.00
Subordinated debentures	3,240	2,448	2,052	63.33
Preferred stock	1,080	0	0	0.00
Common stock	7,560	0	0	0.00
Trustee	1,440	1,440	1,440	100.00
Total	$24,660	$14,040	$14,040	56.93%

Explanation of the columns:
(1) Values are taken from the balance sheet.

(2) Since the firm's total debt is $16,020 and only $14,040 is received from the sale of assets, the preferred and common stockholders are wiped out. These stockholders receive nothing.

The $5,400 from the sale of fixed assets is immediately allocated to the mortgage bonds. The holders of the first mortgage bonds are paid off first, so they receive $2,700. The remaining $2,700 from the sale of fixed assets is allocated to the second mortgage bonds, so these bondholders are also paid off.

By law, trustee expenses have first claim on the remaining available funds, wages have second priority, and taxes have third priority. Thus, these claims are paid in full.

We now have $6,120 remaining and claims of $8,100, so the general creditors will receive 75.56 cents on the dollar:

$$\frac{\text{Funds available}}{\text{Unsatisfied debt}} = \frac{\$14,040 - \$5,400 - \$1,080 - \$1,440}{\$3,240 + \$1,620 + \$3,240} = 0.7556.$$

General creditors are now initially allocated 75.56 percent of their original claims.

(3) This column reflects a transfer of funds from the subordinated debentures to the notes payable to the bank. Since subordinated debentures are subordinate to bank debt, notes payable to the bank must be paid in full before the debentures receive anything. The notes are paid in full by transferring the difference between their book value and initial allocation ($1,620 − $1,224 = $396) from subordinated debentures to notes payable. This reduces the allocation to subordinated debentures and increases the allocation to notes payable by $396.

CHAPTER 8
STOCKS AND THEIR VALUATION

OVERVIEW

Common stock constitutes the ownership position in a firm. As owners, common stockholders have certain rights and privileges, including the right to control the firm through election of directors and the right to the residual earnings of the firm.

Firms generally begin their corporate life as closely held companies, with all the common stock held by the founding managers. Then, as the company grows, it is often necessary to sell stock to the general public (that is, go public) to raise more funds. Eventually, the firm may choose to list its stock on one of the organized exchanges.

A common stock is valued as the present value of its expected future dividend stream. The total rate of return on a stock is comprised of a dividend yield plus a capital gains yield. If a stock is in equilibrium, its total expected return must equal the average investor's required rate of return.

Preferred stock is a hybrid--it is similar to bonds in some respects and to common stock in others. The value of a share of preferred stock which is expected to pay a constant dividend forever is found as the dividend divided by the discount rate.

OUTLINE

The corporation's common stockholders are the owners of the corporation, and as such, they have certain rights and privileges.

■ Common stockholders have control of the firm through their election of the firm's directors, who in turn select officers to manage the business.

  □ In a large, publicly owned firm, neither the managers nor any individual shareholders normally have the 51 percent necessary for absolute control of the company.

  □ Thus, stockholders must vote for directors, and the voting process is regulated by both state and federal laws.

  □ Stockholders who are unable to attend annual meetings may still vote by means of a *proxy*. Proxies can be solicited by any party seeking to control the firm.

■ The *preemptive right* gives the current shareholders the right to purchase any new shares issued in proportion to their current holdings.
  □ The preemptive right may or may not be required by state law.
  □ When granted, the preemptive right enables current owners to maintain their proportionate share of ownership and control of the business.
  □ It also prevents the sale of shares at low prices to new stockholders which would dilute the value of the previously issued shares.

Special classes of common stock are sometimes created by a firm to meet special needs and circumstances. If two classes of stock are desired, one would normally be called "Class A" and the other "Class B."

■ Class A might be entitled to receive dividends before dividends can be paid on Class B stock.

■ Class B might have the exclusive right to vote.
  □ Note that Class A and Class B have no standard meanings.

■ *Founders' shares* are stock owned by the firm's founders that have sole voting rights but restricted dividends for a specified number of years.

Stock financing has both advantages and disadvantages which can be examined from the viewpoint of the corporation as well as from a social perspective.

■ Financing with common stock has the following advantages to the corporation:
  □ Common stock does not obligate the firm to make fixed payments to stockholders.
  □ Common stock carries no fixed maturity date.
  □ Common stock increases the creditworthiness of the firm, thus increasing the future availability of debt at a lower cost.
  □ Common stock can often be sold more easily than debt if the firm's prospects look potentially good but risky.
  □ Financing with common stock serves as a *reserve of borrowing capacity*.

■ Financing with common stock has the following disadvantages to the corporation:
  □ Issuing common stock extends voting rights, and perhaps even control, to new stockholders.
  □ Common stock gives new stockholders the right to a percentage of profits rather than to a fixed payment in the case of creditors.
  □ The cost of underwriting and distributing common stock is high.

□ If common stock is sold to the point where the equity ratio exceeds that in the optimal capital structure, a firm's average cost of capital will increase, and its stock price will not be maximized.

□ Dividends paid to stockholders are not tax deductible as is interest paid to creditors.

■ From a social viewpoint, common stock is a desirable form of financing because it makes businesses less vulnerable to the consequences of declines in sales and earnings.

Some companies are so small that their common stocks are not actively traded; they are owned by only a few people, usually the companies' managers. Such firms are said to be closely held corporations. In contrast, the stocks of most larger companies are owned by a large number of investors, most of whom are not active in management. Such companies are said to be publicly held corporations.

■ Stock market transactions may be separated into three distinct categories.

□ The *secondary market* deals with trading in previously issued, or outstanding, shares of established, publicly owned companies. The company receives no new money when sales are made in the secondary market.

□ The *primary market* handles additional shares sold by established, publicly owned companies. Companies can raise additional capital by selling in this market.

□ The primary market also handles new public offerings of shares in firms that were formerly closely held. Capital for the firm can be raised by *going public*, and this market is often termed the *initial public offering (IPO) market*.

Common stocks are valued by finding the present value of the expected future cash flow stream.

■ People typically buy common stock expecting to earn *dividends* plus a *capital gain* when they sell their shares at the end of some holding period. The capital gain may or may not be realized, but most people expect a gain or else they would not buy stocks.

■ The expected dividend yield on a stock during the coming year is equal to the expected dividend, D_1, divided by the current stock price, P_0. $(\hat{P}_1 - P_0)/P_0$ is the expected capital gains yield. The expected dividend yield plus the expected capital gains yield equals the expected total return.

■ The value of the stock today is calculated as the present value of an infinite stream of dividends. For any investor, cash flows consist of dividends plus the expected future sales price of the stock. This sales price, however, depends on dividends expected by future investors:

Here k_s is the discount rate used to find the present value of the dividends.

Value of stock $= \hat{P}_0 =$ PV of expected dividends

$$= \frac{D_1}{(1 + k_s)^1} + \frac{D_2}{(1 + k_s)^2} + \cdots + \frac{D_\infty}{(1 + k_s)^\infty}$$

$$= \sum_{t=1}^{\infty} \frac{D_t}{(1 + k_s)^t}.$$

■ Dividends are not expected to remain constant in the future, and dividends are harder to predict than bond interest payments. Thus, stock valuation is a more complex task than bond valuation.

■ If expected dividend growth is zero (g = 0), the value of the stock is found as follows: $\hat{P}_0 = D/k_s$. Since a zero growth stock is expected to pay a constant dividend, it can be thought of as a *perpetuity*. The expected rate of return is simply the dividend yield: $\hat{k}_s = D/P_0$.

■ For many companies, earnings and dividends are expected to grow at some normal, or constant, rate. Dividends in any future Year t may be forecasted as $D_t = D_0(1 + g)^t$, where D_0 is the last dividend paid and g is the expected growth rate. For a company which last paid a \$2.00 dividend and which has an expected 6 percent constant growth rate, the estimated dividend one year from now would be D_1 = \$2.00(1.06) = \$2.12; D_2 would be $2.00(1.06)^2$ = \$2.25, and the estimated dividend 4 years hence would be $D_t = D_0(1 + g)^t$ = $2.00(1.06)^4$ = \$2.525. Using this method of estimating future dividends, the current price, P_0, is determined as follows:

$$\hat{P}_0 = \frac{D_0(1 + g)}{k_s - g} = \frac{D_1}{k_s - g}.$$

This equation for valuing a constant growth stock is often called the Gordon Model, after Myron J. Gordon, who developed it.

■ For all stocks, the total expected return is composed of an expected dividend yield plus an expected capital gains yield. For a constant growth stock, the formula for the total expected return can be written as:

$$\hat{k}_s = \frac{D_1}{P_0} + g.$$

■ Firms typically go through periods of nonconstant growth, after which time their growth rate settles to a rate close to that of the economy as a whole. The value of such a firm is equal to the present value of its expected future dividends. To find the value of such a stock, we proceed in three steps:

☐ Find the present value of the dividends during the period of nonconstant growth.

☐ Find the price of the stock at the end of the nonconstant growth period, at which point it has become a constant growth stock, and discount this price back to the present.

☐ Add these two components to find the present value of the stock.

The relationship between a stock's required and expected rates of return determines the equilibrium price level where buying and selling pressures will just offset each other.

■ If the expected rate of return is less than the required rate, investors will desire to sell the stock; there will also be a tendency for the price to decline.

■ When the expected rate of return is greater than the required rate, investors will try to purchase shares of the stock; this will drive the price upward.

■ Only at the equilibrium price, where the expected and required rates are equal, will the stock be stable.

■ Equilibrium will generally exist for a given stock because security prices adjust rapidly to new developments.

■ Changes in the equilibrium price can be brought about (1) by a change in risk aversion, (2) by a change in the risk-free rate, (3) by a change in the stock's beta coefficient, or (4) by a change in the stock's expected growth rate.

■ The *Efficient Markets Hypothesis (EMH)* hypothesizes that stocks are always in equilibrium and that it is impossible for an investor to consistently "beat the market."

☐ The *weak-form* of the EMH states that all information contained in past price movements is fully reflected in current market prices.

☐ The *semistrong-form* of the EMH states that current market prices reflect all *publicly available* information. If this is true, no abnormal returns can be gained by analyzing stocks. Another implication of semistrong-form efficiency is that whenever information is released to the public, stock prices will respond only if the information is different from what had been expected.

☐ The *strong-form* of the EMH states that current market prices reflect all pertinent information, whether publicly available or privately held (inside information). If this form holds, even insiders would find it impossible to earn abnormal returns in the stock market.

■ EMH means that stocks in general are neither overvalued nor undervalued--they are fairly priced and in equilibrium.

Anyone who has ever invested in the stock market knows that there can be, and generally are, large differences between expected and realized prices and returns.

■ Investors always expect positive returns from stock investments or else they would not buy them. However, in some years negative returns are actually earned.

■ Even in bad years, some individual stocks do well, and the "name of the game" in security analysis is to pick the winners. Financial managers are trying to take those actions that will help put their companies in the winner's column.

Preferred stock is a hybrid——it is similar to bonds in some respects and to common stock in other respects.

■ Preferred dividends are similar to interest payments on bonds in that they are fixed in amount and generally must be paid before common stock dividends can be paid.

■ Preferred stock has the following important features:
  □ Preferred stockholders have priority over common stockholders with regard to earnings and assets.
  □ Unlike common stock, preferred stock always has a par value.
  □ Most preferred stock provides for *cumulative dividends*; that is, all preferred dividends in arrears must be paid before common dividends can be paid.
  □ Some preferred stock is *convertible* into common stock.
  □ Other provisions such as voting rights and participating stock are encountered sometimes with preferred stock.

■ There are advantages and disadvantages to financing with preferred stock:
  □ Preferred stock is a fixed cost form of financing, yet the firm avoids the danger of bankruptcy if earnings are too low to pay the preferred dividend. Preferred also allows a firm to avoid sharing control, as it must do when selling common stock.
  □ Although advantageous to a firm, preferred stock does have a higher after-tax cost of capital than debt, mainly because preferred dividends are not tax deductible.
  □ For the investor, preferred stock provides reasonably assured income. Also, for corporate investors, 70 percent of preferred dividends received are not taxable.
  □ The disadvantages to the investors are (a) that returns are limited on preferred stock even though a substantial portion of ownership risk is borne by the preferred stockholders and (b) that there are no legal rights to dividends even if a company earns a profit.

Most preferred stocks entitle their owners to regular fixed dividend payments. If the payments last forever, the issue is a perpetuity whose value, V_{ps}, is found as follows:

$$V_{ps} = \frac{D_{ps}}{k_{ps}}.$$

Here D_{ps} is the dividend to be received in each year and k_{ps} is the required rate of return on the preferred stock.

SELF-TEST QUESTIONS

Definitional

1. One of the fundamental rights of common stockholders is to elect a firm's _____, who in turn select the firm's operating management.

2. If a stockholder cannot vote in person, participation in the annual meeting is still possible through a(n) _____.

3. The preemptive right protects stockholders against loss of _____ of the corporation as well as _____ of market value from the sale of new shares below market value.

4. Firms may find it desirable to separate the common stock into different _____. Generally, this classification is designed to differentiate stock in terms of the right to receive _____ and the right to _____.

5. A(n) _____ _____ or _____ _____ corporation is one whose stock is held by a small group, normally its management.

6. The trading of previously issued shares of a corporation takes place in the _____ market, while new issues are offered in the _____ market.

7. _____ _____ refers to the sale of shares of a closely held business to the general public.

8. Securities traded on the organized exchanges are known as _____ securities.

9. Like other financial assets, the value of common stock is the _____ value of a future stream of income.

10. The income stream expected from a common stock consists of a(n) _____ yield and a(n) _____ _____ yield.

11. If the future growth rate of dividends is expected to be _____, the rate of return is simply the _____ yield.

12. Investors always expect a(n) _____ return on stock investments, but in some years _____ returns may actually be earned.

13. Preferred stock is referred to as a hybrid because it is similar to _____ in some respects and to _____ _____ in others.

14. Most preferred stock dividends are _____ and thus must be paid before any dividends can be paid to common stockholders.

15. Preferred stocks are attractive to _____ investors because of the 70 percent dividend exclusion.

Conceptual

16. According to the valuation model developed in this chapter, the value that an investor assigns to a share of stock is independent of the length of time the investor plans to hold the stock.

    a. True   b. False

17. Which of the following assumptions would cause the constant growth stock valuation model to be invalid? The constant growth model is given below:

$$\hat{P}_0 = \frac{D_0(1 + g)}{k_s - g}.$$

    a. The growth rate is negative.
    b. The growth rate is zero.
    c. The growth rate is less than the required rate of return.
    d. The required rate of return is above 30 percent.
    e. None of the above assumptions would invalidate the model.

18. Assume that a company's dividends are expected to grow at a rate of 25 percent per year for 5 years and then to slow down and to grow at a constant rate of 5 percent thereafter.

The required (and expected) total return, k_s, is expected to remain constant at 12 percent. Which of the following statements is most *correct*?

a. The dividend yield will be higher in the early years and then will decline as the annual capital gains yield gets larger and larger, other things held constant.

b. Right now, it would be easier (require fewer calculations) to find the dividend yield expected in Year 7 than the dividend yield expected in Year 3.

c. The stock price will grow each year at the same rate as the dividends.

d. The stock price will grow at a different rate each year during the first 5 years, but its average growth rate over this period will be the same as the average growth rate in dividends; that is, the average stock price growth rate will be $(25 + 5)/2$.

e. Statements a, b, c, and d are all false.

19. Which of the following statements is most *correct*?

a. According to the text, the constant growth stock valuation model is especially useful in situations where g is greater than 15 percent and k_s is 10 percent or less.

b. According to the text, the constant growth model can be used as one part of the process of finding the value of a stock which is expected to experience a very rapid rate of growth for a few years and then to grow at a constant ("normal") rate.

c. According to the text, the constant growth model cannot be used unless g is greater than zero.

d. According to the text, the constant growth model cannot be used unless the constant g is greater than k.

e. Statements a, b, c, and d are all true.

20. When stockholders assign their right to vote to another party, this is called

a. A privilege.

b. A preemptive right.

c. An ex right.

d. A proxy.

e. A prospectus.

SELF-TEST PROBLEMS

1. Stability Inc. has maintained a dividend rate of $4 per share for many years. The same rate is expected to be paid in future years. If investors require a 12 percent rate of return on similar investments, determine the present value of the company's stock.

   a. $15.00   **b.** $30.00   **c.** $33.33   **d.** $35.00   **e.** $40.00

2. Your sister-in-law, a stockbroker at Invest Inc., is trying to sell you a stock with a current market price of $25. The stock's last dividend (D_0) was $2.00, and earnings and dividends are expected to increase at a constant growth rate of 10 percent. Your required return on this stock is 20 percent. From a strict valuation standpoint, you should:

   a. Buy the stock; it is fairly valued.
   b. Buy the stock; it is undervalued by $3.00.
   c. Buy the stock; it is undervalued by $2.00.
   d. Not buy the stock; it is overvalued by $2.00.
   e. Not buy the stock; it is overvalued by $3.00.

3. Lucas Laboratories' last dividend was $1.50. Its current equilibrium stock price is $15.75, and its expected growth rate is a constant 5 percent. If the stockholders' required rate of return is 15 percent, what is the expected dividend yield and expected capital gains yield for the coming year?

   a. 0%; 15%   **b.** 5%; 10%   **c.** 10%; 5%   **d.** 15%; 0%   **e.** 15%; 15%

4. The Canning Company has been hard hit by increased competition. Analysts predict that earnings (and dividends) will decline at a rate of 5 percent annually into the foreseeable future. If Canning's last dividend (D_0) was $2.00, and investors' required rate of return is 15 percent, what will be Canning's stock price *in 3 years*?

   a. $8.15   **b.** $9.50   **c.** $10.00   **d.** $10.42   **e.** $10.96

(The following data relate to Self-Test Problems 5 through 7.)

The Club Auto Parts Company has just recently been organized. It is expected to experience no growth for the next 2 years as it identifies its market and acquires its inventory. However, Club will grow at an annual rate of 5 percent in the third year and, beginning with the fourth year, should attain a 10 percent growth rate which it will sustain thereafter. The first dividend (D_1) to be paid at the end of the first year is expected to be $0.50 per share. Investors require a 15 percent rate of return on Club's stock.

5. What is the current equilibrium stock price?

   a. $5.00   **b.** $8.75   **c.** $9.56   **d.** $12.43   **e.** $15.00

6. What will Club's stock price be at the end of the first year (P_1)?

   a. $5.00   **b.** $8.75   **c.** $9.56   **d.** $12.43   **e.** $15.00

7. What dividend yield and capital gains yield should an investor in Club expect for the first year?

   a. 7.5%; 7.5%   **b.** 4.7%; 10.3%   **c.** 5.7%; 9.3%   **d.** 10.5%; 4.5%   **e.** 11.5%; 3.5%

8. Johnson Corporation's stock is currently selling at $45.83 per share. The last dividend paid (D_0) was $2.50. Johnson is a constant growth firm. If investors require a return of 16 percent on Johnson's stock, what do they think Johnson's growth rate will be?

   a. 6%   **b.** 7%   **c.** 8%   **d.** 9%   **e.** 10%

9. Assume that the average firm in your company's industry is expected to grow at a constant rate of 7 percent and its dividend yield is 8 percent. Your company is about as risky as the average firm in the industry, but it has just successfully completed some R&D work which leads you to expect that its earnings and dividends will grow at a rate of 40 percent [$D_1 = D_0(1 + g) = D_0(1.40)$] this year and 20 percent the following year, after which growth should match the 7 percent industry average rate. The last dividend paid (D_0) was $1. What is the value per share of your firm's stock?

   a. $22.47   **b.** $24.15   **c.** $21.00   **d.** $19.48   **e.** $22.00

10. Assume that as investment manager of Maine Electric Company's pension plan (which is exempt from income taxes), you must choose between Exxon bonds and GM preferred stock. The bonds have a $1,000 par value; they mature in 20 years; they pay $35 each 6 months; they are callable at Exxon's option at a price of $1,150 after 5 years (ten 6-month periods); and they sell at a price of $815.98 per bond. The preferred stock is a perpetuity; it pays a dividend of $1.50 each quarter, and it sells for $75 per share. Assume interest rates do not change. What is the most likely *effective annual rate of return (EAR)* on the *higher* yielding security? (Hint: You will need a financial calculator to work this problem.)

   a. 9.20%   b. 8.24%   c. 9.00%   d. 8.00%   e. 8.50%

11. Chadmark Corporation is expanding rapidly, and it currently needs to retain all of its earnings, hence it does not pay any dividends. However, investors expect Chadmark to begin paying dividends, with the first dividend of $0.75 coming 2 years from today. The dividend should grow rapidly, at a rate of 40 percent per year, during Years 3 and 4. After Year 4, the company should grow at a constant rate of 10 percent per year. If the required return on the stock is 16 percent, what is the value of the stock today?

   a. $16.93   b. $17.54   c. $15.78   d. $18.87   e. $16.05

12. Some investors expect Endicott Industries to have an irregular dividend pattern for several years, and then to grow at a constant rate. Suppose Endicott has $D_0 = \$2.00$; no growth is expected for 2 years ($g_1 = 0$); then the expected growth rate is 8 percent for 2 years; and finally the growth rate is expected to be constant at 15 percent thereafter. If the required return is 20 percent, what will be the value of the stock?

   a. $28.53   b. $25.14   c. $31.31   d. $21.24   e. $23.84

ANSWERS TO SELF-TEST QUESTIONS

1. directors
2. proxy
3. control; dilution
4. classes; dividends; vote
5. closely held; privately owned
6. secondary; primary
7. Going public
8. listed

9. present
10. dividend; capital gains
11. zero; dividend
12. positive; negative
13. debt; common stock
14. cumulative
15. corporate

16. a. The model considers all future dividends. This produces a current value which is appropriate for all investors independent of their expected holding period.

17. e. The model would be invalid, however, if the growth rate *exceeded* the required rate of return.

18. b. Statement b is correct. We know that after Year 5, the stock will have a constant growth rate, and the capital gains yield will be equal to that growth rate. We also know that the total return is expected to be constant. Therefore, we could find the expected dividend yield in Year 7 simply by subtracting the growth rate from the total return: yield = 12% − 5% = 7% in Year 7.

    The other statements are all false. This could be confirmed by thinking about how the dividend growth rate starts high, ends up at the constant growth rate, and must lie between these two rates and be declining between Years 1 and 5. The average growth rate in dividends during Years 1 through 5 will be (25 + 5)/2 = 15%, which is above k_s = 12%, so statements c and d must be false.

19. b. Statement b is correct. In the case of a nonconstant growth stock which is expected to grow at a constant rate after Year N, we would find the value of D_{N+1} and use it in the constant growth model to find P_N. The other statements are all false. Note that the constant growth model can be used for g = 0 or g < 0.

20. d. Recently, there has been a spate of proxy fights, whereby a dissident group of stockholders solicits proxies in competition with the firm's management. If the dissident group gets a majority of the proxies, then it can gain control of the board of directors and oust existing management.

SOLUTIONS TO SELF-TEST PROBLEMS

1. c. This is a zero-growth stock, or perpetuity: $\hat{P}_0 = D/k_s = \$4.00/0.12 = \$33.33$.

2. e. $\hat{P}_0 = \dfrac{D_0(1 + g)}{k_s - g} = \dfrac{\$2.00(1.10)}{0.20 - 0.10} = \$22.00$.

    Since the stock is currently selling for $25.00, the stock is not in equilibrium and is overvalued by $3.00.

3. c. $\text{Dividend yield} = \dfrac{D_1}{P_0} = \dfrac{D_0(1 + g)}{P_0} = \dfrac{\$1.50(1.05)}{\$15.75} = 0.10 = 10\%.$

$\text{Capital gains yield} = \dfrac{\hat{P}_1 - P_0}{P_0} = \dfrac{P_0(1 + g) - P_0}{P_0} = \dfrac{\$16.54 - \$15.75}{\$15.75} = g = 5\%.$

For a constant growth stock, the capital gains yield is equal to g.

4. a. $\hat{P}_0 = \dfrac{D_0(1 + g)}{k_s - g} = \dfrac{\$2.00(0.95)}{0.15 - (-0.05)} = \dfrac{\$1.90}{0.20} = \$9.50.$

$\hat{P}_3 = \hat{P}_0(1 + g)^3 = \$9.50(0.95)^3 = \$9.50(0.8574) = \$8.15.$

The Gordon model can also be used:

$\hat{P}_3 = \dfrac{D_4}{k_s - g} = \dfrac{D_0(1 + g)^4}{0.15 - (-0.05)} = \dfrac{\$2.00(0.95)^4}{0.20} = \dfrac{\$2.00(0.8145)}{0.20} = \$8.15.$

5. b. To calculate the current value of a nonconstant growth stock, follow these steps:

1. Determine the expected stream of dividends during the nonconstant growth period. Also, calculate the expected dividend at the end of the first year of constant growth that will be used later to calculate stock price.

$D_1 = \$0.50.$
$D_2 = D_1(1 + g) = \$0.50(1 + 0.0) = \$0.50.$
$D_3 = D_2(1 + g) = \$0.50(1.05) = \$0.525.$
$D_4 = D_3(1 + g) = \$0.525(1.10) = \$0.5775.$

2. Discount the expected dividends during the nonconstant growth period at the investor's required rate of return to find their present value.

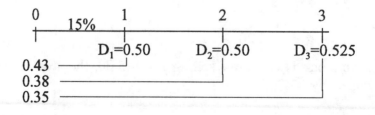

3. Calculate the expected stock price at the end of the final year of nonconstant growth. This occurs at the end of Year 3. Use the Gordon model for this calculation.

$$\hat{P}_3 = \frac{D_4}{k_s - g} = \frac{\$0.5775}{0.15 - 0.10} = \$11.55.$$

Then discount this stock price back 3 periods at the investor's required rate of return to find its present value.

$$PV = \$11.55(PVIF_{15\%,3}) = \$11.55(0.6575) = \$7.59.$$

4. Add the present value of the stock price expected at the end of Year 3 plus the dividends expected in Years 1, 2, and 3 to find the present value of the stock, P_0.

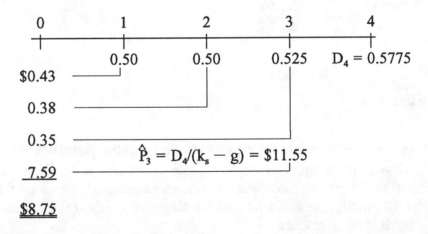

Alternatively, input 0, 0.5, 0.5, 12.075 (0.525 + 11.55) into the cash flow register, input I = 15, and then solve for NPV = $8.75.

6. c. To calculate the expected stock price at the end of Year 1, P_1, follow the same procedure you did to find the value of the nonconstant growth stock in Self-Test Problem 5. However, discount values to Year 1 instead of Year 0. Also, remember that the dividend in Year 1, D_1, is not included in the valuation because it has already been paid and therefore adds nothing to the wealth of the investor buying the stock at the end of Year 1.

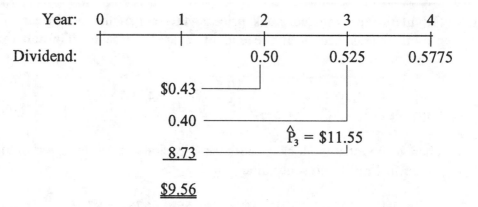

Alternatively, input 0, 0.5, 12.075 (0.525 + 11.55) into the cash flow register, input I = 15, and then solve for NPV = $9.57.

---

7. c.

$$\text{Dividend yield} = \frac{D_1}{P_0} = \frac{\$0.50}{\$8.75} = 5.7\%.$$

$$\text{Capital gains yield} = \frac{\hat{P}_1 - P_0}{P_0} = \frac{\$9.56 - \$8.75}{\$8.75} = 9.3\%.$$

The Total yield = Dividend yield + Capital gains yield = 5.7% + 9.3% = 15%. The total yield must equal the required rate of return. Also, the capital gains yield is not equal to the growth rate during the nonconstant growth phase of a nonconstant growth stock. Finally, the dividend and capital gains yields are not constant until the constant growth state is reached.

8. e.

$$P_0 = \frac{D_0(1 + g)}{k_s - g}$$

$$\$45.83 = \frac{\$2.50(1 + g)}{0.16 - g}$$

$$\$7.33 - \$45.83g = \$2.50 + \$2.50g$$

$$\$48.33g = \$4.83$$

$$g = 0.0999 \approx 10\%.$$

9.   **d.** $D_0 = \$1.00$; $k_s = 8\% + 7\% = 15\%$; $g_1 = 40\%$; $g_2 = 20\%$; $g_n = 7\%$.

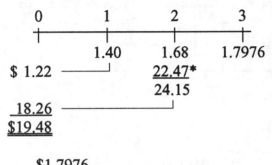

$$*\hat{P}_2 = \frac{\$1.7976}{0.15 - 0.07} = \$22.47.$$

10.   **a.**   Exxon bonds: Price = \$815.98, Maturity = 20 years, PMT = \$35 per 6 months, and they are callable at \$1,150 after 10 periods (5 years).

Will the bond's YTM or YTC be applicable?   The bond is selling at a discount, so k_d > Coupon interest rate.   Therefore, the bond is not likely to be called, so calculate the YTM.

Input N = 40, PV = -815.98, PMT = 35, FV = 1000, and solve for I = $k_d/2$ = 4.5%. EAR = $(1.045)^2 - 1 = 9.2\%$.

Preferred: D = \$1.50 per quarter and P_0 = \$75.
$k_{ps} = \$1.50/\$75 = 2\% = $ periodic rate.   EAR = $(1.02)^4 - 1 = 8.24\%$.

Thus, the Exxon bonds provide the higher effective annual rate of return.

11.   **a.**   To calculate Chadmark's current stock price, follow the following steps: (1) Determine the expected stream of dividends during the nonconstant growth period. You will need to calculate the expected dividend at the end of Year 5, which is the first year of constant growth. This dividend will be used in the next step to calculate the stock price. (2) Calculate the expected stock price at the end of the final year of nonconstant growth. This occurs at the end of Year 4. Use the Gordon model for this calculation. (3) Add the value obtained in Step 2 to the dividend expected in Year 4. (4) Put the values obtained in the prior steps on a time line and discount them at the required rate of return to find the present value of Chadmark's stock. These steps are shown below.

$D_0 = \$0$; $D_1 = \$0$; $D_2 = \$0.75$; $D_3 = \$0.75(1.4) = \$1.05$; $D_4 = \$0.75(1.4)^2 = \$1.47$; $D_5 = \$0.75(1.4)^2(1.10) = \$1.617$.

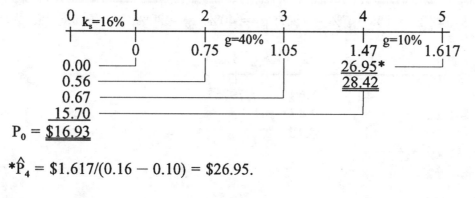

$P_0 = \$16.93$

$*\hat{P}_4 = \$1.617/(0.16 - 0.10) = \$26.95$.

$CF_0 = 0$; $CF_1 = 0$; $CF_2 = 0.75$; $CF_3 = 1.05$; $CF_4 = 28.42$.

Alternatively, using a financial calculator you could input the cash flows as shown above into the cash flow register, input I = 16, and press NPV to obtain the stock's value today of $16.93.

12. c.   First, set up the time line as follows. Note that D_5 is used to find $\hat{P}_4$, which is treated as part of the cash flow at t = 4:

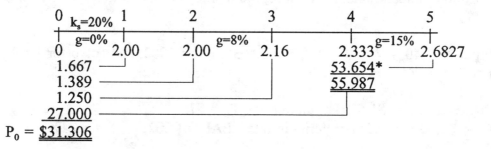

$P_0 = \$31.306$

$*\hat{P}_4 = \$2.6827/(0.20 - 0.15) = \$53.654$.

Enter the time line values into the cash flow register, with I = 20, to find NPV = $31.31. Be sure to enter $CF_0 = 0$. Note that P_4 is the PV, at t = 4, of dividends from t = 5 to infinity; that is, the PV of the dividends after the stock is expected to become a constant growth stock.

OVERVIEW

The firm's marginal cost of capital (MCC) schedule is developed in the following manner: First, the cost of capital must be estimated for each component of the firm's capital structure. These components are normally debt, preferred stock, and common equity. The next task is to combine the component costs to form a weighted average cost of capital. The weights are based on the firm's target capital structure. Capital typically has an increasing cost if the firm expands beyond certain limits. The point at which the cost of capital increases is called a break point, and the MCC schedule is often drawn as a step-function which increases due to increases in one or more of the capital components.

The investment opportunity schedule (IOS) is a plot of the firm's potential projects arrayed in descending order of their rates of return. The intersection of the MCC and the IOS schedules defines the firm's optimal capital budget as well as the relevant marginal cost of capital, the "corporate cost of capital," used to evaluate all new projects with the same risk as the firm's other assets.

OUTLINE

Determining the firm's cost of capital, or the proper discount rate for use in calculating the present value of the cash inflows for the firm's projects, is an important element of the capital budgeting process.

■ *Capital components* are items on the right-hand side of the balance sheet such as debt, preferred stock, common stock, and retained earnings.
  ☐ Each element of capital has a *component cost* which can be identified as follows:
  • k_d = interest rate on the firm's new debt, before tax.
  • $k_d(1 - T)$ = after-tax cost of debt where T is the marginal tax rate.
  • k_{ps} = component cost of preferred stock.
  • k_s = component cost of retained earnings; it is equal to the required rate of return on common stock.

- k_e = cost of external capital obtained by issuing additional common stock; it must be distinguished from equity raised through retained earnings due to the flotation costs when new stock is issued.
- WACC = the weighted average cost of capital.

The cost of each capital component can be determined as follows:

■ The after-tax cost of debt, $k_d(1 - T)$, is defined as the interest rate on debt, k_d, less the tax savings that result because interest is tax deductible.
  □ For example, if a firm has a tax rate of 40 percent and can borrow at a rate of 10 percent, then its after-tax cost of debt is $k_d = 10\%(1 - 0.40) = 10\%(0.60) = 6.0\%$.
  □ The tax deductibility of interest payments has the effect of causing the federal government to pay part of the interest charges.
    - k_d is the interest rate on new debt, not that on already outstanding debt.

■ The component cost of preferred stock, k_{ps}, is the preferred dividend, D_{ps}, divided by the net issuing price, P_n, or the price the firm receives after deducting flotation costs: $k_{ps} = D_{ps}/P_n$. No tax adjustments are made when calculating k_{ps} because preferred dividends, unlike interest expense on debt, are not deductible, and hence there are no tax savings.

■ The cost of retained earnings, k_s, is the rate of return stockholders require on equity capital the firm obtains from earnings. There are three approaches used to estimate k_s:
  □ The *Capital Asset Pricing Model (CAPM)* works as follows:
    - Estimate the risk-free rate, k_{RF}, usually based on U.S. Treasury securities.
    - Estimate the stock's beta coefficient as an index of risk.
    - Estimate the expected rate of return on the market, or on an "average" stock, k_M.
    - Substitute the preceding values into the CAPM equation, $k_s = k_{RF} + (k_M - k_{RF})b$, to estimate the required rate of return on the stock in question.
    - Thus, if $k_{RF} = 8\%$, $k_M = 13\%$, and the beta is 0.7, then $k_s = 8\% + (13\% - 8\%)0.7 = 11.5\%$.
  □ The *bond-yield-plus-risk-premium approach* estimates k_s by adding a risk premium of three to five percentage points to the firm's own bond yield. Thus, k_s = Bond yield + Risk premium.
    - If the firm uses a risk premium of 4 percentage points, and its bond rate is 9 percent, then $k_s = 9\% + 4\% = 13\%$.
    - Because the risk premium is a judgmental estimate, this method is not likely to produce a precise cost of equity; however, it does get us "into the right ballpark."
  □ The required rate of return, k_s, may also be estimated by the *discounted cash flow (DCF) approach*. This approach combines the expected dividend yield, D_1/P_0, with the expected future growth rate, g, of earnings and dividends, or

$$k_s = \hat{k}_s = \frac{D_1}{P_0} + \text{Expected g.}$$

- The DCF approach assumes that stocks are normally in equilibrium and that growth is expected to be at a constant rate. If growth is not constant, then a nonconstant growth model must be used.
- The expected growth rate may be based on projections of past growth rates, if they have been relatively stable, or on expected future growth rates as estimated in some other manner.
- If the firm's next expected dividend is $1.24, its expected growth rate is 8 percent per year, and its stock is selling for $23 per share, then

$$k_s = \hat{k}_s = \frac{\$1.24}{\$23} + 8.0\% = 13.4\%.$$

☐ If the firm cannot earn about 13.4 percent on reinvested equity capital, then it should pay its earnings to stockholders and let them invest directly in other assets that do provide this return. Thus, k_s is an *opportunity cost*.

☐ It is recommended that all three approaches be used in estimating the required rate of return on common stock. When the methods produce widely different results, judgment must be used in selecting the best estimate.

■ The cost of new common equity, or external equity, k_e, is higher than the cost of retained earnings, k_s, because of *flotation costs* involved in selling new common stock.

☐ To allow for flotation costs, F, we must adjust the DCF formula for the required rate of return as follows:

$$k_e = \frac{D_1}{P_0(1-F)} + g.$$

☐ If the firm has a flotation cost of 10 percent, its cost of new outside equity is computed as follows:

$$k_e = \frac{\$1.24}{\$23(1-0.10)} + 8.0\% = 14.0\%.$$

☐ If the firm can earn 14 percent on investments financed by new common stock, then earnings, dividends, and the growth rate will be maintained, and the price per share will not fall. If it earns more than 14 percent, the price will rise; while if it earns less, the price will fall.

The target proportions of debt, preferred stock, and common equity, along with the component costs of capital, are used to calculate the firm's weighted average cost of capital (WACC).

■ The calculation of the weighted average cost of capital is shown below for a firm which finances 30 percent with debt, 10 percent with preferred stock, and 60 percent with common equity and which has the following after-tax component costs:

Component	Weight	×	After-tax Cost	=	Weighted Cost
Debt	0.3	×	8.4%	=	2.52%
Preferred	0.1	×	12.6	=	1.26
Common	0.6	×	16.0	=	9.60
				WACC =	13.38%

■ In more general terms, and in equation format,

$$WACC = w_d k_d (1 - T) + w_{ps} k_{ps} + w_{ce}(k_s \text{ or } k_e).$$

■ The capital structure that minimizes a firm's weighted average cost of capital also maximizes its stock price.

The marginal cost of capital (MCC) is defined as the cost of the last dollar of new capital that the firm raises, and the marginal cost rises as more and more capital is raised during a given period.

■ Firms raise capital in accordance with their target capital structures.

■ As companies raise larger and larger sums during a given time period, the component costs begin to rise. This causes an increase in the weighted average cost of each additional dollar of new capital.

■ Suppose that a firm needs $500,000 in new capital. Its capital structure is 60 percent common equity, 30 percent debt and 10 percent preferred stock, and its marginal tax rate is 40 percent. The before-tax cost of debt is 14 percent and the cost of preferred stock is 12.6 percent. The firm will need to raise 0.6($500,000) = $300,000 in common equity. It expects retained earnings for the year to be $100,000; therefore, it needs to sell $300,000 - $100,000 = $200,000 of new common stock. The cost of retained earnings is 16.0 percent, but the cost of new equity is 16.8 percent. The average cost of capital, using new equity, is:

$$\text{WACC} = w_d k_d (1 - T) + w_{ps} k_{ps} + w_{ce} k_e$$
$$= 0.3(14\%)(0.60) + 0.1(12.6\%) + 0.6(16.8\%) = 13.86\%.$$

■ The point at which the marginal cost of capital increases is called a *break point*. The retained earnings break point is calculated as Retained earnings/Equity fraction. For the firm discussed above, this break point is $100,000/0.6 = $166,667. That is, when $166,667 of new capital is raised, the firm will have used 0.6($166,667) = $100,000 of retained earnings. After that, more costly new common equity must be used.

■ The cost of capital could also rise due to increases in the cost of debt or the cost of preferred stock, or as a result of further increases in flotation costs as the firm issues more and more common stock.

The marginal cost of capital (MCC) schedule shows the relationship between the cost of each dollar raised, WACC, and the total amount of capital raised during the year. The MCC schedule can be used to help determine the discount rate to be used in the capital budgeting process.

■ The optimal capital structure is the one that produces the lowest MCC schedule.

■ As a result of firms facing increasing MCC schedules, in this chapter a specific retained earnings break point is identified, but additional break points are not precisely identified. The MCC schedule is shown to be upward sloping, reflecting (1) a positive relationship between capital raised and capital costs and (2) a band of costs is used to indicate our inability to measure capital costs precisely.

The cost of capital is affected by a variety of factors.

■ The two most important factors which are beyond the firm's direct control are the level of interest rates and taxes.
   □ If interest rates in the economy rise, the cost of debt capital increases because firms will have to pay bondholders a higher rate of interest. Higher interest rates also increase the cost of common and preferred equity capital.
   □ Tax rates are used in the calculation of the cost of debt as used to develop the WACC, but there are other less apparent ways in which tax policy can affect the cost of capital. For example, lowering the capital gains tax rate relative to the rate on ordinary income would make stocks more attractive, which would reduce the cost of equity relative to that of debt. This would lead to a change in the optimal capital structure.

■ A firm can affect its cost of capital through its capital structure policy, its dividend policy, and its investment policy.

☐ The firm can change its capital structure, and such a change can affect its cost of capital. If a firm decides to use more debt and less common equity, this change in the weights in the WACC equation will tend to lower the WACC. However, an increase in the use of debt will increase the riskiness of both debt and equity, and these increases will tend to increase the WACC, and thus, offset the effects of the change in weights.

☐ For any given level of earnings, the higher the dividend payout ratio, the lower the level of retained earnings, and the lower the retained earnings break point in the MCC schedule.

☐ When we estimate the cost of capital, we use as the starting point the required rate of return on the firm's stock and its cost of new debt as reflected in the yield on its outstanding bonds. The cost rates reflect the riskiness of the firm's assets. Therefore, we implicitly assume that new capital will be invested in assets of the same type and with the same degree of risk as is embedded in the existing assets. This assumption will be incorrect if the firm dramatically changes its investment policy.

The Investment Opportunity Schedule (IOS) shows the rate of return that is expected on each potential investment opportunity.

■ The Investment Opportunity Schedule (IOS) is a plot of the firm's potential projects in descending order of each project's rate of return.

■ The WACC at the point where the IOS intersects the MCC curve is defined as the "corporate cost of capital," which reflects the marginal cost of capital to the corporation.

A number of difficult issues relating to the cost of capital are listed below. These topics are covered in advanced finance courses.

■ *Depreciation-generated funds* are the largest single source of capital for many firms. The cost of depreciation-generated funds is approximately equal to the weighted average cost of capital in the interval in which capital comes from retained earnings and low-cost debt.

■ As a general rule, the same principles of cost of capital estimation apply to both *privately held* and publicly owned firms, but the problems of obtaining input data are somewhat difficult for each.

■ One cannot overemphasize the practical difficulties encountered when one actually attempts to estimate the cost of equity.

■ It is difficult to assign proper risk-adjusted discount rates to capital budgeting projects of differing degrees of riskiness.

■ Establishing the target capital structure is a major task in itself.

SELF-TEST QUESTIONS

Definitional

1. The firm should calculate its cost of capital as a(n) _weighted average_ of the after-tax costs of the various types of funds it uses.

2. Capital components are items on the right-hand side of the balance sheet such as the following: (1) _debt_, (2) _pref stock_, (3) _common stock_, and (4) _retain. earnings_

3. The cost of equity capital is defined as the _rate of return_ stockholders require on the firm's common stock.

4. There are ___3___ approaches that can be used to determine the cost of retained earnings.

5. Assigning a cost to retained earnings is based on the _opportunity cost_ principle.

6. The cost of external equity capital is higher than the cost of retained earnings due to _flotation costs_.

7. Using the Capital Asset Pricing Model (CAPM), the required rate of return on common stock is found as a function of the _risk - free rate_, the firm's _beta coefficient_, and the required rate of return on an average _stock_.

8. The cost of common equity may also be found by adding a(n) _risk premium_ to the interest rate on the firm's own _bond yield_.

9. The required rate of return may also be estimated as the _dividend yield_ on the common stock plus the expected future _growth rate_ of the dividends.

10. The proportions of _debt_ , _preferred stock_ , and _common equity_ in the target capital structure should be used to calculate the _weighted average_ cost of capital.

11. The _marginal_ cost of capital is the cost of raising another dollar of new capital.

12. The MCC schedule can be used to help determine the _discount rate_ to be used in the capital budgeting process.

13. The _Investment Opport Schedule_ graphs a firm's capital projects in descending order of each project's _rate of return_.

Conceptual

14. Funds acquired by the firm through preferred stock have a cost to the firm equal to the preferred dividend divided by the price investors paid for one share.

    a. True   **b.** False   _Flotation $_

15. Which of the following statements could be true concerning the costs of debt and equity?

    a. The cost of debt for Firm A is greater than the cost of equity for Firm A.
    b. The cost of debt for Firm A is greater than the cost of equity for Firm B.
    c. The cost of retained earnings for Firm A is less than its cost of external equity.
    d. The cost of retained earnings for Firm A is less than its cost of debt.
    e. Statements b and c could both be true.

16. Which of the following statements is most _correct_?

    a. If Congress raised the corporate tax rate, this would lower the effective cost of debt but probably would also reduce the amount of retained earnings available to corporations, so the effect on the marginal cost of capital is uncertain.
    b. For corporate investors, 70 percent of the dividends received on both common and preferred stocks is exempt from taxes. However, neither preferred nor common dividends may be deducted by the issuing company. Therefore, the dividend exclusion has no effect on a company's cost of capital, so its WACC would probably not change at all if the dividend exclusion rule were rescinded by Congress.
    c. Normally, the MCC schedule is drawn with an upward slope, reflecting the fact that as more capital is raised, the cost of capital increases. However, if the firm uses a lot of short-term debt, then its MCC schedule could, according to the text, have a U shape.
    d. Each of the above statements is true.
    e. Each of the above statements is false.

17. Which of the following statements is most *correct*?

a. Three procedures for determining the cost of retained earnings were discussed in the text: the CAPM, the DCF, and the WACC.

b. One reason why new common stock has a higher cost than retained earnings is because, to raise capital by selling stock, the firm must attract new investors who are less sanguine (that is, less optimistic) about the firm's prospects. This requires that the price of the stock be reduced, and this price reduction is built into the flotation cost. Therefore, the steeper the demand curve for the stock, the greater the differential between the cost of new equity and the cost of retained earnings.

c. Logically, one can think of a high dividend payout stock as being similar to a shorter-term bond, and of a low payout stock as being similar to a longer-term bond, because cash flows come in faster if the payout is higher. Because of this factor, the differential between the cost of retained earnings and the cost of new outside equity should normally be *greater* for a low payout stock, other things held constant.

d. When calculating the WACC for a firm which will obtain equity both from retained earnings and by selling new stock, the cost of equity used in the WACC formula should normally be a weighted average of k_s and k_e, that is, the equity component will be $w_{ce}(k_s + k_e)$.

e. Each of the above statements is false.

SELF-TEST PROBLEMS

1. Roland Corporation's next expected dividend (D_1) is $2.50. The firm has maintained a constant payout ratio of 50 percent during the past 7 years. Seven years ago its EPS was $1.50. The firm's beta coefficient is 1.2. The required return on an average stock in the market is 13 percent, and the risk-free rate is 7 percent. Roland's A-rated bonds are yielding 10 percent, and its current stock price is $30. Which of the following values is the most reasonable estimate of Roland's cost of retained earnings, k_s?

  a. 10%　　　　b. 12%　　　　c. 14%　　　　d. 20%　　　　e. 26%

2. The director of capital budgeting for See-Saw Inc., manufacturers of playground equipment, is considering a plan to expand production facilities in order to meet an increase in demand. He estimates that this expansion will produce a rate of return of 11 percent. The firm's target capital structure calls for a debt/equity ratio of 0.8. See-Saw currently has a bond issue outstanding which will mature in 25 years and has a 7 percent annual coupon rate. The bonds are currently selling for $804. The firm has maintained a constant growth rate of 6 percent. See-Saw's next expected dividend is $2 and its current stock price is $40. Its tax rate is 40 percent. Should it undertake the expansion? (Assume that there is no preferred stock outstanding and that any new debt will have a 25-year maturity.)

a. No; the expected return is 2.5 percentage points lower than the cost of capital.
b. No; the expected return is 1.0 percentage points lower than the cost of capital.
c. Yes; the expected return is 0.5 percentage points higher than the cost of capital.
d. Yes; the expected return is 1.0 percentage points higher than the cost of capital.
e. Yes; the expected return is 2.5 percentage points higher than the cost of capital.

3. Midterm Corporation's present capital structure, which is also its target capital structure, calls for 50 percent debt and 50 percent common equity. The firm has only one potential project, an expansion program with a 10.2 percent rate of return and a cost of $20 million but which is completely divisible; that is, Midterm can invest any amount up to $20 million. Midterm expects to retain $3 million of earnings next year. It can raise new debt at a before-tax cost of 10 percent. The cost of retained earnings is 12 percent; Midterm can sell any amount of new common stock desired at a constant cost of new equity of 15 percent. The firm's marginal tax rate is 40 percent. What is Midterm's optimal capital budget?

a. $0 million   **b.** $5 million   **c.** $6 million   **d.** $10 million   **e.** $20 million

4. The management of Florida Phosphate Industries (FPI) is planning next year's capital budget. FPI projects net income of $10,500, and its payout ratio is 40 percent. The company's earnings and dividends are growing at a constant rate of 5 percent. The last dividend, D_0, was $0.90; and the current equilibrium stock price is $8.59. FPI can raise new debt at a 14 percent before-tax cost. If FPI issues new common stock, a 10 percent flotation cost will be incurred. FPI is at its optimal capital structure, which is 40 percent debt and 60 percent equity, and the firm's marginal tax rate is 40 percent. FPI has the following independent, indivisible, and equally risky investment opportunities:

Project	Cost	Rate of Return
A	$15,000	17%
B	15,000	16
C	12,000	15
D	20,000	13

What is FPI's optimal capital budget?

a. $62,000   **b.** $42,000   **c.** $30,000   **d.** $15,000   **e.** $0

5. Gator Products Company (GPC) is at its optimal capital structure of 70 percent common equity and 30 percent debt. GPC's MCC and IOS schedules for next year intersect at a 14 percent marginal cost of capital. At the intersection, the IOS schedule is vertical and the MCC schedule is horizontal. GPC has a marginal tax rate of 40 percent. Next year's dividend is expected to be $2.00 per share, and GPC has a constant growth in earnings and dividends of 6 percent. The after-tax cost of equity used in the MCC at the intersection is based on new equity with a flotation cost of 10 percent, while the before-tax cost of debt is 12 percent. What is GPC's current equilibrium stock price?

    a. $12.73   **b.** $17.23   **c.** $20.37   **d.** $23.70   **e.** $37.20

(The following data apply to Self-Test Problems 6 and 7.)

Sun Products Company (SPC) uses only debt and equity. It can borrow unlimited amounts at an interest rate of 12 percent so long as it finances at its target capital structure, which calls for 45 percent debt and 55 percent common equity. Its last dividend was $2.40, its expected constant growth rate is 5 percent, its stock sells for $30 per share, and new stock would net the company $24 per share after flotation costs. SPC's tax rate is 40 percent, and it expects to have $120 million of retained earnings this year. Two projects are available: Project A has a cost of $240 million and a rate of return of 13 percent, while Project B has a cost of $150 million and a rate of return of 10 percent. All of the company's potential projects are equally risky.

6. What is SPC's cost of equity from newly issued stock?

    a. 15.50%   **b.** 13.40%   **c.** 7.20%   **d.** 12.50%   **e.** 16.00%

7. What is SPC's marginal cost of capital? In other words, what WACC cost rate should it use to evaluate capital budgeting projects (these two projects plus any others that might arise during the year, provided the cost of capital schedule remains as it is currently)?

    a. 12.05%   **b.** 13.40%   **c.** 11.77%   **d.** 12.50%   **e.** 10.61%

ANSWERS TO SELF-TEST QUESTIONS

1. weighted average
2. debt; preferred stock; common stock; retained earnings

3. rate of return
4. three
5. opportunity cost

6. flotation costs
7. risk-free rate (k_{RF}); beta coefficient (b); stock (k_M)
8. risk premium; bond yield
9. dividend yield; growth rate
10. debt; preferred stock; common equity; weighted average
11. marginal
12. discount rate
13. Investment Opportunity Schedule (IOS); rate of return

14. b. Flotation costs must be subtracted from the investor's cost to get the net issuance price, which is then used to calculate the cost of preferred stock.

15. e. If Firm A has more business risk than Firm B, Firm A's cost of debt could be greater than Firm B's cost of equity. Also, the cost of retained earnings is less than the cost of external equity because of flotation costs.

16. a. Statement a is correct. If Congress were to raise the tax rate, this would lower the cost of debt; however, a bigger chunk of the firm's earnings would go to Uncle Sam. The effect on the MCC would depend on which had the greater effect on the MCC. Statement b is false. Preferred stock generally has a lower before-tax cost than debt due to the dividend exclusion; however, if the dividend exclusion were omitted, preferred stock would have an increased before-tax cost. Statement c is false because short-term debt is not considered in the MCC schedule. The MCC schedule is usually drawn as a step function; however, at some point numerous break points would occur and the MCC would rise almost continuously beyond some level of new financing.

17. b. Statement a is false. The three methods for determining the cost of equity are the DCF, the CAPM, and the Bond-yield-plus-risk-premium. Statement b is correct. Statement c is false. The differential for the cost of retained earnings and the cost of new stock is discussed in statement b. Statement d is false. The MCC will contain a break where retained earnings are used up and new common stock is used, and there would be 2 different MCC's calculated—one using k_s and one using k_e.

SOLUTIONS TO SELF-TEST PROBLEMS

1. c. Use all three methods to estimate k_s.

   CAPM: $k_s = k_{RF} + (k_M - k_{RF})b = 7\% + (13\% - 7\%)1.2 = 14.2\%$.

   Risk Premium: k_s = Bond yield + Risk premium = $10\% + 4\% = 14\%$.

DCF: $k_s = D_1/P_0 + g = \$2.50/\$30 + g$, where g can be estimated as follows:

$\$0.75 = \$2.50(\text{PVIF}_{k,7})$
$\text{PVIF}_{k,7} = \$0.75/\$2.50 = 0.3000.$

Thus k, which is the compound growth rate, g, is about 19%, or, using a calculator, 18.8%. Therefore, $k_s = 0.083 + 0.188 = 27.1\%.$

Roland Corporation has apparently been experiencing supernormal growth during the past 7 years, and it is not reasonable to assume that this growth will continue. The first two methods yield a k_s of about 14 percent, which appears reasonable.

2. e. Cost of equity $= k_s = \$2/\$40 + 0.06 = 0.11 = 11\%.$

Cost of debt $= k_d =$ Yield to maturity on outstanding bonds based on current market price.

$$V_B = \text{INT}(\text{PVIFA}_{k_d,25}) + M(\text{PVIF}_{k_d,25}),$$
$$\$804 = \$70(\text{PVIFA}_{k_d,25}) + \$1,000(\text{PVIF}_{k_d,25}).$$

Solving by trial and error gives $k_d = 9\%$. Alternatively, with a financial calculator: Input N = 25, PV = -804, PMT = 70, FV = 1000, and solve for I = k_d = 9%.

In determining the capital structure weights, note that debt/equity = 0.8 or, for example, 4/5. Therefore, debt/assets is

$$\frac{D}{A} = \frac{\text{Debt}}{\text{Debt} + \text{Equity}} = \frac{4}{4 + 5} = \frac{4}{9},$$

and equity/assets = 5/9. Hence, the weighted average cost of capital is calculated as follows:

$$\begin{aligned}
\text{WACC} &= k_d(1 - T)(D/A) + k_s(1 - D/A) \\
&= 0.09(1 - 0.4)(4/9) + 0.11(5/9) \\
&= 0.024 + 0.061 = 0.085 = 8.5\%.
\end{aligned}$$

The cost of capital is 8.5 percent, while the expansion project's rate of return is 11.0 percent. Since the expected return is 2.5 percentage points higher than the cost, the expansion should be undertaken.

3. **c.** First, look only at equity (in millions of dollars):

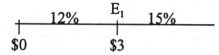

Now look at total capital (in millions of dollars):

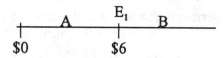

The retained earnings break point is calculated as follows:

$E_1 = \$3,000,000/0.5 = \$6,000,000.$

Now, determine the weighted average cost of capital for intervals A and B:

$WACC = w_d(k_d)(1 - T) + w_{ce}(k_s \text{ or } k_e).$

A = 0.5(10%)(0.6) + 0.5(12%) = 9.0%.
B = 0.5(10%)(0.6) + 0.5(15%) = 10.5%.

Finally, graph the IOS and MCC schedules.

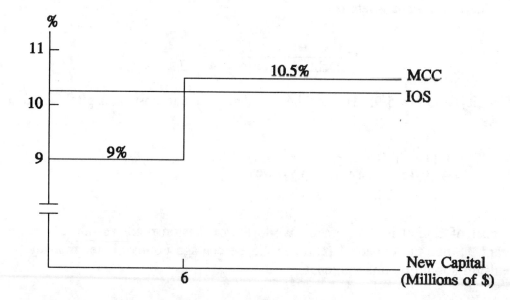

Thus, the optimal capital budget is $6 million.

4. b. Now, look only at equity:

$$\underset{\$0}{\vdash}\ \overset{16\%}{\underset{}{}}\ \overset{E_1}{\underset{\$6,300}{\vdash}}\ \overset{17.22\%}{\underline{\hspace{2cm}}}$$

Retained earnings are forecast to be $\$10,500(0.6) = \$6,300$. The cost of retained earnings is as follows:

$$k_s = \frac{D_0(1 + g)}{P_0} + g = \frac{\$0.90(1.05)}{\$8.59} + 0.05 = 0.16 = 16.0\%.$$

The cost of new equity is as follows:

$$k_{e1} = \frac{D_0(1 + g)}{P_0(1 - F)} + g = \frac{\$0.90(1.05)}{\$8.59(1 - 0.10)} + 0.05 = 0.1722 = 17.22\%.$$

Now, look at total capital:

$$\underset{\$0}{\vdash}\ \overset{A}{\underset{}{}}\ \overset{E_1}{\underset{\$10,500}{\vdash}}\ \overset{B}{\underline{\hspace{2cm}}}$$

The retained earnings break point is calculated as follows:

$E_1 = \$6,300/0.60 = \$10,500.$

Now, determine the weighted average cost of capital for intervals A and B:

$$WACC = w_d(k_d)(1 - T) + w_{ce}(k_s \text{ or } k_e)$$

$A = 0.4(14\%)(0.6) + 0.6(16.00\%) = 12.96\%.$
$B = 0.4(14\%)(0.6) + 0.6(17.22\%) = 13.69\%.$

Finally, graph the MCC and IOS schedules:

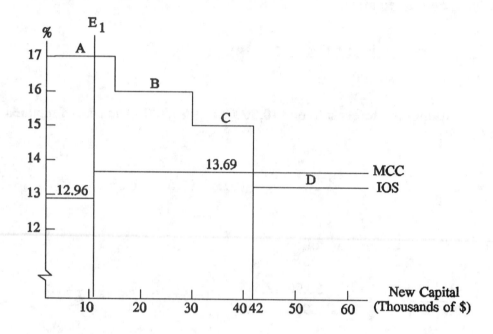

Therefore, the optimal capital budget is $42,000. Projects A, B, and C are accepted.

5. c. At the intersection of the IOS and MCC schedules, WACC = 14%. Therefore,

$$WACC = 14\% = w_d(k_d)(1 - T) + w_{ce}(k_e)$$
$$14\% = 0.3(12\%)(0.6) + 0.7(k_e)$$
$$k_e = 16.91\%.$$

Now, at equilibrium:

$$\hat{k}_e = k_e = \frac{D_1}{P_0(1 - F)} + g$$

$$0.1691 = \frac{\$2.00}{P_0(1 - 0.10)} + 0.06$$

$$0.1091 = \frac{\$2.222}{P_0}$$

$$P_0 = \$20.37.$$

6. a. $k_e = [\$2.40(1.05)]/\$24 + 5\% = 0.1050 + 0.05 = 0.1550 = 15.50\%.$

7. c. $k_d = 12\%$; $k_d(1 - T) = 12\%(0.6) = 7.2\%$.
   $k_s = [\$2.40(1.05)]/\$30 + 5\% = 13.40\%$.
   $k_e = 15.50\%$.

   RE = \$120 million; BP_{RE} = \$120/0.55 = \$218.18 million.
   D/A = 45%; E/A = 55%.

   0 - \$218.18 million: $WACC_1 = 0.45(7.2\%) + 0.55(13.40\%) = 10.61\%$.
   > \$218.18 million: $WACC_2 = 0.45(7.2\%) + 0.55(15.50\%) = 11.77\%$.

OVERVIEW

Capital budgeting is similar in principle to security valuation in that future cash flows are estimated, risks are appraised and reflected in a cost of capital discount rate, and all cash flows are evaluated on a present value basis. Five primary methods can be used to determine which projects should be included in a firm's capital budget: (1) payback, (2) discounted payback, (3) net present value (NPV), (4) internal rate of return (IRR), and (5) modified IRR (MIRR). Both payback methods have deficiencies, and thus should not be used as the sole criterion for making capital budgeting decisions. The NPV, IRR, and MIRR methods all lead to the same accept/reject decisions on independent projects. However, the methods may conflict when ranking mutually exclusive projects which differ in scale or timing. Under these circumstances, the NPV method should be used to make the final decision.

OUTLINE

Capital budgeting is the process of analyzing fixed asset investment proposals.

■ A number of factors combine to make capital budgeting decisions perhaps the most important ones financial managers must make. Since the results of such decisions continue for many years, capital budgeting decisions have long-term consequences. Timing is also important since capital assets must be ready to come on line at the time they are needed.

■ The same general concepts that are used in security valuation are also used in capital budgeting; however, whereas a set of stocks and bonds exists in the securities market from which investors select, capital budgeting projects are created by the firm.

■ Analyzing capital expenditure proposals has a cost, so firms classify projects into different categories to help differentiate the level of analysis required:
  ☐ Replacement: maintenance of business

- ☐ Replacement: cost reduction
- ☐ Expansion of existing products or markets
- ☐ Expansion into new products or markets
- ☐ Safety and/or environmental projects
- ☐ Other miscellaneous projects

■ Normally, a more detailed analysis is required for expansion and new product decisions than for simple replacement and maintenance decisions. Also, projects requiring larger investments will be analyzed more carefully than smaller projects.

■ Once a potential capital budgeting project has been identified, its evaluation involves the same steps that are used in security analysis.
- ☐ The cost of the project must be determined.
- ☐ Cash flows from the project are estimated.
- ☐ The riskiness of these projected cash flows is determined.
- ☐ Given the riskiness of the projected cash flows, the appropriate cost of capital is determined at which cash flows are to be discounted.
- ☐ Cash flows are discounted to their present value to obtain an estimate of the asset's value to the firm.
- ☐ The present value of the benefits is compared with the required outlay, or cost. If the asset's value exceeds its cost, the project should be accepted; otherwise, it should be rejected.

Five primary methods are currently used to rank projects and to decide whether or not they should be accepted for inclusion in the capital budget: (1) payback, (2) discounted payback, (3) net present value (NPV), (4) internal rate of return (IRR), and (5) modified internal rate of return (MIRR). The MIRR is discussed in a later section.

■ The *payback period* is defined as the expected number of years required to recover the original investment in the project. Payback is a type of "breakeven" calculation in the sense that if cash flows come in at the expected rate until the payback year, then the project will break even.
- ☐ The payback method's flaws are that cash flows beyond the payback period are ignored and it does not take into account the cost of capital.
- ☐ Although the payback method has some serious faults as a project ranking criterion, it does provide information on how long funds will be tied up in a project. Thus, the shorter the payback period, other things held constant, the greater the project's *liquidity*.

■ A variant of the regular payback, the *discounted payback period* discounts the expected cash flows by the project's cost of capital, thus taking into account the effects of capital costs.

Thus, the discounted payback period is defined as the number of years required to recover the investment from discounted net cash flows.

- ■ The *net present value (NPV)* method of evaluating investment proposals is a discounted cash flow (DCF) technique that accounts for the time value of all cash flows from a project.
  - □ To implement the NPV, proceed as follows: (a) Find the present value of each cash flow, discounted at the project's cost of capital, (b) sum these discounted cash flows to obtain the project's NPV, and (c) accept the project if the NPV is positive.
  - □ The NPV is defined as follows:

$$\text{NPV} = \sum_{t=0}^{n} \frac{CF_t}{(1 + k)^t}.$$

  Here, CF_t is the expected net cash flow in Period t and k is the project's cost of capital. Cash outflows are treated as negative cash flows.
  - □ If the NPV is positive, the project should be accepted; if negative, it should be rejected. If two projects are mutually exclusive (that is, only one can be accepted), the one with the higher NPV should be chosen, assuming that the NPV is positive. If both projects have negative NPVs, neither should be chosen.
  - □ Finding the NPV with a financial calculator is efficient and easy. Simply enter the different cash flows into the "cash flow register" along with the value of k = i, and then press the NPV key for the solution.

- ■ The *internal rate of return (IRR)* is defined as the discount rate which equates the present value of a project's expected cash inflows to the present value of its expected costs.
  - □ The equation for calculating the IRR is shown below:

$$\sum_{t=0}^{n} \frac{CF_t}{(1 + IRR)^t} = 0.$$

  This equation has one unknown, the IRR, and we can solve for the value of the IRR that will make the equation equal to zero. The solution value of IRR is defined as the internal rate of return.
  - □ The IRR formula is simply the NPV formula solved for the particular discount rate that causes the NPV to equal zero.
  - □ The IRR can be found by trial and error, but most financial calculators and computers with financial analysis software can easily calculate IRRs and NPVs.
  - □ To find the IRR with a financial calculator, simply enter the different cash flows into the cash flow register, making sure to input the t=0 cash flow, and then press the IRR key for the solution.

■ The same basic equation is used for both the NPV and the IRR methods, but in the NPV method, the discount rate, k, is specified and the NPV is found, whereas in the IRR method, the NPV is specified to equal zero, and the value of IRR that forces this equality is determined.

■ In many respects the NPV method is better than the IRR method. However, the IRR is widely used in business. Therefore, it is important to understand the IRR method including its problems.

■ A *net present value profile* is a graph which relates a project's NPV to the discount rate used to calculate its NPV.
   □ The NPV profile crosses the Y-axis at the *undiscounted* NPV, while it crosses the X-axis at the IRR.
   □ If an *independent* project is being evaluated, then the NPV and IRR criteria always lead to the same accept/reject decision.
   □ If two *mutually exclusive* projects have NPV profiles which intersect in the upper right-hand quadrant, then there may be a conflict in rankings between NPV and IRR methods. Two basic conditions can lead to conflicts between NPV and IRR:
      • Project size (or scale) differences exist; that is, the cost of one project is larger than that of the other.
      • Timing differences exist such that cash flows from one project come in the early years and most of the cash flows from the other project come in the later years.
   □ The critical issue in resolving conflicts between mutually exclusive projects is to determine how useful it is to generate cash flows earlier rather than later. Thus, the value of early cash flows depends on the rate at which we can reinvest these cash flows.
      • The NPV method implicitly assumes that project cash flows are reinvested at the project's cost of capital.
      • The IRR method implicitly assumes that project cash flows are reinvested at the project's IRR.
      • The opportunity cost of a project's cash flows is the project's cost of capital. If these cash flows were not available to the firm and if the firm needed capital to invest in new projects, then the funds would be obtained from the firm's capital suppliers; the cost would be the overall cost of capital. Thus, the assumption of reinvestment at the cost of capital is the correct assumption, and NPV is the preferred method.
   □ In summary, when projects are independent, the NPV and IRR methods both make exactly the same accept/reject decision. However, when evaluating mutually exclusive projects, especially those that differ in scale and/or timing, the NPV method should be used.

Multiple IRRs can result when the IRR criterion is used with a project that has nonnormal cash flows. Projects with nonnormal cash flows call for a large cash outflow either

sometime during or at the end of its life. In such cases, the NPV criterion can be easily applied, and this method leads to conceptually correct capital budgeting decisions.

Business executives often prefer to work with percentage rates of return, such as IRR, rather than dollar amounts of NPV when analyzing investments. To overcome some of the IRR's limitations a modified IRR, or MIRR, has been devised.

■ The MIRR is defined as the discount rate which forces PV costs = PV terminal value, where *terminal value (TV)* is the future value of the inflows compounded at the project's cost of capital. Thus,

$$\sum_{t=0}^{n} \frac{COF_t}{(1 + k)^t} = \frac{\sum_{t=0}^{n} CIF_t(1 + k)^{n-t}}{(1 + MIRR)^n}$$

$$PV \text{ costs} = \frac{TV}{(1 + MIRR)^n}.$$

■ MIRR assumes that cash flows are reinvested at the cost of capital rather than the project's own IRR, making it a better indicator of a project's true profitability.

■ NPV and MIRR will lead to the same project selection decision if the two projects are of equal size. However, conflicts can still occur when projects differ in scale, and in this case, NPV should be used.

■ MIRR also avoids the problem of multiple IRRs, which can arise when a project has nonnormal cash flows or has negative cash flows after the project has gone into operation. NPV can be easily applied to such situations; however, MIRR can also overcome the multiple IRR problem because there is only one MIRR for any set of cash flows.

In making the accept/reject decision, each of the five capital budgeting decision methods provides decision makers with a somewhat different piece of relevant information.

■ Payback and discounted payback provide an indication of both the risk and the liquidity of a project.

■ NPV is important because it gives a direct measure of the dollar benefit (on a present value basis) of the project to the firm's shareholders, so it is regarded as the best single measure of profitability.

■ IRR also measures profitability, but expressed as a percentage rate of return, which many decision makers seem to prefer. Further, IRR contains information regarding a project's "safety margin" which is not inherent in NPV.

■ The modified IRR has all the virtues of the IRR, but it also incorporates the correct reinvestment rate assumption, and it avoids problems the IRR can have when applied to projects with nonnormal cash flows.

An important aspect of the capital budgeting process is the post-audit, which involves comparing actual results with those predicted by the project's sponsors and explaining why any differences occurred. The results of the post-audit help to improve forecasts and to increase efficiency of the firm's operations.

■ The post-audit is not a simple process--a number of factors can cause complications.
   □ Each element of the cash flow forecast is subject to uncertainty, so a percentage of all projects undertaken by any reasonably aggressive firm will necessarily go awry.
   □ Projects sometime fail to meet expectations for reasons beyond the control of the operating executives and for reasons that no one could realistically be expected to anticipate.
   □ It is often difficult to separate the operating results of one investment from those of a larger system.
   □ It is often hard to hand out blame or praise, because the executives who were responsible for launching a given long-term investment may have moved on by the time the results are known.

SELF-TEST QUESTIONS

Definitional

1. A firm's _____ _____ outlines its planned expenditures on fixed assets.

2. The most difficult step in the analysis of capital expenditure proposals involves estimating future _____ _____.

3. The number of years necessary to return the original investment in a project is known as the _____ _____.

4. The primary advantage of payback analysis is its _____.

5. One important weakness of payback analysis is the fact that _____ _____ beyond the payback period are _____.

6. The net present value (NPV) method of evaluating investment proposals is a(n) _____ cash flow (DCF) technique.

7. A capital investment proposal should be accepted if its NPV is _____.

8. If two projects are _____ _____, the one with the _____ positive NPV should be selected.

9. In the IRR approach, a discount rate is sought which makes the NPV equal to _____.

10. A net present value profile shows the relationship between a project's _____ and the _____ _____ used to calculate the NPV.

11. If an independent project's _____ is greater than the project's cost of capital, it should be accepted.

12. If two mutually exclusive projects are being evaluated and one project has a higher NPV while the other project has a higher IRR, the project with the higher _____ should be preferred.

13. The NPV method implicitly assumes reinvestment at the project's _____ _____ _____, while the IRR method implicitly assumes reinvestment at the _____ _____ _____ _____.

14. The MIRR method assumes reinvestment at the _____ _____ _____, making it a better indicator of a project's profitability than IRR.

15. The process of comparing a project's actual results with its projected results is known as a(n) _____ - _____.

16. The objective of the post-audit is to improve both _____ and _____.

17. The internal rate of return (IRR) is the _____ rate that equates the present value of the _____ _____ with the present value of the _____ _____.

18. The MIRR is defined as the discount rate which forces the present value of costs to equal the present value of the _____ _____.

Conceptual

19. The NPV of a project with cash flows that accrue relatively slowly is *more sensitive* to changes in the discount rate than is the NPV of a project with cash flows that come in more rapidly.

    a. True   **b.** False

20. The NPV method is preferred over the IRR method because the NPV method's reinvestment rate assumption is better.

    a. True   **b.** False

21. When you find the yield to maturity on a bond, you are finding the bond's net present value (NPV).

    a. True   **b.** False

22. Other things held constant, a decrease in the cost of capital (discount rate) will cause an *increase* in a project's IRR.

    a. True   **b.** False

23. The IRR method can be used in place of the NPV method for all independent projects.

    a. True   **b.** False

24. The NPV and MIRR methods lead to the same decision for mutually exclusive projects regardless of the projects' relative sizes.

    a. True   **b.** False

25. Projects with nonnormal cash flows sometimes have multiple MIRRs.

    a. True   **b.** False

26. Projects A and B each have an initial cost of $5,000, followed by a series of positive cash inflows. Project A has total undiscounted cash inflows of $12,000, while B has total

undiscounted inflows of $10,000. Further, at a discount rate of 10 percent, the two projects have identical NPVs. Which project's NPV will be *more sensitive* to changes in the discount rate? (Hint: Projects with steeper NPV profiles are more sensitive to discount rate changes.)

a. Project A.
b. Project B.
c. Both projects are equally sensitive to changes in the discount rate since their NPVs are equal at all costs of capital.
d. Neither project is sensitive to changes in the discount rate, since both have NPV profiles which are horizontal.
e. The solution cannot be determined unless the timing of the cash flows is known.

27. Which of the following statements is most *correct*?

a. The IRR of a project whose cash flows accrue relatively rapidly is more sensitive to changes in the discount rate than is the IRR of a project whose cash flows come in more slowly.
b. There are many conditions under which a project can have more than one IRR. One such condition is where an otherwise normal project has a negative cash flow at the end of its life.
c. The phenomenon called "multiple internal rates of return" arises when two or more mutually exclusive projects which have different lives are being compared.
d. The modified IRR (MIRR) method has wide appeal to professors, but most business executives prefer the NPV method to either the regular or modified IRR.
e. Each of the above statements is false.

28. Which of the following statements is most *correct*?

a. If a project has an IRR greater than zero, then taking on the project will increase the value of the company's common stock because the project will make a positive contribution to net income.
b. If a project has an NPV greater than zero, then taking on the project will increase the value of the firm's stock.
c. Assume that you plot the NPV profiles of two mutually exclusive, projects with normal cash flows and that the cost of capital is *greater* than the rate at which the profiles cross one another. In this case, the NPV and IRR methods will lead to contradictory rankings of the two projects.
d. For independent (as opposed to mutually exclusive) normal projects, the NPV and IRR methods will generally lead to conflicting accept/reject decisions.
e. Statements b, c, and d are all true.

29. Which of the following statements is most *correct*?

   a. Underlying the MIRR is the assumption that cash flows can be reinvested at the firm's cost of capital.
   b. Underlying the IRR is the assumption that cash flows can be reinvested at the firm's cost of capital.
   c. Underlying the NPV is the assumption that cash flows can be reinvested at the firm's cost of capital.
   d. The discounted payback method always leads to the same accept/reject decisions as the NPV method.
   e. Statements a and c are both correct.

SELF-TEST PROBLEMS

1. Your firm is considering a fast-food concession at the World's Fair. The cash flow pattern is somewhat unusual since you must build the stands, operate them for 2 years, and then tear the stands down and restore the sites to their original condition. You estimate the net cash flows to be as follows:

Time	Expected Net Cash Flows
0	($800,000)
1	700,000
2	700,000
3	(400,000)

What is the approximate IRR of this venture?

   a. 5%   b. 15%   c. 25%   d. 35%   e. 45%

(The following data apply to the next three Self-Test Problems.)

Toya Motors needs a new machine for production of its new models. The financial vice president has appointed you to do the capital budgeting analysis. You have identified two different machines that are capable of performing the job. You have completed the cash flow analysis, and the expected net cash flows are as follows:

	Expected Net Cash Flow	
Year	Machine B	Machine O
0	($5,000)	($5,000)
1	2,085	0
2	2,085	0
3	2,085	0
4	2,085	9,677

2. What is the payback period for Machine B?

    a. 1.0 year   **b.** 2.0 years   **c.** 2.4 years   **d.** 2.6 years   **e.** 3.0 years

3. The cost of capital is uncertain at this time, so you construct NPV profiles to assist in the final decision. The profiles for Machines B and O cross at what cost of capital?

    a. 6%   **d.** 24%
    b. 10%   **e.** They do not cross in the upper righthand quadrant.
    c. 18%

4. If the cost of capital for both projects is 14 percent at the time the decision is made, which project would you choose?

    a. Project B; it has the higher positive NPV.
    b. Project 0; it has the higher positive NPV.
    c. Neither; both have negative NPVs.
    d. Either; both have the same NPV.
    e. Project B; it has the higher IRR.

(The following data apply to the next six Self-Test Problems.)

The director of capital budgeting for Giant Inc. has identified two mutually exclusive projects, L and S, with the following expected net cash flows:

	Expected Net Cash Flows	
Year	Project L	Project S
0	($100)	($100)
1	10	70
2	60	50
3	80	20

Both projects have a cost of capital of 10 percent.

5. What is the payback period for Project S?

    a. 1.6 years **b.** 1.8 years **c.** 2.1 years **d.** 2.5 years **e.** 2.8 years

6. What is Project L's NPV?

    a. $50.00   **b.** $34.25   **c.** $22.64   **d.** $18.79   **e.** $10.06

7. What is Project L's IRR?

    a. 18.1%   **b.** 19.7%   **c.** 21.4%   **d.** 23.6%   **e.** 24.2%

8. What is Project L's MIRR?

    a. 15.3%   **b.** 16.5%   **c.** 16.9%   **d.** 17.1%   **e.** 17.4%

9. What is Project S's MIRR?

    a. 15.3%   **b.** 16.5%   **c.** 16.9%   **d.** 17.1%   **e.** 17.4%

10. Plot the NPV profiles for the two projects. Where is the crossover point?

    a. 6.9%   **b.** 7.8%   **c.** 8.7%   **d.** 9.6%   **e.** 9.9%

11. Your company is considering two mutually exclusive projects, X and Y, whose costs and cash flows are shown below:

Year	Project X	Project Y
0	($2,000)	($2,000)
1	200	2,000
2	600	200
3	800	100
4	1,400	100

The projects are equally risky, and their cost of capital is 10 percent. You must make a recommendation, and you must base it on the modified IRR. What is the MIRR of the better project?

    a. 11.50%   **b.** 12.00%   **c.** 11.70%   **d.** 12.50%   **e.** 13.10%

12. A company is analyzing two mutually exclusive projects, S and L, whose cash flows are shown below:

Year	Project S	Project L
0	($2,000)	($2,000)
1	1,800	0
2	500	500
3	20	800
4	20	1,600

The company's cost of capital is 9 percent, and it can get an unlimited amount of capital at that cost. What is the regular IRR (not MIRR) of the better project? (Hint: Note that the better project may or may not be the one with the higher IRR.)

a. 11.45%   b. 11.74%   c. 13.02%   d. 13.49%   e. 12.67%

13. The stock of Barkley Inc. and "the market" provided the following returns over the last 5 years:

Year	Barkley	Market
1991	(5)	(3)
1992	21	10
1993	9	4
1994	23	11
1995	31	15

Barkley finances only with retained earnings, and it uses the CAPM with a historical beta to determine its cost of equity. The risk-free rate is 7 percent, and the market risk premium is 5 percent. Barkley is considering a project which has a cost at t = 0 of $2,000 and which is expected to provide cash inflows of $1,000 per year for 3 years. What is the project's MIRR?

a. 23.46%   b. 18.25%   c. 22.92%   d. 20.95%   e. 21.82%

14. CDH Worldwide's stock returns versus the market were as follows, and the same relative volatility is expected in the future:

Year	CDH	Market
1992	12	15
1993	(6)	(3)
1994	25	19
1995	18	12

The T-bond rate is 6 percent; the market risk premium is 7 percent; CDH finances only with equity from retained earnings; and it uses the CAPM to estimate its cost of capital. Now CDH is considering two alternative trucks. Truck S has a cost of $12,000 and is expected to produce cash flows of $4,500 per year for 4 years. Truck L has a cost of $20,000 and is expected to produce cash flows of $7,500 per year for 4 years. By how much would CDH's value rise if it buys the better truck, and what is the MIRR of the better truck?

a. $803.35; 17.05%   **d.** $1,338.91; 16.06%
b. $1,338.91; 17.05%   **e.** $803.35; 14.41%
c. $1,896.47; 16.06%

15. Assume that your company has a cost of capital of 14 percent and that it is analyzing the following project:

```
             0    14%    1        2        3        4
Project M:   +----------+--------+--------+--------+
            -250       140      140      170      -100
```

What are the project's IRR and MIRR?

a. 24.26%; 16.28%   **d.** 24.26%; 17.19%
b. 23.12%; 17.19%   **e.** None of the above
c. 23.12%; 16.28%

ANSWERS TO SELF-TEST QUESTIONS

1. capital budget
2. cash flows
3. payback period
4. simplicity

5. cash flows; ignored
6. discounted
7. positive
8. mutually exclusive; higher

9. zero
10. NPV; discount rate
11. IRR
12. NPV
13. cost of capital; internal rate of return

14. cost of capital
15. post-audit
16. forecasts; operations
17. discount; cash inflows; cash outflows (or initial cost)
18. terminal value

19. a. The more the cash flows are spread over time, the greater is the effect of a change in discount rate. This is because the compounding process has a greater effect as the number of years increases.

20. a. Project cash flows are substitutes for outside capital. Thus, the opportunity cost of these cash flows is the firm's cost of capital, adjusted for risk. The NPV method uses this cost as the reinvestment rate, while the IRR method assumes reinvestment at the IRR.

21. b. The yield to maturity on a bond is the bond's IRR.

22. b. The computation of IRR is independent of the project's cost of capital.

23. a. Both the NPV and IRR methods lead to the same accept/reject decisions for independent projects. Thus, the IRR method can be used as a proxy for the NPV method when choosing independent projects.

24. b. NPV and MIRR may not lead to the same decision when the projects differ in scale.

25. b. Multiple IRRs occur in projects with nonnormal cash flows, but there is only one MIRR for each project.

26. a. If we were to begin graphing the NPV profiles for each of these projects, we would know 2 of the points for each project. The Y-intercepts for Projects A and B would be $7,000 and $5,000, respectively, and the crossover rate would be 10 percent. Thus, from this information we can conclude that Project A's NPV profile would have the steeper slope and would be more sensitive to changes in the discount rate.

27. b. Statement a is false because the IRR is independent of the discount rate. Statement b is true; the situation identified is that of a project with nonnormal cash flows, which has multiple IRRs. Statement c is false; multiple IRRs occur with projects with nonnormal cash flows, not with mutually exclusive projects with different lives. Statement d is false; business executives tend to prefer the IRR because it gives a measure of the project's safety margin.

28. b. Statement b is true; the others are all false. Note that IRR must be greater than the cost of capital; that conflicts arise if the cost of capital is to the left of the crossover rate; and that for some projects with nonnormal cash flows there are two IRRs, so NPV and IRR could lead to conflicting accept/reject decisions, depending on which IRR we examine.

29. e. Statement e is correct, because both statements a and c are true. The IRR assumes reinvestment at the IRR, and since the discounted payback ignores cash flows beyond the payback period, it could lead to rejections of projects with high late cash flows and hence NPV > 0.

SOLUTIONS TO SELF-TEST PROBLEMS

1. c. Unless you have a calculator that performs IRR calculations, the IRR must be obtained by trial and error or graphically. (Calculator solution: Input CF_0 = -800000, CF_{1-2} = 700000, CF_3 = -400000. Output: IRR = 25.48%.) Note that this project actually has multiple IRRs, with a second IRR at about -53 percent.

2. c. After Year 1, there is $5,000 − $2,085 = $2,915 remaining to pay back. After Year 2, only $2,915 − $2,085 = $830 is remaining. In Year 3, another $2,085 is collected. Assuming that the Year 3 cash flow occurs evenly over time, then payback occurs $830/$2,085 = 0.4 of the way through Year 3. Thus, the payback period is 2.4 years.

3. b. To solve graphically, construct the NPV profiles:

The Y-intercept is the NPV when k = 0%. For B, 4($2,085) − $5,000 = $3,340. For O, $9,677 − $5,000 = $4,677. The X-intercept is the discount rate when NPV = $0, or the IRR. For B, $5,000 = $2,085 × $PVIFA_{IRR,4}$; IRR ≈ 24%. For O, $5,000 = $9,677 × $PVIF_{IRR,4}$; IRR ≈ 18%. The graph is an approximation since we are only using two points to plot lines that are curvilinear. However, it shows that there is a crossover point and that it occurs somewhere in the vicinity of k =

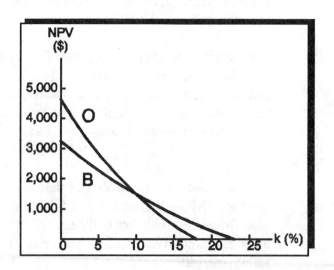

10%. (Note that other data points for the NPV profiles could be obtained by calculating the NPVs for the two projects at different discount rates.)

Alternatively,

Year	B	O	Project Δ (B − O)
0	($5,000)	($5,000)	$ 0
1	2,085	0	2,085
2	2,085	0	2,085
3	2,085	0	2,085
4	2,085	9,677	(7,592)

The IRR of Project Δ, 10.00 percent, is the crossover point.

4. a. Refer to the NPV profiles. When k = 14%, we are to the right of the crossover point and Project B has the higher NPV. You can verify this fact by calculating the NPVs. When k = 14%, NPV_B = $1,075 and NPV_O = $730. Note that Project B also has the higher IRR. However, the NPV method should be used when evaluating mutually exclusive projects. Note that had the project cost of capital been 8 percent, then Project O would be chosen on the basis of the higher NPV.

5. a. After the first year, there is only $30 remaining to be repaid, and $50 is received in Year 2. Assuming an even cash flow throughout the year, the payback period is 1 + $30/$50 = 1.6 years.

6. d. NPV_L = -$100 + $10/1.10 + $60/(1.10)^2 + $80/(1.10)^3 = -$100 + $9.09 + $49.59 + $60.11 = $18.79. Financial calculator solution: Input the cash flows into the cash flow register, I = k = 10, and solve for NPV = $18.78.

7. a. Input the cash flows into the cash flow register and solve for IRR = 18.1%.

8. b. $$\sum_{t=0}^{n} \frac{COF_t}{(1+k)^t} = \frac{\sum_{t=0}^{n} CIF_t(1+k)^{n-t}}{(1+MIRR)^n}.$$

$$\text{PV costs} = \frac{TV}{(1 + MIRR)^n}$$

$$\$100 = \frac{\$10(1.10)^2 + \$60(1.10)^1 + \$80(1.10)^0}{(1 + MIRR)^3}$$

$$= \frac{\$12.10 + \$66.00 + \$80.00}{(1 + MIRR)^3}$$

$$= \frac{\$158.10}{(1 + MIRR)^3}$$

$$MIRR_L = 16.50\%.$$

Alternatively, input N = 3, PV = -100, PMT = 0, FV = 158.10, and solve for I = MIRR = 16.50%.

9. c.
$$\$100 = \frac{\$70(1.10)^2 + \$50(1.10)^1 + \$20(1.10)^0}{(1 + MIRR)^3}$$

$$= \frac{\$84.70 + \$55.00 + \$20.00}{(1 + MIRR)^3}$$

$$= \frac{\$159.70}{(1 + MIRR)^3}$$

$$MIRR_S = 16.89\% \approx 16.9\%.$$

Alternatively, input N = 3, PV = -100, PMT = 0, FV = 159.70, and solve for I = MIRR = 16.89%.

10. c. The NPV profiles plot as follows:

k	NPV_L	NPV_S
0%	$50	$40
5	33	29
10	19	20
15	7	12
20	(4)	5
25	(13)	(2)

By looking at the graph, the approximate crossover point is 8 to 9 percent. Now, to find the precise

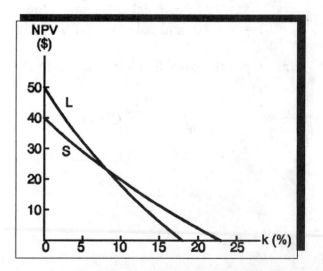

crossover point, determine the cash flows for Project Δ, which is the difference between the two projects' cash flows:

Year	L	S	Project Δ (L − S)
0	($100)	($100)	$ 0
1	10	70	(60)
2	60	50	10
3	80	20	60

The crossover point is the IRR of Project Δ, or 8.7 percent.

11. e. Project X:

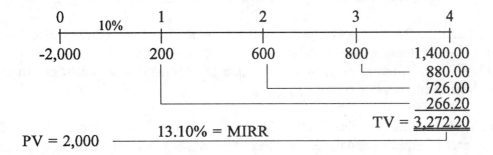

$$\$2,000 = \frac{\$3,272.20}{(1 + MIRR_X)^4}$$

Project Y:

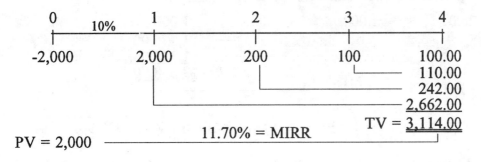

$$\$2,000 = \frac{\$3,114.00}{(1 + MIRR_Y)^4}$$

Project X has the higher MIRR; $MIRR_X = 13.10\%$.

Alternate step: You could calculate NPVs, see that X has the higher NPV, and just calculate MIRR_X. $\text{NPV}_X = \$234.96$ and $\text{NPV}_Y = \$126.90$.

12. b. Put the cash flows into the cash flow register, and then calculate NPV at 9% and IRR:

Project S: $\text{NPV}_S = \$101.83$; $\text{IRR}_S = 13.49\%$.

Project L: $\text{NPV}_L = \$172.07$; $\text{IRR}_L = 11.74\%$.

Because $\text{NPV}_L > \text{NPV}_S$, it is the better project. $\text{IRR}_L = 11.74\%$.

Alternatively, the PVIF table could be used to calculate the NPVs of both projects; however, calculating the IRR by trial and error would be tedious.

13. d. First, calculate the beta coefficient. Barkley's stock has been exactly twice as volatile as the market; thus, beta = 2.0. This can be calculated as $[21 - (-5)]/[10 - (-3)] = 26/13 = 2.0$. (Alternatively, you could use a calculator with statistical functions to determine the beta.)

Next, enter the known values in the CAPM equation to find the required rate of return, or the cost of equity capital. Since the company finances only with equity, this is the cost of capital:

$$\text{CAPM} = k_{RF} + (k_M - k_{RF})b = 7\% + (5\%)b = 7\% + 5\%(2.0) = 17\% = k_s.$$

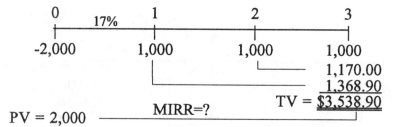

Find TV: N = 3; I = 17; PV = 0; PMT = -1000; FV = 3,538.90.

Find MIRR: N = 3; PV = -2000; PMT = 0; FV = 3538.90; I = MIRR = 20.95%.

14. b. First, we must find the cost of capital. Run a regression between the market and CDH stock returns to get beta = 1.31. Then apply the SML:

$$k_{CDH} = 6\% + 1.31(7) = 15.17\%.$$

(1) Now set up the time lines, insert the proper data into the cash flow register of the calculator, and find the NPV and IRRs for the trucks.

Truck S: NPV = $803.35; IRR = 18.45%.

```
    0          1          2          3          4
    +----------+----------+----------+----------+
       15.17%
 -12,000      4,500      4,500      4,500      4,500
```

Truck L: NPV = $1,338.91; IRR = 18.45%.

```
    0          1          2          3          4
    +----------+----------+----------+----------+
       15.17%
 -20,000      7,500      7,500      7,500      7,500
```

$NPV_L > NPV_S$, thus $Truck_L$ is the better truck.

(2) To find Truck L's MIRR, compound its cash inflows at 15.17 percent to find the TV, then find the MIRR = I that causes PV of TV = $20,000:

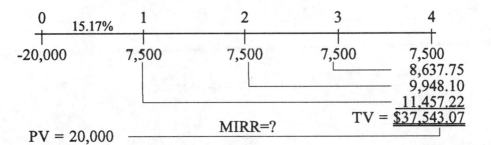

Find TV: Enter N = 4; I = 15.17; PV = 0; PMT = -7500; and solve for FV = $37,543.07.

Find MIRR: Enter N = 4; PV = -20000; PMT = 0; FV = 37543.07; and solve for I = MIRR = 17.05%.

It is interesting to note that both trucks have the same IRR and MIRR; however, the NPV rule should be used so Truck L is the better truck. This problem shows that the NPV method is superior when choosing among competing projects that differ in size.

15. d. IRR = 24.26%; MIRR = 17.19%.

To calculate the IRR, enter the given values into the cash flow register and press the IRR key to get IRR = 24.26%.

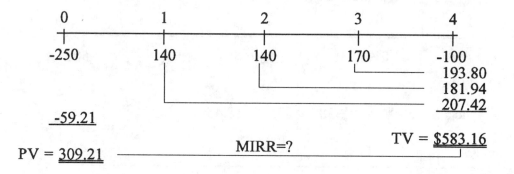

Enter N = 4, PV = -309.21, PMT = 0, FV = 583.16, and solve for MIRR = I = 17.19%.

CHAPTER 11
RISK AND OTHER TOPICS IN CAPITAL BUDGETING

OVERVIEW

One of the most critical steps in capital budgeting analysis is *cash flow estimation*. The key to correct cash flow estimation is to consider only *incremental cash flows*. However, the process is complicated by such factors as sunk costs, opportunity costs, externalities, net working capital changes, and salvage values. Cash flow estimation for replacement projects is similar to that for expansion projects, except that there are more flows to consider when analyzing replacement projects. Adjustments to the analysis must be made for projects with unequal lives as well as for the effects of inflation.

Capital budgeting can affect a firm's market risk, its corporate risk, or both, but it is extremely difficult to quantify either type of risk. Two methods are used to incorporate project risk into capital budgeting: the *certainty equivalent approach* and the *risk-adjusted discount rate approach*.

Capital budgeting and the cost of capital are interrelated--we cannot determine the cost of capital until we determine the size of the capital budget, and we cannot determine the size of the capital budget until we determine the cost of capital. Therefore, the cost of capital and the capital budget must be determined simultaneously.

OUTLINE

The most important, and also the most difficult, step in the analysis of a capital project is estimating its cash flows. Two key concepts in the process are important to recognize: (1) capital decisions must be based on cash flows, not accounting income, and (2) only incremental cash flows are relevant to the accept/reject decision.

■ In capital budgeting analysis, *annual cash flows, not accounting profits,* are used. While accounting profits are important for some purposes, determining the net cash flow (net income plus depreciation) is the most relevant for capital budgeting purposes.

■ In evaluating a capital project, we are concerned only with those cash flows that result directly from the project. These *incremental cash flows* represent the changes in the firm's total cash flows that occur as a direct result of accepting or rejecting the project. Four special problems in determining incremental cash flows follow:

  □ A *sunk cost* is an outlay that has already occurred or has been committed and hence is not affected by the accept/reject decision. Sunk costs are not incremental, and hence should not be included in the analysis.

  □ *Opportunity costs*, which are cash flows that can be generated from assets the firm already owns provided they are not used for the project in question, must be included in the analysis.

  □ *Externalities* are the effects of a project on other parts of the firm, and their effects need to be considered in the incremental cash flows.

  □ *Shipping and installation costs* must be taken into account since they are part of the full cost of the equipment and are included in the depreciable basis when depreciation charges are calculated.

The difference between the required increase in current assets and the spontaneous increase in current liabilities is the change in net working capital.

■ If this change is positive, as it generally is for expansion projects, this indicates that additional financing, over and above the cost of the fixed assets, will be needed to fund the increase in current assets.

■ As the project approaches completion, inventories will be sold off and not replaced, and receivables will be collected. As these changes occur, the firm will receive an end-of-project cash inflow that is equal to the net working capital requirement that occurred when the project was begun.

Two types of capital budgeting decisions are (1) expansion project analysis and (2) replacement project analysis.

■ An expansion project is one that calls for the firm to invest in new facilities to increase sales. Steps in the capital budgeting analysis for an expansion project include:

  □ Summarize the investment outlays required for the project. Changes in net working capital should be included as an outflow here; however, they should be considered as an inflow at the end of the project.

  □ Estimate the cash flows that will occur once production begins, including effects of depreciation and salvage values.

  □ Summarize the data by combining all the net cash flows on a time line and evaluate the project by payback period, IRR, MIRR, and NPV (at the appropriate cost of capital). If the project has a positive NPV, the project should be accepted.

☐ The cost of capital may need to be increased if the project is deemed riskier than the firm's average project.

■ Replacement project analysis is different from that for expansion projects because the cash flows from the old asset must be considered.
  ☐ The following additional cash flows must be considered at time 0:
    • The cash received from the sale of the old equipment is an inflow.
    • However, the sale of the old machine will usually have tax effects. If the old equipment is sold below book value, there will be a tax savings; if the equipment is sold at a profit, taxes must be paid. The tax effect is equal to the loss or gain on the sale times the firm's marginal tax rate.
  ☐ The cash flow from operations calculation must also be modified.
    • First, look at the effects of the new equipment on revenues and costs. An incremental increase in revenues would produce a cash inflow, while an incremental increase in costs would produce a cash outflow, just as before. After combining the revenue and cost effects into a single incremental cash inflow, multiply by $(1 - T)$ to obtain the after-tax cash inflow.
    • The depreciation expense on the old equipment must be subtracted from the depreciation expense on the new equipment to get the net change in depreciation. This amount is then multiplied by the tax rate to find the tax savings or loss from the change in depreciation.
    • Any salvage value on the old machine, including tax effects, must be included as a cash outflow at the end of the project's life. Accepting the new project causes the firm to forgo the old machine's salvage value. Thus, it must be included as an opportunity cost. Of course, any salvage value on the new machine must also be included in the analysis.

If two mutually exclusive projects have significantly different lives, the analysis must include an adjustment. Two procedures have been developed to deal with this problem: (1) the replacement chain method and (2) the equivalent annual annuity method.

■ The replacement chain method extends one, or both, projects until an equal life is achieved.
  ☐ Suppose two mutually exclusive projects are being considered: Project A with a 2-year life, and Project B with a 3-year life. The projects' lives would be extended to a 6-year common life.
  ☐ Project A would have an extended NPV equal to NPV_A plus NPV_A discounted for 2 years at the project's cost of capital, plus NPV_A discounted for 4 years at the project's cost of capital. Project B would have an extended NPV equal to NPV_B plus NPV_B discounted for 3 years at the project's cost of capital.
  ☐ The project with the highest adjusted NPV would be chosen.

☐ This method assumes that the project can be repeated and that there is no change in cash flows.

■ Another way to deal with unequal lives is the equivalent annual annuity (EAA) method.
☐ First, find each project's NPV over its original life. Then find the constant annuity cash flow that has the same present value.
- This can be done by dividing the original NPV of each project by the PVIFA for the project's original life and cost of capital to find the equivalent annual annuity.
- With a financial calculator, enter N, I, and PV to solve for PMT.
☐ The project with the higher EAA would be chosen, because the project with the higher EAA will always have the higher NPV when extended out to any common life.

■ As a general rule, the unequal life issue does not arise for independent projects. Also, common life techniques can only be applied when the shorter-life project is actually expected to be replicated.

Inflationary effects need to be recognized in capital budgeting decisions.

■ Inflationary expectations are built into interest rates and money costs (through the inflation premium). It is reflected in the WACC, which is used to find NPVs, and in the hurdle rate, if the IRR (or MIRR) method is used. The higher the inflation rate, the higher the k (or WACC), and the smaller will be the NPV.

■ If expected inflation is not built into the forecasted cash flows, then the calculated NPV will be incorrect; that is, it will be downwardly biased. Adjusting forecasted cash flows for inflation will produce an unbiased NPV.

Capital budgeting can affect a firm's market risk, its corporate risk, or both, but it is extremely difficult to quantify either type of risk. This makes it difficult to incorporate differential risk into capital budgeting decisions.

■ Two methods are used to incorporate project risk into capital budgeting.
☐ In the *certainty equivalent approach* all cash flows that are not known with certainty are scaled down, and the riskier the flows, the lower their certainty equivalent values.
☐ In the *risk-adjusted discount rate approach* differential project risk is dealt with by changing the discount rate. Average-risk projects are discounted at the firm's average cost of capital, higher-risk projects are discounted at a higher cost of capital, and lower-risk projects are discounted at a rate below the firm's average cost of capital.

■ Diversified companies with divisions of varying risk may use a two-step process to determine a project's risk-adjusted discount rate.

☐ First, divisional costs of capital are established for each of the major operating divisions.

☐ Then, within the division, projects classified as high-risk would have an increased discount rate while low-risk projects would have a lowered discount rate.

Both the firm's investment opportunity schedule (IOS) and its marginal cost of capital (MCC) schedule are important elements in determining the optimal capital budget. The IOS is a plot of the firm's potential projects in descending order of IRR. The MCC is a plot of the firm's weighted average cost of capital.

■ The optimal capital budget, along with the firm's marginal cost of capital, is found by combining the IOS and MCC schedules. The intersection of the IOS and MCC schedules defines the firm's marginal cost of capital.

☐ All projects that have "average" risk should be evaluated at this cost of capital. Note that for independent projects, the IRR method can be used as a proxy for the NPV method since both lead to the same accept/reject decision. Thus, all projects of average risk with IRRs exceeding the firm's marginal cost of capital should be accepted.

☐ However, for mutually exclusive projects, the NPV method should be used, and the appropriate discount rate for average-risk projects is the firm's marginal cost of capital.

■ The procedures set forth above are conceptually correct; however, most companies actually use a more judgmental, less quantitative process for establishing its final capital budget.

☐ A reasonably good estimate of the MCC is obtained from the treasurer, and the director of capital budgeting can get a "good fix" on the IOS schedule.

☐ The IOS and MCC schedules are combined to get a reasonably good approximation of the corporation's marginal cost of capital.

☐ The corporate MCC is scaled up or down to reflect each division's target capital structure and riskiness.

☐ Each project within each division is classified into one of three risk groups: high-, low-, or average-risk.

☐ Each project's NPV is then determined, using its risk-adjusted project cost of capital. The optimal capital budget consists of all independent projects with positive risk-adjusted NPVs plus those mutually exclusive projects with the highest positive risk-adjusted NPVs.

Under ordinary circumstances, a firm should expand to the point where its marginal return is just equal to its marginal cost. Capital rationing occurs when a constraint is placed on the total size of the firm's capital budget.

Appendix 11A reviews depreciation concepts covered in accounting courses. The MACRS classes and asset lives are given, as well as the recovery allowance percentages for 3-year, 5-year, 7-year, and 10-year class personal property.

Appendix 11B discusses refunding operations--whether to call a bond issue now or to postpone the call to a later date. The analysis requires that the NPV of refunding the issue be calculated.

SELF-TEST QUESTIONS

Definitional

1. An increase in net working capital would show up as a cash _____ at time 0 and then again as a cash _____ at the _____ of the project's life.

2. A(n) _____ _____ is a cash outlay which has already occurred or has been committed.

3. In general, a project's operating cash flow in any year is equal to the project's _____ _____ plus its _____ expense.

4. In replacement analysis, two cash flows that occur at t=0 that are not present in expansion projects are the price received from the sale of the _____ equipment and the _____ effects of the sale.

5. In replacement analysis, the depreciation tax savings or loss is based on the _____ in depreciation expense between the old and new asset.

6. A(n) _____ cash flow represents the change in the firm's total cash flow that occurs as a direct result of project acceptance.

7. If two projects are _____, the fact that they have unequal lives will not affect the analysis.

8. If two mutually exclusive projects have unequal lives, either the _____ _____ or the _____ _____ _____ method may be used for the analysis.

9. If the cash flows are real, but the cost of capital is nominal, there will be a(n) _____ bias to the calculated NPV.

10. Riskier projects should be evaluated with a higher _____ ____ _____ than average-risk projects.

12. The marginal cost of capital schedule is a plot of the firm's _____ _____ _____ _____ _____ versus the dollars of new capital raised.

13. The firm's _____ _____ ____ _____ is defined by the intersection of the MCC and IOS schedules.

14. All projects of _____ risk should be evaluated at the firm's marginal cost of capital.

15. In general, projects can be evaluated using the IRR method; however, _____ _____ projects must be evaluated by the NPV method.

16. _____ _____ occurs when firms set an absolute limit on the dollar amount of investment capital.

Conceptual

17. In general, the value of land currently owned by a firm is irrelevant to a capital budgeting decision because the cost of that property is a sunk cost.

    a. True   **b.** False

18. McDonald's is planning to open a new store across from the student union. Annual revenues are expected to be $5 million. However, opening the new location will cause annual revenues to drop by $3 million at McDonald's existing stadium location. The relevant sales revenues for the capital budgeting analysis are $2 million per year.

    a. True   **b.** False

19. In replacement project analysis, the salvage value of the old asset need not be considered since the current market value of the asset is included in the analysis.

    a. True   **b.** False

20. When independent projects of different risk are to be considered in capital budgeting, any project will be acceptable to the firm if the project's IRR is greater than the firm's weighted average cost of capital.

    a. True   **b.** False

21. The equivalent annual annuity (EAA) for a project is determined by dividing the project's original NPV by

   a. The PVIF for the project's original life and cost of capital.
   b. The cost of the project.
   c. The cost of capital.
   d. The PVIFA for the project's original life and cost of capital.
   e. The number of years of the project's life.

22. Two corporations are formed. They are identical in all respects except for their methods of depreciation. Firm A uses MACRS depreciation, while Firm B uses the straight line method. Both plan to depreciate their assets for tax purposes over a 5-year life (6 calendar years), which is equal to the useful life, and both pay a 35 percent tax rate. (Note: The half-year convention will apply, so the firm using the straight line method will take 10 percent depreciation in Year 1 and 10 percent in Year 6.) Which of the following statements is *false*?

   a. Firm A will generate higher cash flows from operations in the first year than B.
   b. Firm A will pay more Federal corporate income taxes in the first year than B.
   c. If there is no change in tax rates over the 6-year period, and if we disregard the time value of money, the total amount of funds generated from operations by these projects for each corporation will be the same over the 6 years.
   d. Firm B will pay the same amount of federal corporate income taxes, over the 6-year period, as A.
   e. Firm A could, if it chose to, use straight line depreciation for stockholder reporting even if it used MACRS for tax purposes.

23. Which of the following steps are commonly used in practice to establish a firm's optimal capital budget?

   a. Rough estimates of the MCC and IOS schedules are used to obtain the firm's MCC.
   b. The corporate MCC is scaled up or down to reflect each division's capital structure and risk characteristics.
   c. Each division's MCC is scaled up or down to reflect differential project risk.
   d. Each project's NPV is then determined using its appropriate risk-adjusted cost of capital.
   e. All the above steps are used.

SELF-TEST PROBLEMS

1. The capital budgeting director of National Products Inc. is evaluating a new project that would decrease operating costs by $30,000 per year without affecting revenues. The project's cost is $50,000. The project will be depreciated using the MACRS method over its 3-year class life. It will have a *zero salvage value* after 3 years. The marginal tax rate of National Products is 35 percent, and the project's cost of capital is 12 percent. What is the project's NPV?

   a. $7,068   **b.** $8,324   **c.** $10,214   **d.** $11,010   **e.** $12,387

2. Your firm has a marginal tax rate of 40 percent and a cost of capital of 14 percent. You are performing a capital budgeting analysis on a new project that will cost $500,000. The project is expected to have a useful life of 10 years, although its MACRS class life is only 5 years. The project is expected to increase the firm's net income by $61,257 per year and to have a salvage value of $35,000 at the end of 10 years. What is the project's NPV?

   a. $95,356   **b.** $108,359   **c.** $135,256   **d.** $162,185   **e.** $177,902

3. The Board of Directors of National Brewing Inc. is considering the acquisition of a new still. The still is priced at $600,000 but would require $60,000 in transportation costs and $40,000 for installation. The still has a useful life of 10 years but will be depreciated over its 5-year MACRS life. It is expected to have a salvage value of $10,000 at the end of 10 years. The still would increase revenues by $120,000 per year and increase yearly operating costs by $20,000 per year. Additionally, the still would require a $30,000 increase in net working capital. The firm's marginal tax rate is 40 percent, and the project's cost of capital is 10 percent. What is the NPV of the still?

   a. $18,430   **b.** -$12,352   **c.** -$65,204   **d.** -$130,961   **e.** -$203,450

(The following data apply to Self-Test Problems 4 through 6.)

As the capital budgeting director of Union Mills Inc. you are analyzing the replacement of an automated loom system. The old system was purchased 5 years ago for $200,000; it falls into the MACRS 5-year class; and it has 5 years of remaining life and a $50,000 salvage value five years from now. The current market value of the old system is $100,000. The new system has a price of $300,000, plus an additional $50,000 in installation costs. The new system falls into the MACRS 5-year class, has a 5-year economic life, and a $100,000 salvage value. The new system will require a $40,000 increase in the spare parts inventory. The primary advantage of the new system is that it will decrease operating costs by $40,000 per year. Union Mills has a 12 percent cost of capital and a marginal tax rate of 35 percent.

4. What is the net cash investment at Year 0?

 a. $350,000   **b.** $320,800   **c.** $295,000   **d.** $40,000   **e.** $23,200

5. What is the annual net operating cash inflow in Year 1?

 a. $46,300   **b.** $43,950   **c.** $39,825   **d.** $33,350   **e.** $50,200

6. What is the net cash flow in the final year (Year 5)?

 a. $31,360   **b.** $43,060   **c.** $119,325   **d.** $121,930   **e.** $117,200

(The following data apply to Self-Test Problems 7 and 8.)

Buckeye Foundries builds railroad cars and then leases them to railroads and shippers. The company has some old boxcars which it plans to convert into specialized carriers. Its analysts foresee demand in two areas—cars to carry coal and cars to carry livestock. Each type of car will cost $50,000 per car to convert. Because of the greater weight they will carry, the coal cars will last only 10 years but will provide an after-tax cash flow of $9,500 per year. The livestock cars will last for 15 years, and their annual after-tax cash flow is estimated at $8,140. Buckeye's cost of capital is 10 percent. At the end of each car's original life, it can be rebuilt into "like new" condition at a cost expected to equal the original conversion cost. Also, since Buckeye has only a limited number of cars to convert, regard the two types of cars as being mutually exclusive.

7. Using the replacement chain method of evaluation, find the adjusted NPV for each alternative.

 a. $8,373; $11,913   **c.** $8,373; $16,212   **e.** $12,846; $14,765
 b. $8,373; $14,765   **d.** $12,846; $11,913

8. Which alternative should be taken according to the equivalent annual annuity method?

 a. Livestock cars, since their EAA equals $1,363 versus the coal cars' EAA of $1,200.
 b. Coal cars, since their EAA equals $1,363 versus the livestock cars' EAA of $1,200.
 c. Livestock cars, since their EAA equals $1,566 versus the coal cars' EAA of $1,363.
 d. Coal cars, since their EAA equals $1,566 versus the livestock cars' EAA of $1,363.
 e. Coal cars, since their EAA equals $2,000 versus the livestock cars' EAA of $1,566.

9. Central City Electric is considering two alternative ways to meet demand: It can build a coal-fired plant (Project C) at a cost of $1,000 million. This plant would have a 20-year life and would provide net cash flows of $120 million per year over its life. Alternatively, the company can build a gas-fired plant (Project G) that would cost $400 million and would produce net cash flows of $68 million per year for 10 years, after which the plant would have to be replaced. The power will be needed for exactly 20 years; the cost of capital for either plant is 10 percent; and inflation and productivity gains are expected to offset one another so as to leave expected costs and cash flows constant over time. What is the NPV of the better project, that is, how much (in millions) will the better project add to Central City's total value?

   a. $17.83   b. $21.63   c. $20.03   d. $24.70   e. $19.57

10. Consolidated Inc. uses a weighted average cost of capital of 12 percent to evaluate average-risk projects and adds/subtracts two percentage points to evaluate projects of greater/lesser risk. Currently, two mutually exclusive projects are under consideration. Both have a net cost of $200,000 and last 4 years. Project A, which is riskier than average, will produce yearly after-tax net cash flows of $71,000. Project B, which has less-than-average risk, will produce an after-tax net cash flow of $146,000 in Years 3 and 4 only. What should Consolidated do?

   a. Accept Project B with an NPV of $9,412.
   b. Accept both projects since both NPVs are greater than zero.
   c. Accept Project A with an NPV of $6,874.
   d. Accept neither project since both NPVs are less than zero.
   e. Accept Project A with an NPV of $15,652.

11. Consolidated Industries' overall cost of capital (WACC) is 10 percent. Division HR is riskier than average, Division AR has average risk, and Division LR is less risky than average. Consolidated adjusts for risk by adding or subtracting 2 percentage points. What is the risk-adjusted project cost of capital for a low-risk project in the HR division?

   a. 6%   b. 8%   c. 10%   d. 12%   e. 14%

(The following data apply to Self-Test Problems 12 through 14.)

The Braxton Corp. has the following investment opportunities in the coming planning period:

Project	Net Investment	IRR
F	$300,000	18%
G	100,000	15
H	200,000	13
H*	200,000	12
I	100,000	10

Projects H and H* are mutually exclusive. The firm's MCC schedule is 10 percent up to $500,000 of new capital, and 11 percent thereafter.

12. What is the firm's marginal cost of capital?

   a. 10%   **b.** 11%   **c.** 12%   **d.** 13%   **e.** 15%

13. Assume that all projects have average risk. What is the dollar total of the firm's optimal capital budget?

   a. $300,000   **b.** $400,000   **c.** $500,000   **d.** $600,000   **e.** $700,000

14. Now assume that Project F is riskier than average and that Project I is less risky than average. The remaining projects have average risk. Braxton's policy is to adjust the marginal cost of capital up or down by 2 percentage points to account for risk. What is the effect of differential risk on Braxton's optimal capital budget?

   a. The capital budget is not changed.
   b. Project F is now unacceptable.
   c. The capital budget is now $700,000.
   d. Project I becomes acceptable.
   e. Both c and d are correct.

Appendix 11B

B-1. The city of Tampa issued $1,000,000 of 12 percent coupon, 25-year, semiannual payment, tax-exempt muni bonds 10 years ago. The bonds had 10 years of call protection, but now Tampa can call the bonds if it chooses to do so. The call premium would be 11 percent of the face amount. New 15-year, 10 percent, semiannual payment bonds can be sold at par, but flotation costs on this issue would be 3 percent, or $30,000. What is the net present value of the refunding?

    a. $13,011   **b.** $12,262   **c.** $15,121   **d.** $13,725   **e.** $14,545

B-2.   Assume that the Tennessee Valley Power Authority (which is exempt from income taxes) issued $100,000 of 30-year maturity, 10 percent coupon, semiannual payment, tax-exempt bonds on January 1, 1986. The bonds were callable after 10 years, or after January 1, 1996, at a price that is 10 percent above the bonds' par value. On January 1, 1996, the Power Authority learns that it can issue $100,000 of new 20-year, semiannual payment, 8 percent coupon bonds at par. Costs associated with selling the new issue will amount to $2,000. What is the NPV of the refunding decision?

    a. -$7,485.46   **b.** $9,285.48   **c.** -$4,334.60   **d.** $7,792.77   **e.** $6,982.74

B-3.   Assume that the city of Pensacola has $10 million of 12 percent, 20-year, $1,000 par value, semiannual payment bonds outstanding that can be called at a price of $1,100 per bond. New 20-year, 10 percent, semiannual payment bonds can be sold at a flotation cost of $600,000, or 6 percent. What is the NPV of the refunding operation?

    a. $115,909   **b.** $120,606   **c.** $125,505   **d.** $130,707   **e.** $135,808

ANSWERS TO SELF-TEST QUESTIONS

1. outflow; inflow; end
2. sunk cost
3. net income; depreciation
4. old; tax
5. difference
6. incremental
7. independent
8. replacement chain; equivalent annual annuity

9. downward
10. cost of capital
11. investment opportunity schedule
12. weighted average cost of capital
13. marginal cost of capital
14. average
15. mutually exclusive
16. Capital rationing

17. b. The net market value of land currently owned is an opportunity cost of the project. If the project is not undertaken, the land could be sold to realize its current market value less any taxes and expenses. Thus, project acceptance means forgoing this cash inflow.

18. a. Incremental revenues, which are relevant in a capital budgeting decision, must consider the effects on other parts of the firm.

19. b. In an incremental analysis, the cash flows assuming replacement are compared with the cash flows assuming the old asset is retained. If the old asset is retained, it will produce a salvage value cash flow which must be included, with tax effects, in the replacement analysis.

20. b. The only time this statement holds is when all independent projects being evaluated have the same risk as the firm's current average project. Otherwise, the cost of capital must be adjusted for project risk.

21. d. The EAA is the annual constant cash flow which, over the project's original life, produces the project's original NPV. Thus, the divisor is the PVIFA.

22. b. Statement a is true; MACRS is an accelerated depreciation method, so Firm A will have a higher depreciation expense than Firm B. We are also given that both firms are identical except for depreciation methods used. Net cash flow is equal to net income plus depreciation. In Year 1, Firm A's depreciation expense is twice as great as Firm B's; however, Firm A's lower net income is more than compensated for by the addition of depreciation (which is twice as high as Firm B's). Thus, in Year 1, Firm A's net cash flow is greater than Firm B's. Statement b is false; because Firm A's depreciation expense is larger, it's earnings before taxes will be lower, and thus it will pay less income taxes than Firm B. Statements c, d, and e are all true.

23. e. In fact, responses (a) through (d) are the steps normally followed, in the correct sequence.

SOLUTIONS TO SELF-TEST PROBLEMS

1. d. Cash flow = Net income + Depreciation. The first step is to set up the income statement for Years 1 through 3. (Note that a reduction in operating costs increases revenues.)

	1	2	3
Revenues	$30,000	$30,000	$30,000
- Depreciation[a]	16,500	22,500	7,500
EBT	$13,500	$ 7,500	$22,500
- Taxes (35%)	4,725	2,625	7,875
Net income	$ 8,775	$ 4,875	$14,625
+ Depreciation	16,500	22,500	7,500
	$25,275	$27,375	$22,125
SV tax savings[b]			1,225
Net cash flow	$25,275	$27,375	$23,350

[a]Depreciation schedule: Cost basis = $50,000.

Year	Allowance Percentage	Depreciation	Ending Book Value
1	0.33	$16,500	$33,500
2	0.45	22,500	11,000
3	0.15	7,500	3,500
4	0.07	3,500	0
		$50,000	

[b]At the end of Year 3, the project will not be fully depreciated to its book value of $3,500; however, its salvage value is zero. Thus, National can reduce its taxable income by $3,500, producing a 0.35($3,500) = $1,225 tax savings.

The project's cash flows are then placed on a time line as follows and discounted at the project's cost of capital:

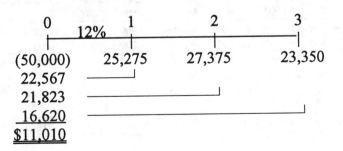

Alternatively, input the cash flows into the cash flow register, input I = 12, and then solve for NPV = $11,010.

2. e. In this case, the *net income* of the project is \$61,257. Net cash flow = Net income + Depreciation = \$61,257 + Depreciation. The depreciation allowed in each year is calculated as follows:

$Dep_1 = \$500,000(0.20) = \$100,000.$
$Dep_2 = \$500,000(0.32) = \$160,000.$
$Dep_3 = \$500,000(0.19) = \$95,000.$
$Dep_4 = \$500,000(0.12) = \$60,000.$
$Dep_5 = \$500,000(0.11) = \$55,000.$
$Dep_6 = \$500,000(0.06) = \$30,000.$
$Dep_{7-10} = \$0.$

In the final year (Year 10), the firm receives \$35,000 from the sale of the machine. However, the book value of the machine is \$0. Thus, the firm would have to pay 0.4(\$35,000) = \$14,000 in taxes; and the net salvage value is \$35,000 - \$14,000 = \$21,000. The time line is as follows:

0 14%	1	2	3	4	5	6	7	8	9	10
(500,000)	61,257	61,257	61,257	61,257	61,257	61,257	61,257	61,257	61,257	61,257
	100,000	160,000	95,000	60,000	55,000	30,000				21,000
(500,000)	161,257	221,257	156,257	121,257	116,257	91,257	61,257	61,257	61,257	82,257

The project's NPV can be found by discounting each of the cash flows at the firm's 14 percent cost of capital. The project's NPV, found by using a financial calculator, is \$177,902.

3. d. Cash flow = Net income + Depreciation. The first step to this problem is to set up the income statement for Years 1 through 10. (Note that the return of NWC is not shown in the income statement here, but is shown on the time line that follows.)

	1	2	3	4	5	6	7-9	10
Revenues	120,000	120,000	120,000	120,000	120,000	120,000	120,000	120,000
- Operating costs	20,000	20,000	20,000	20,000	20,000	20,000	20,000	20,000
- Depreciation[a]	140,000	224,000	133,000	84,000	77,000	42,000		
EBT	(40,000)	(124,000)	(33,000)	16,000	23,000	58,000	100,000	100,000
- Taxes (40%)	(16,000)	(49,600)	(13,200)	6,400	9,200	23,200	40,000	40,000
Net income	(24,000)	(74,400)	(19,800)	9,600	13,800	34,800	60,000	60,000
+ Depreciation	140,000	224,000	133,000	84,000	77,000	42,000		
	116,000	149,600	113,200	93,600	90,800	76,800	60,000	60,000
SV (AT)[b]								6,000
Cash flow	116,000	149,600	113,200	93,600	90,800	76,800	60,000	66,000

[a]Depreciation schedule:

Cost basis = Price + Transportation + Installation = \$600,000 + \$60,000 + \$40,000 = \$700,000.

Year	Allowance Percentage	Depreciation	Ending Book Value
1	0.20	$140,000	$560,000
2	0.32	224,000	336,000
3	0.19	133,000	203,000
4	0.12	84,000	119,000
5	0.11	77,000	42,000
6	0.06	42,000	0
		$700,000	

[b]At the end of Year 10 the still has a salvage value of $10,000; however, it has been fully depreciated so the firm must pay taxes of 0.4($10,000) = $4,000. Therefore, the still's after-tax salvage value is $10,000 - $4,000 = $6,000. The still's cash flows are then placed on a time line as follows and discounted at the project's cost of capital:

```
    0  10%  1        2        3        4       5       6       7       8       9        10
    +------+--------+--------+--------+-------+-------+-------+-------+-------+--------+
(700,000) 116,000 149,600 113,200  93,600  90,800  76,800  60,000  60,000  60,000  66,000
 (30,000)*                                                                         +30,000*

(730,000) 116,000 149,600 113,200  93,600  90,800  76,800  60,000  60,000  60,000  96,000
```

*An increase in net working capital is required in Year 0, so this must be added back to the cash flow at the end of the project's life.

4. b.

Price of new machine	($300,000)
Installation	(50,000)
Sale of old machine	+100,000
Tax on sale*	(30,800)
Increase in net working capital	(40,000)
	($320,800)

*The old machine has been depreciated down to $12,000, since it falls into the MACRS 5-year class and it has been in operation for 5 years. Now, the old machine has a market value of $100,000. The $88,000 (market value minus book value) is treated as ordinary income and is taxed at 35 percent. Thus, Union Mills must pay a tax of 0.35($88,000) = $30,800 on the sale of the old asset.

5. a. The after-tax revenue/cost component is 0.65($40,000) = $26,000. As for the tax savings due to depreciation, the depreciable basis for the new machine is $350,000. Further, the MACRS depreciation allowance for Year 1 of a 5-year class asset is 20 percent. Thus, the depreciation expense on the new machine is 0.20($350,000) = $70,000. The old machine has not been fully depreciated, so its depreciation expense in Year 1 is $12,000, and the change in depreciation due to the replacement decision is an increase of $58,000. The tax savings is 0.35($58,000) = $20,300. Therefore, the Year 1 net cash flow from operations is $26,000 + $20,300 = $46,300.

6. c. In the final year, Year 5, the net cash flow is composed of 0.65($40,000) = $26,000 in after-tax cost decrease and 0.35(0.11)($350,000) = $13,475 in depreciation tax savings, for a total of $39,475, plus the applicable nonoperating cash flows. Thus, we have the following:

From operations	$ 39,475
Salvage value of new machine	100,000
Tax on new machine salvage value	(27,650)
Salvage value of old machine	(50,000)
Tax on old machine salvage value	17,500
Change in working capital	40,000
Net cash flow	$119,325

Note that the salvage value of the old machine is a cash outflow. This is an opportunity cost, since buying the new machine deprives Union Mills of the salvage value of the old machine. Additionally, salvage tax effects must be considered. Also note that the change in working capital considered at $t = 0$, an outflow, is exactly offset by an inflow at the end of the project. This is because it is assumed that the project will terminate and the increase in working capital is no longer required.

7. e. First, find each car's original NPV as follows:

$$NPV_C = \$9,500(PVIFA_{10\%,10}) - \$50,000 = \$8,373.$$
$$NPV_L = \$8,140(PVIFA_{10\%,15}) - \$50,000 = \$11,913.$$

Now look at the projects at a common life of 30 years:

$$Adjusted\ NPV_C = \$8,373 + \$8,373(PVIF_{10\%,10}) + \$8,373(PVIF_{10\%,20}) = \$12,846.$$
$$Adjusted\ NPV_L = \$11,913 + \$11,913(PVIF_{10\%,15}) = \$14,765.$$

Alternatively, once you've found the original NPV of each car, then the replication of the cars can be shown on the time line.

Coal:

```
        0                    10                  20
        |—————— 10% ————————|———————————————————|
        8,373               8,373               8,373
        3,228
        1,245
       12,846
```

Livestock:

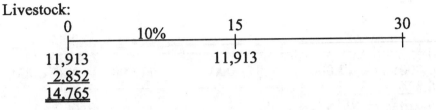

8. c. The original NPVs were calculated above. Now:

EAA_C = \$8,373/$PVIFA_{10\%,10}$ = \$8,373/6.1446 = \$1,363. Alternatively, input N = 10, I = 10, PV = -8373, FV = 0, and solve for PMT = \$1,363.

EAA_L = \$11,913/$PVIFA_{10\%,15}$ = \$11,913/7.6061 = \$1,566. Alternatively, input N = 15, I = 10, PV = -11913, FV = 0, and solve for PMT = \$1,566.

Because $EAA_L > EAA_C$ the livestock cars should be chosen.

9. d. Project C:

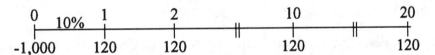

With a financial calculator, input the cash flows into the cash flow register, input I = 10, and then solve for NPV = \$21.63 million.

Project G:

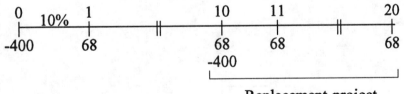

Replacement project

With a financial calculator input the cash flows for the first replication of the project into the cash flow register, input I = 10, and then solve for NPV = \$17.83 million. However, this NPV must be adjusted for a 20-year common life. The NPV for the next replication can be calculated by inputting N = 10, I = 10, PMT = 0, FV = 17.83, and then solving for NPV = \$6.87. Thus, the extended NPV for Project G = \$17.83 + \$6.87 = \$24.70 million:

$$\text{Extended NPV}_G = \$17.83 + (PVIF_{10\%,10})\$17.83$$
$$= \$17.83 + \$6.87 = \$24.70 \text{ million.}$$

10. a. Look at the time lines:

A:

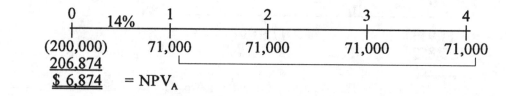

Alternatively, input the cash flows in the cash flow register, I = 14, and then solve for $NPV_A = \$6,873.57$.

B:

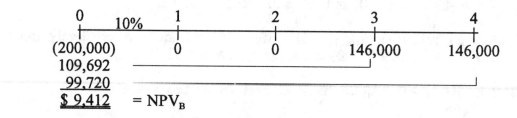

Alternatively, input the cash flows in the cash flow register, I = 10, and then solve for $NPV_B = \$9,411.93$.

Note that both discount rates are adjusted for risk. Since the projects are mutually exclusive, the project with the higher NPV is chosen.

11. c. $k_{HR} = 10\% + 2\% = 12\%$; $k_{Project} = 12\% - 2\% = 10\%$.

12. b. First, plot the MCC and IOS schedules:

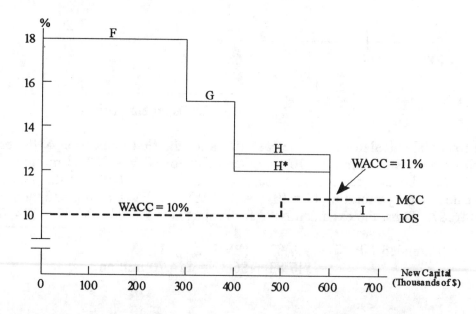

The intersection of the schedules defines the firm's marginal cost of capital. Thus, Braxton's MCC is 11 percent.

13. d. Since all projects have average risk, they are all evaluated at a project cost of capital of 11 percent. Clearly, Projects F and G are acceptable since their IRRs exceed 11 percent. (Since they are independent projects, it is permissible to use the IRR method as a proxy for the NPV method.) The decision between Projects H and H* must be made according to the NPV rule. Since we do not know the project cash flows, we cannot calculate their NPVs. However, one of the two would be chosen since both will have positive NPVs. Thus, the optimal capital budget consists of Projects F and G, and either Project H or H*, and totals $600,000.

14. e. Since Project F is riskier than average, its cost of capital must be adjusted upward to 11% + 2% = 13%. However, its IRR is 18 percent so Project F remains acceptable. On the other hand, Project I's cost of capital is adjusted downward to 9 percent, and hence it becomes acceptable. Thus, the optimal capital budget increases to $700,000. Note that Braxton's MCC remains at 11 percent.

Appendix 11B

B-1. d. Interest on old bond per 6 months: $120,000/2 = $60,000
Interest on new bond per 6 months: $100,000/2 =   50,000
Savings per six months $10,000

Cost: Call premium = 11% − $110,000
      Flotation cost = 3% =   30,000
      Total investment outlay $140,000

$k_d/2 = 10\%/2 = 5\%$ per 6 months.

$$NPV = \sum_{t=1}^{30} \frac{\$10,000}{(1+k)^t} - \$140,000 = \$153,725 - \$140,000 = \$13,725.$$

Alternatively, input the cash flows into the cash flow register, enter I = 5, and then solve for NPV = $13,725.

B-2. d.   Cost of refunding = Call premium + Flotation cost
        = 0.10($100,000) + $2,000 = $12,000.

    Savings each 6 months = Interest on old bonds − Interest on new bonds
        = 0.05($100,000) − 0.04($100,000)
        = $5,000 − $4,000 = $1,000.

$k_d/2 = 8.0\%/2 = 4.0\%$ = Discount rate for NPV.

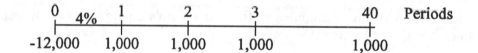

$$NPV = \sum_{t=1}^{40} \frac{\$1,000}{(1.04)^t} - \$12,000 = \$19,792.77 - \$12,000 = \$7,792.77.$$

B-3. a. Cost of refunding = Call premium + Flotation cost
= ($1,100 − $1,000)10,000 + $600,000 = $1,600,000.

Savings each 6 months = Interest on old bonds − Interest on new bonds
= 0.06($1,000)(10,000) − 0.05($1,000)(10,000)
= $100,000.

Using a time line, the cash flows are shown below:

```
  0       5%      1             2          ...  40    Periods
  +---------------+-------------+---------------+
-1,600,000     100,000       100,000         100,000
```

$$NPV = \sum_{t=1}^{40} \frac{\$100,000}{(1.05)^t} - \$1,600,000.$$

Using a financial calculator, input the cash flows into the cash flow register, enter
I = 5, and then solve for NPV = $115,908.64 ≈ $115,909.

CHAPTER 12
CAPITAL STRUCTURE AND LEVERAGE

OVERVIEW

Capital structure theory suggests that some optimal capital structure exists which simultaneously maximizes a firm's stock price and minimizes its cost of capital. The use of debt tends to increase earnings per share, which will lead to a higher stock price; but, at the same time, the use of debt also increases the risk borne by stockholders, which lowers the stock price. The optimal capital structure strikes a balance between these risk and return effects. While it is difficult to determine the optimal capital structure with precision, it is possible to identify the factors that influence it. A firm's target capital structure is generally set equal to the estimated optimal capital structure. The target may change over time as conditions vary, but, at any given moment, a well-managed firm's management has a specific structure in mind; and financing decisions are made so as to be consistent with this target structure.

OUTLINE

Capital structure policy involves a tradeoff between risk and return: Using more debt raises the riskiness of the firm's earnings stream; however, a higher debt ratio generally leads to a higher expected rate of return.

■ The optimal capital structure is the one that strikes the optimal balance between risk and return and thereby maximizes the price of the stock.

■ Four primary factors influence capital structure decisions:
   ☐ Business risk is the amount of risk in a firm's operations if no debt is used. The greater the firm's business risk, the lower its optimal debt ratio.
   ☐ A major reason for using debt is the fact that interest is tax deductible. Therefore, the higher a firm's tax rate, the more advantageous debt is to the firm.

❑ Financial flexibility, which is the ability to raise capital on reasonable terms under adverse conditions, is another consideration. The potential future availability of funds, and the consequences of a funds shortage, have a major influence on the target capital structure.

❑ Managerial conservatism or aggressiveness influences the target capital structures firms actually establish.

Business risk is the uncertainty inherent in estimates of future returns on assets, or of returns on equity if the firm uses no debt, and is the single most important determinant of a firm's capital structure.

■ Business risk varies from one industry to another and also among firms in a given industry. It can also change over time.

■ Business risk depends on the following factors: (1) demand variability, (2) sales price variability, (3) input price variability, (4) ability to adjust output prices for changes in input prices, and (5) operating leverage (the extent to which costs are fixed).

■ Operating leverage is the degree to which a firm uses fixed costs in its production processes.

❑ High operating leverage implies that a relatively small change in sales will result in a large change in operating income.

❑ The higher a firm's degree of operating leverage, the higher its breakeven point tends to be.

• The breakeven point is defined as the volume of sales at which total costs equal total revenues, so profits equal zero.

• The breakeven point is calculated as fixed costs divided by the difference in sales price and variable cost per unit: $Q_{BE} = F/(P - V)$.

❑ The higher a firm's operating leverage, the higher its business risk, other things held constant.

❑ Production technology limits control over the amount of fixed costs and operating leverage. However, firms do have some control over the type of production processes they employ, and so the firm's capital budgeting decisions will have an impact on its operating leverage and business risk.

Financial leverage refers to the firm's use of fixed-income securities, such as debt and preferred stock, and financial risk is the additional risk placed on the common stockholders as a result of using financial leverage.

■ The degree to which a firm employs financial leverage will affect its expected earnings per share (EPS) and the riskiness of these earnings. Financial leverage will cause EPS to rise if the return on assets is greater than the cost of debt. However, the degree of risk associated with the firm will also increase as leverage increases.

■ The optimal capital structure is the one that maximizes the price of the firm's stock, and this always calls for a debt ratio which is lower than the one that maximizes expected EPS.

■ At first, EPS will rise as the use of debt increases. Interest charges rise, but the number of outstanding shares will decrease as equity is replaced by debt. At some point EPS will peak. Beyond this point interest rates will rise so fast that EPS is depressed in spite of the fact that the number of shares outstanding is decreasing.

■ Risk, as measured by the standard deviation of EPS, rises continuously as the use of debt increases.

■ The expected stock price will at first increase with financial leverage, will then reach a peak, and finally will decline as financial leverage becomes excessive due to the importance of potential bankruptcy costs.
   □ The optimal capital structure is found when the expected stock price is maximized.
   □ Management should set its target capital structure at this ratio of debt/assets.

■ The financial structure that maximizes EPS usually has more debt than the one which results in the highest stock price.

Operating leverage and financial leverage are interrelated: A reduction in operating leverage would normally lead to an increase in the optimal amount of financial leverage, while an increase in operating leverage would lead to a decrease in the optimal amount of debt.

■ The degree of operating leverage (DOL) is defined as the percentage change in operating income (EBIT) that results from a given percentage change in sales.
   □ The formula used to analyze the DOL for a single product is shown below:

$$DOL = \frac{Q(P - V)}{Q(P - V) - F}.$$

   Here, Q = units of output, P = sales price per unit, V = variable cost per unit, and F = fixed operating costs.
   □ The formula to analyze the DOL for an entire firm is shown below:

$$DOL = \frac{S - VC}{S - VC - F}.$$

   Here, S = sales in dollars, VC = total variable costs, and F = fixed operating costs.

■ Financial leverage affects earnings after interest and taxes. The degree of financial leverage (DFL) is the percentage change in earnings available to common stockholders (EPS) that results from a given percentage change in EBIT.

  ☐ The formula for DFL is:

$$DFL = \frac{\%\Delta EPS}{\%\Delta EBIT} = \frac{EBIT}{EBIT - I}.$$

  ☐ To find the effects on income available to common stockholders, multiply the percentage change in EBIT by DFL. The greater the degree of financial leverage, the greater the impact of a given change in EBIT on EPS.

■ Degree of total leverage (DTL) combines DOL and DFL to show how a given change in sales will affect EPS.

  ☐ One formula for DTL is: DTL = DOL × DFL. Equivalent formulas include:

$$DTL = \frac{Q(P - V)}{Q(P - V) - F - I} = \frac{S - VC}{S - VC - F - I}.$$

  ☐ DTL shows the interrelationship between operating and financial leverage.
  ☐ The DTL number can be used to find the new earnings per share for any given percentage increase in sales:

$$EPS_1 = EPS_0[1 + DTL(\%\Delta Sales)].$$

There are problems with using the type of leverage analyses described in the text.

■ It is extremely difficult to determine the relationships among financial leverage, P/E ratios, and cost of equity, k_s. Therefore, it is frequently difficult to use stock price analysis to determine a target capital structure.

■ Established management teams are often conservative; they may be more interested in survival than in maximizing expected stock prices.

■ Firms that provide vital services (utilities) must put long-run viability above short-run stock price maximization or cost of capital minimization.

■ Because of these factors, management may place considerable emphasis on the times-interest-earned ratio and the fixed charge coverage ratio when establishing the firm's financial structure. The higher these ratios, the less likely it is that a firm will be unable to meet all of its fixed charge obligations and thus face bankruptcy.

Modern capital structure theory began in 1958, when Professors Franco Modigliani and Merton Miller (MM) published what has been called the most influential finance article ever written.

■ MM proved, under a very restrictive set of assumptions, that a firm's value is unaffected by its capital structure. Their theory produces what is often referred to as the "irrelevance result."

■ MM provided us with some clues about what is required for capital structure to be relevant and hence to have an effect on a firm's value. Consequently, MM's work was only the beginning of capital structure research.

■ MM published a follow-up paper in 1963 in which they relaxed the assumption that there are no corporate taxes. MM demonstrated that if all of their other assumptions hold, the asymmetry of the tax deductibility of interest versus the non-deductibility of dividend payments leads to a situation which calls for 100 percent debt financing.

■ Merton Miller than analyzed the effects of personal taxes. While an increase in the corporate tax rate makes debt look better to corporations, an increase in the personal tax rate encourages additional equity financing.

■ Bankruptcy-related problems are more likely to arise the more debt a firm includes in its capital structure. Therefore, bankruptcy costs discourage firms from pushing their use of debt to excessive levels.
  ☐ Bankruptcy-related costs have two components: the probability of their occurring and the costs they produce given that financial distress has arisen.

■ The "trade-off theory of leverage" recognizes that firms trade off the *benefits* of debt financing (favorable corporate tax treatment) against the *costs* of debt financing (higher interest rates and bankruptcy costs).

■ Signaling theory recognizes the fact that investors and managers do *not* have the same information regarding a firm's prospects, as was assumed by tradeoff theory. This is called *asymmetric information,* and it has an important effect on the optimal capital structure.
  ☐ As a result, one would expect a firm with very favorable prospects to try to avoid selling stock and to attempt to raise any required new capital by other means, including using debt beyond the normal target capital structure.
  ☐ The announcement of a stock offering by a mature firm that seems to have financing alternatives is taken as a signal that the firm's prospects as seen by its management are not bright.

☐ The implications of the signaling theory for capital structure decisions is that firms should, in normal times, maintain a *reserve borrowing capacity* which can be used in the event that some especially good investment opportunity comes along.

■ Agency conflicts are particularly likely when the firm's managers have too much cash at their disposal. Firms can reduce excess cash flow in a variety of ways:
☐ Funnel cash back to shareholders through higher dividends or stock repurchases.
☐ Shift the capital structure toward more debt in the hope that higher debt service requirements will force managers to become more disciplined. A leveraged buyout (LBO) is one way to achieve this.

■ Increasing debt and reducing free cash flow has its downside: It increases the risk of bankruptcy, which can be costly.

■ In practice, capital structure decisions must be made using a combination of judgment and numerical analysis.

The following factors will all have some influence on the firm's choice of a target capital structure.

■ *Sales stability.* If sales are stable, a firm will be more likely to take on increased debt and higher fixed charges.

■ *Asset structure.* Firms whose assets can readily be pledged as collateral for loans will tend to operate with a higher degree of financial leverage.

■ *Operating leverage.* Lower operating leverage generally permits a firm to employ more debt.

■ *Growth rate.* Firms that are growing rapidly generally need large amounts of external capital. The flotation costs associated with debt are generally less than those for common stock, so rapidly growing firms tend to use more debt.

■ *Profitability.* A high degree of profitability would indicate an ability to carry a high level of debt. However, many profitable firms are able to meet most of their financing needs with retained earnings, and do so.

■ *Taxes.* Interest charges are tax deductible, while dividend payments are not. This factor favors the use of debt over equity for firms in high tax brackets.

■ *Control.* Management controls issues such as voting, job security, and fear of takeover, all of which influence the capital structure of a firm in various ways.

■ *Management attitudes.* Managements vary in their attitudes toward risk. More conservative managers will use stock rather than debt for financing, while less conservative managers will use more debt.

■ *Lender and rating agency attitudes.* This factor will penalize firms that go beyond the average for their industry in the use of financial leverage.

■ *Market conditions.* At any point in time, securities markets may favor either debt or equity.

■ *Firm's internal conditions.* Expected future earnings patterns and internal factors will influence management's choice of debt versus equity.

■ *Financial flexibility.* Most treasurers have as a goal to always be in a position to raise the capital needed to support operations, even under bad conditions. Therefore, they want to always maintain some reserve borrowing capacity.

There are wide variations in the use of financial leverage both among industries and among individual firms within each industry. The times-interest-earned ratio is a good tool to gauge the degree of financial leverage used by a particular firm. It gives a measure of how safe the debt is and how vulnerable the company is to financial distress. TIE ratios depend on three factors: (1) the percentage of debt, (2) the interest rate on debt, and (3) the company's profitability.

SELF-TEST QUESTIONS

Definitional

1. Determination of a(n) _____ capital structure requires consideration of both _____ and _____.

2. A firm's _____ capital structure is generally set equal to the estimated optimal structure.

3. Business risk refers to the uncertainty about expected _____ _____ _____, or of returns on equity, if the firm uses no debt.

4. Some of the factors that influence a firm's business risk include: (1) _____ variability, (2) sales price variability, and (3) _____ leverage.

5. Business risk represents the riskiness of the firm's operations if it uses no _____; financial risk represents the additional risk borne by common stockholders as a result of using _____.

6. Common stockholders are compensated for bearing financial risk by a higher _____ _____.

7. Expected EPS generally _____ as the debt/assets ratio increases.

8. As financial leverage increases, the stock price will first begin to rise, but it will then decline as financial leverage becomes excessive because potential _____ _____ become increasingly important.

9. Financial leverage refers to the use of _____ financing.

10. Difficulties in determining the relationship between ___ /___ ratios, the cost of _____, and the degree of _____ _____ have made some managers reluctant to rely heavily on stock price analysis to help determine the optimal capital structure.

11. Conservative financial managers may try to maintain a target _____ _____ that does not maximize the firm's _____ _____.

12. Established management teams are often conservative; they may be more concerned with _____ than with maximizing stock prices.

13. The _____ ratio and the _____ - _____ - _____ ratio give some indication of a firm's risk of default on its fixed charges.

14. The _____ ___ _____ _____ is defined as the percentage change in EBIT associated with a given change in sales volume.

15. The _____ ___ _____ _____ is defined as the percentage change in EPS associated with a given change in EBIT.

16. The _____ ___ _____ _____ is defined as the percentage change in EPS associated with a given change in sales volume.

17. Debt has a(n) _____ advantage over equity in that _____ is a deductible expense while _____ are not.

18. Management may prefer additional _____ as opposed to common stock in order to help maintain _____ of the company.

Conceptual

19. Firm A has a higher degree of business risk than Firm B. Firm A can offset this by increasing its operating leverage.

   a. True   **b.** False

20. Two firms operate in different industries, but they have the same expected EPS and the same standard deviation of expected EPS. Thus, the two firms must have the same financial risk.

   a. True   **b.** False

21. Two firms could have identical financial and operating leverage yet have different degrees of business risk.

   a. True   **b.** False

22. As a general rule, the capital structure that maximizes stock price also

   a. Maximizes the weighted average cost of capital.
   b. Maximizes EPS.
   c. Maximizes bankruptcy costs.
   d. Minimizes the weighted average cost of capital.
   e. Minimizes the required rate of return on equity.

23. A decrease in the debt ratio will normally have no effect on

   a. Financial risk.   **d.** Systematic risk.
   b. Total risk.   **e.** Firm-unique risk.
   c. Business risk.

24. Which of the following statements is most *correct*?

   a. If a firm is exposed to a high degree of business risk as a result of its high operating leverage, then it probably should offset this risk by using a larger-than-average amount of financial leverage. This follows because debt has a lower after-tax cost than equity.
   b. Financial risk can be reduced by replacing common equity with preferred stock.

c. As explained in the text, one of the advantages of the degree of leverage concept is that it takes account of market risk, so if a firm's stockholders hold diversified portfolios of stocks, as opposed to holding only the stock of the one firm, this fact is accounted for by the use of the degree of total leverage.

d. In the text it was stated that the capital structure which minimizes the WACC also maximizes the firm's stock price and its total value, but generally not its expected EPS. One reason given for why debt is beneficial is that it shelters operating income from taxes, while it was stated that a disadvantage of excessive debt has to do with costs associated with bankruptcy and financial distress generally.

e. All of the above statements are false.

SELF-TEST PROBLEMS

1. The Fisher Company will produce 50,000 10-gallon aquariums next year. Variable costs will equal 40 percent of dollar sales, while fixed costs total $100,000. At what price must each aquarium be sold for the firm's EBIT to be $90,000?

   a. $5.00   **b.** $5.33   **c.** $5.50   **d.** $6.00   **e.** $6.33

(The following data apply to the next four Self-Test Problems.)

Brown Products is a new firm just starting operations. The firm will produce backpacks which will sell for $22.00 each. Fixed costs are $500,000 per year, and variable costs are $2.00 per unit of production. The company expects to sell 50,000 backpacks per year, and its effective federal-plus-state tax rate is 40 percent. Brown needs $2 million to build facilities, obtain working capital, and start operations. If Brown borrows part of the money, the interest charges will depend on the amount borrowed as follows:

Amount Borrowed	Percentage of Debt in Capital Structure	Interest Rate on Total Amount Borrowed
$ 200,000	10%	9.00%
400,000	20	9.50
600,000	30	10.00
800,000	40	15.00
1,000,000	50	19.00
1,200,000	60	26.00

Assume that stock can be sold at a price of $20 per share on the initial offering, regardless of how much debt the company uses. Then after the company begins operating, its price will be determined as a multiple of its earnings per share. The multiple (or the P/E ratio) will depend upon the capital structure as follows:

Debt/Assets	P/E	Debt/Assets	P/E
0.0	12.5	40.0	8.0
10.0	12.0	50.0	6.0
20.0	11.5	60.0	5.0
30.0	10.0		

2. What is Brown's optimal capital structure, which maximizes stock price, as measured by the debt/assets ratio?

   a. 10%   **b.** 20%   **c.** 30%   **d.** 40%   **e.** 50%

3. What is Brown's degree of operating leverage at the expected level of sales?

   a. 1.00   **b.** 1.08   **c.** 2.00   **d.** 2.16   **e.** 3.00

4. What is Brown's degree of financial leverage at the expected level of sales and optimal capital structure?

   a. 1.00   **b.** 1.08   **c.** 2.00   **d.** 2.16   **e.** 3.00

5. What is Brown's degree of total leverage at the expected level of sales and optimal capital structure?

   a. 1.00   **b.** 1.08   **c.** 2.00   **d.** 2.16   **e.** 3.00

6. Bicycles Inc. currently sells 75,000 units annually. At this sales level, its net operating income (EBIT) is $4 million and the degree of total leverage is 2.0. The firm's debt consists of $20 million in bonds with a 10 percent coupon. The company is considering a new assembly line which would entail an increase in fixed costs, resulting in a degree of operating leverage of 1.8. However, the firm desires to maintain the degree of total leverage at 2.0. Assuming that EBIT remains at $4 million, what dollar amount of bonds must be retired to accomplish adding the assembly line yet retain the old degree of total leverage?

   a. $10 million **b.** $12 million **c.** $14 million **d.** $16 million **e.** $18 million

7. Tapley Dental Supplies Inc. is in a stable, no-growth situation. Its $1,000,000 of debt consists of perpetuities which have a 10 percent coupon and sell at par. Tapley's EBIT is

$500,000, its cost of equity is 15 percent, it has 100,000 shares outstanding, all earnings are paid out as dividends, and its federal-plus-state tax rate is 40 percent. Tapley could borrow an additional $500,000 at an interest rate of 13 percent without having to retire the original debt, and it would use the proceeds to repurchase stock *at the current price*, not at the new equilibrium price. The increased risk from the additional leverage will raise the cost of equity to 17 percent. If Tapley does recapitalize, what will the new stock price be?

a. $17.20   b. $16.00   c. $16.50   d. $17.00   e. $16.75

ANSWERS TO SELF-TEST QUESTIONS

1. optimal; risk; return
2. target
3. returns on assets
4. demand; operating
5. debt; debt
6. expected return
7. increases
8. bankruptcy costs
9. debt (or fixed charge)
10. P/E; equity; financial leverage

11. capital structure; stock price
12. survival
13. debt; times-interest-earned (or fixed charge coverage)
14. degree of operating leverage (DOL)
15. degree of financial leverage (DFL)
16. degree of total leverage (DTL)
17. tax; interest; dividends
18. debt; control

19. b. Increasing operating leverage will increase Firm A's business risk; therefore, Firm A should use less operating leverage.

20. b. The two firms would have the same total risk. However, they could have different combinations of business and financial risk.

21. a. Business risk consists of several elements in addition to operating leverage, for example, sales variability, and it does not depend on financial risk at all.

22. d. The optimal capital structure balances risk and return to maximize the stock price. The structure that maximizes stock price also minimizes the firm's cost of capital.

23. c. Business risk measures the riskiness of a firm's operations assuming no debt is used.

24. d. Statement a is false; if a firm is exposed to a high degree of business risk this implies that it should offset this risk by using a lower amount of financial leverage. Statement b is false; preferred stock is a fixed-income security, and as such, would increase

financial risk. Statement c is false; the degree of total leverage is equal to the DOL ×
DFL——which takes into account both business risk and financial risk. Statement d is the
correct choice.

SOLUTIONS TO SELF-TEST PROBLEMS

1. e. $\text{EBIT} = PQ - VQP - F$
       $\$90,000 = P(50,000) - 0.4(50,000)P - \$100,000$
       $30,000P = \$190,000$
            $P = \$6.33.$

2. b. The first step is to calculate EBIT:

Sales in dollars [50,000($22)]	$1,100,000
Less: Fixed costs	500,000
Variable costs [50,000($2)]	100,000
EBIT	$ 500,000

The second step is to calculate the EPS at each debt/assets ratio using the formula:

$$\text{EPS} = \frac{(\text{EBIT} - I)(1 - T)}{\text{Shares outstanding}}.$$

Recognize (1) that I = Interest charges = (Dollars of debt)(Interest rate at each D/A
ratio), and (2) that shares outstanding = (Assets − Debt)/Initial price per share =
($2,000,000 − Debt)/$20.00.

D/A	EPS	D/A	EPS
0%	$3.00	40%	$3.80
10	3.21	50	3.72
20	3.47	60	2.82
30	3.77		

Finally, the third step is to calculate the stock price at each debt/assets ratio using the following formula: Price = (P/E)(EPS).

D/A	Price	D/A	Price
0%	$37.50	40%	$30.40
10	38.52	50	22.32
20	39.91	60	14.10
30	37.70		

Thus, a debt/assets ratio of 20 percent maximizes stock price. This is the optimal capital structure.

3. c. $$DOL = \frac{Q(P - V)}{Q(P - V) - F} = \frac{50,000(\$22 - \$2)}{50,000(\$22 - \$2) - \$500,000} = \frac{\$1,000,000}{\$500,000} = 2.0.$$

4. b. $$DFL = \frac{EBIT}{EBIT - I} = \frac{PQ - VQ - F}{PQ - VQ - F - I}$$

$$= \frac{\$1,100,000 - \$100,000 - \$500,000}{\$1,100,000 - \$100,000 - \$500,000 - \$38,000} = \frac{\$500,000}{\$462,000} = 1.08.$$

5. d. $$DTL = \frac{PQ - VQ}{PQ - VQ - F - I}$$

$$= \frac{\$1,100,000 - \$100,000}{\$1,100,000 - \$100,000 - \$500,000 - \$38,000} = \frac{\$1,000,000}{\$462,000} = 2.16,$$

or DTL = (DOL)(DFL) = (2.00)(1.08) = 2.16.

6. d. DTL = DOL × DFL
    DFL = DTL/DOL = 2.0/1.8 = 1.11.

$$DFL = EBIT/(EBIT - I)$$
$$1.11 = \$4 \text{ million}/(\$4 \text{ million} - I)$$
$$\$4 = \$4.44 - 1.11(I)$$
$$\$0.44 = 1.11(I)$$
$$I = \$0.4 \text{ million} = \$400,000.$$

Therefore, the new interest payment must be $0.40 million. The current interest payment is 0.10($20 million) = $2.0 million. Thus, the interest payment must be reduced by

$1.60 million by retiring bonds. This would require that $1.60/0.10 = $16 million of bonds be retired.

7. a. Value of stock = [$500,000 − 0.1($1,000,000)](0.6)/0.15 = $1,600,000.

$P_0 = \$1,600,000/100,000 = \$16.$

After the recapitalization, value of stock is equal to [$500,000 − 0.1($1,000,000) − 0.13($500,000)](0.6)/0.17 = $1,182,353.

$P_0 = \$1,182,353/[100,000 − (\$500,000/\$16)] = \$17.20.$

CHAPTER 13
DIVIDEND POLICY

OVERVIEW

Dividend policy involves the decision to pay out earnings as dividends or to retain and reinvest them in the firm. Any change in dividend policy has both favorable and unfavorable effects on the firm's stock price: higher dividends mean higher immediate cash flows to investors, which is good, but lower future growth, which is bad. The optimal dividend policy balances these opposing forces and maximizes stock price. Three theories regarding the relationship between dividend payout and stock price have been proposed: (1) *dividend irrelevance*, which states that dividend policy has no effect on the firm's stock price; (2) the *"bird-in-the-hand"* theory, which states that investors prefer dividends because they are less risky than potential capital gains; and (3) the *tax preference theory*, which states that investors prefer to have companies retain earnings rather than pay them out as dividends because capital gains are subject to less taxes than dividends. In addition, dividend policy is further complicated due to *signaling* and *clientele* effects. It is simply not possible to state that any one dividend policy is correct, and hence it is impossible to develop a precise model for use in establishing dividend policy. Thus, financial managers must consider a number of factors when setting their firms' dividend policies.

OUTLINE

Dividend policy involves the decision to pay out earnings versus retaining them for reinvestment in the firm.

■ The constant growth stock model, $P_0 = D_1/(k_s - g)$, shows that paying out more dividends will increase stock price. However, if this results in insufficient equity funds to meet investment needs, then the firm must sell new common stock and incur flotation costs, which will cause the price of the stock to decrease.

- The optimal dividend policy strikes a balance between investors' desire for current cash flows (dividends) and future expected growth so as to maximize the value of the firm's stock.

A number of theories have been proposed to explain how factors interact to determine a firm's optimal dividend policy. These theories include: (1) the dividend irrelevance theory, (2) the "bird-in-the-hand" theory, and (3) the tax preference theory.

- Modigliani and Miller (MM), the principal proponents of the *dividend irrelevance theory*, argue that the value of the firm depends only on the income produced by its assets, not on how this income is split between dividends and retained earnings (and hence growth).
  - ☐ MM prove their proposition, but only under a set of restrictive assumptions including (1) no personal taxes, (2) independence between dividend policy and equity costs, and (3) zero flotation costs.
  - ☐ Obviously, firms and investors do pay taxes and do incur flotation costs, and investors may apply a different required rate of return on equity (k_s) to firms that pay out more rather than less of their earnings. Thus, the MM conclusions on dividend irrelevance may not be valid under real-world conditions.

- The most critical assumption of MM's dividend irrelevance theory is that dividend policy does not affect the required rate of return on equity, k_s. Relaxing this assumption provides the basis for the "bird-in-the-hand" theory.
  - ☐ Myron Gordon and John Lintner argue that k_s increases as the dividend payout is reduced because investors are more sure of receiving dividend payments than income from capital gains that presumably result from retained earnings.
  - ☐ MM call the Gordon-Lintner argument the *"bird-in-the-hand" theory* because Gordon and Lintner believe that investors view dividends in the hand as being less risky than capital gains in the bush. In MM's view, however, most investors are going to reinvest their dividends in the same or similar firms, and the riskiness of the firm's cash flows to investors in the long run is solely a function of the firm's asset cash flows.

- The *tax preference theory* states that investors may prefer to have companies retain most of their earnings because of various tax advantages. Investors then would be willing to pay more for low payout companies than for otherwise similar high payout companies.

Empirical testing of the dividend theories has not produced definitive results regarding which theory is correct.

There are two other issues which have a bearing on optimal dividend policy: (1) the information content, or signaling, hypothesis and (2) the clientele effect.

■ It has been observed that a dividend increase announcement is often accompanied by an increase in the stock price.
   □ This might be interpreted by some to mean that investors prefer dividends over capital gains, thus supporting the Gordon-Lintner hypothesis.
   □ However, MM argue that a dividend increase is a signal to investors that the firm's management forecasts good future earnings. Thus, MM argue that investors' reactions to dividend announcements do not necessarily show that investors prefer dividends to retained earnings. Rather, the fact that the stock price changes merely indicates that there is an important information content in dividend announcements. This is referred to as the *information content, or signaling, hypothesis.*

■ MM also suggest that a *clientele effect* might exist.
   □ Some stockholders (for example, retirees) prefer current income; therefore, they would want the firm to pay out a high percentage of its earnings as dividends.
   □ Other stockholders have no need for current income (for example, doctors in their peak earning years) and they would simply reinvest any dividends received, after first paying income taxes on the dividend income. Therefore, they would want the firm to retain most of its earnings.
   □ Thus, a firm establishes a dividend policy and then attracts a specific clientele that is drawn to this dividend policy. Those who do not like the dividend policy can simply sell their shares to those that do.

The theories offer conflicting advice, yet managers must take action. Here are the actual dividend policies that firms follow in practice:

■ *Residual dividend policy* is based on the premise that investors prefer to have a firm retain and reinvest earnings rather than pay them out in dividends if the rate of return the firm can earn on reinvested earnings exceeds the rate of return investors can obtain for themselves on other investments of comparable risk. Further, it is less expensive for the firm to use retained earnings than it is to issue new common stock. A firm using the residual policy would follow these four steps:
   □ Determine the optimal capital budget.
   □ Determine the amount of equity required to finance the optimal capital budget, recognizing that the funds used will consist of both equity and debt to preserve the optimal capital structure.
   □ To the extent possible, use retained earnings to supply the equity required.
   □ Pay dividends only if more earnings are available than are needed to support the optimal capital budget.
   □ In an effort to please investors by stabilizing dividends, firms generally use the residual policy to help set their *long-run payout ratios*, not as a guide to the payout in any one year.

■ A company's policy of *constant, or steadily increasing, dividends per share* implies to shareholders that the regular dividend will at least be maintained and, accordingly, that earnings will be sufficient to cover it. Some other features of this policy are as follows:

  ☐ Dividends are increased only when earnings have increased and seem stable enough to maintain the new dividend level.

  ☐ Dividend payments will be maintained, at least temporarily, even if earnings fall below the level of the dividend payment. Firms try very hard never to reduce the regular dividend.

  ☐ Most corporations follow this type of policy.
  - Stable dividends or a stable dividend growth rate will tend to stabilize a firm's stock price movements.
  - Investors who rely on dividends for income normally prefer a stable dividend policy.
  - A stable growth rate policy confirms investors' estimates of the growth factor and hence reduces risk perceptions.

  ☐ Because of these factors, many people think that a stable dividend policy (including a steady growth rate) will maximize a firm's stock price.

■ It would be possible for a firm to pay out a constant percentage of earnings, that is, a *constant payout ratio*. Only a few firms pay out a constant percentage of their yearly earnings. This would normally result in an unpredictable dividend stream and would not please most investors.

■ The policy of paying a *low regular dividend plus extras* is a compromise between a stable dividend (or stable growth rate) and a constant payout rate. It is often followed by firms with relatively volatile earnings from year to year. The low regular dividend can usually be maintained even when earnings decline, and "extra" dividends can be paid when excess funds are available.

Firms usually pay dividends on a quarterly basis in accordance with the following payment procedures:

■ *Declaration date*. This is the day on which the board of directors declares the dividend. At this time they set the amount of the dividend to be paid, the holder-of-record date, and the payment date.

■ *Holder-of-record date*. This is the date the stock transfer books of the corporation are closed. Those shareholders who are listed on the company's books on this date are the holders of record and they receive the announced dividend.

■ *Ex-dividend date*. This date is four days prior to the holder-of-record date. Shares purchased after the ex-dividend date are not entitled to the dividend. This practice is a convention of the brokerage business which allows sufficient time for stock transfers to be made on the books of the corporation.

■ *Payment date.* This is the day when dividend checks are actually mailed to the holders of record.

Many firms have instituted dividend reinvestment plans (DRPs) whereby stockholders can automatically reinvest dividends received in the stock of the paying corporation. Income taxes on the amount of the dividends must be paid even though stock rather than cash is received.

Regardless of the debate on the relevancy of dividend policy, it is possible to identify several factors which influence dividend policy. These factors are grouped into four broad categories.

■ Constraints: (1) bond indentures, (2) impairment of capital rule, (3) availability of cash, and (4) penalty tax on improperly accumulated earnings.

■ Investment opportunities: (1) location of the IOS schedule and (2) ability to accelerate or postpone projects.

■ Alternative sources of capital: (1) cost of selling new stock, (2) ability to substitute debt for equity, and (3) control.

■ Effects of dividend policy on k_s: (1) stockholders' desire for current versus future income, (2) perceived riskiness of dividends versus capital gains, (3) the tax advantage of capital gains over dividends, and (4) the information content of dividends (signaling).

Stock dividends and stock splits are often used to lower a firm's stock price and, at the same time, to conserve its cash resources.

■ The effect of a stock split is an increase in the number of shares outstanding and a reduction in the par, or stated, value of the shares. For example, if a firm had 1,000 shares of stock outstanding with a par value of $100 per share, a 2-for-1 split would reduce the par value to $50 and increase the number of shares to 2,000.
   □ The total net worth of the firm remains unchanged.
   □ The stock split does not involve any cash payment, only additional certificates representing new shares.
   □ Stock splits often occur due to the widespread belief that there is an optimal price range for each stock.

■ A stock dividend requires an accounting entry transfer from retained earnings to the common stock.
   □ Again, no cash is involved with this "dividend." Net worth remains unchanged, and the number of shares is increased.

■ Unless the total amount of dividends paid on shares is increased, any upward movement in the stock price following a stock split or dividend is likely to be temporary. The price will normally fall in proportion to the dilution in earnings and dividends unless earnings and dividends rise.

Stock repurchases are an alternative to dividends for transmitting cash to stockholders.

■ There are two principal types of repurchases: (1) situations in which the firm has cash available for distribution to its stockholders and (2) situations in which the firm concludes that its capital structure is too heavily weighted with equity.

■ Stock repurchased by the issuing firm is called *treasury stock*.

■ Advantages of repurchases include:
   □ The repurchase is often motivated by management's belief that the firm's shares are undervalued.
   □ The stockholder is given a choice of whether or not to sell his stock to the firm.
   □ The repurchase can remove a large block of stock overhanging the market.
   □ If an increase in cash flow is temporary, the cash can be distributed to stockholders as a repurchase rather than as a dividend, which could not be maintained in the future.
   □ Repurchases can be used to produce large-scale changes in capital structures.

■ Disadvantages of repurchases include:
   □ Repurchases are not as dependable as cash dividends; therefore, the price of the stock may benefit more from cash dividends. A dependable repurchase program may not be practical due to the improper accumulation tax.
   □ Selling stockholders may not be aware of all the implications of the repurchase; therefore, repurchases are usually announced in advance.
   □ If a firm pays too high a price for the repurchased stock, it is to the disadvantage of the remaining stockholders.

■ While repurchases on a regular basis do not appear feasible due to various uncertainties, occasional repurchases do offer some significant advantages over dividends, and repurchases can be valuable in making a major change in capital structure within a short period of time.

SELF-TEST QUESTIONS

Definitional

1. MM argue that a firm's dividend policy has _____ _____ on a stock's price.

2. Gordon and Lintner hypothesize that investors value a dollar of _____ more highly than a dollar of expected _____ _____.

3. A company may be forced to increase its _____ ratio in order to avoid a tax on retained earnings deemed to be unnecessary for the conduct of the business.

4. Some stockholders prefer dividends to _____ _____ because of a need for current _____.

5. If the _____ of a firm's stock increases with the announcement of an increase in dividends, it may be due to the _____ content in the dividend announcement rather than to a preference for dividends over capital gains.

6. A firm with _____ earnings is most appropriate for using the policy of "extra" dividends.

7. The stock transfer books of a corporation are closed on the _____-__-_____ date.

8. The ___-_____ date occurs four days prior to the _____-___-_____ date and provides time for stock transfers to be recorded on the books of the firm.

9. Actual payment of a dividend is made on the _____ date as announced by the _____ ____ _____.

10. Many firms have instituted _____ _____ plans whereby stockholders can use their dividends to purchase additional shares of the company's stock.

11. A stock split involves a reduction in the _____ _____ of the common stock, but no accounting transfers are made between accounts.

12. The assumption that some investors prefer a high dividend payout while others prefer a low payout is called the _____ effect.

13. The residual dividend policy is based on the fact that new common stock is _____ _____ than retained earnings.

14. Stock repurchased by the firm which issued it is called _____ _____.

Conceptual

15. An increase in cash dividends will always result in an increase in the price of the common stock because D_1 will increase in the stock valuation model.

    a. True   **b.** False

16. If investors are indifferent between dividends and capital gains, the farther to the left the IOS and MCC schedule intersect, the higher the dividend payout ratio should be.

    a. True   **b.** False

17. A stock split will affect the amounts shown in which of the following balance sheet accounts?

    a. Common stock   **d.** Cash
    b. Paid-in capital   **e.** None of the above accounts
    c. Retained earnings

18. If investors prefer dividends to capital gains, then

    a. The required rate of return on equity, k_s, will not be affected by a change in dividend policy.
    b. The cost of capital will not be affected by a change in dividend policy.
    c. k_s will increase as the payout ratio is reduced.
    d. k_s will decrease as the retention rate increases.
    e. A policy conforming to the residual theory of dividends will maximize stock price.

19. Which of the following statements is most *correct*?

    a. Modigliani and Miller's theory of the effect of dividend policy on the value of a firm has been called the "bird-in-the-hand" theory, because MM argued that a dividend in the hand is less risky than a potential capital gain in the bush. After extensive empirical tests, this theory is now accepted by most financial experts.
    b. According to proponents of the "dividend irrelevance theory," if a company's stock price rises after the firm announces a greater-than-expected dividend increase, the price

increase occurs because of signaling effects, not because of investors' preferences for dividends over capital gains.
   c. Both statements a and b are correct.
   d. Both statements a and b are false.

20. Which of the following statements is most *correct*?

   a. The residual dividend policy calls for the establishment of a fixed, stable dividend (or dividend growth rate) and then for the level of investment each year to be determined as a residual equal to net income minus the established dividends.
   b. According to the residual dividend policy, for any given MCC schedule and level of earnings, the further to the right the IOS schedule cuts the MCC schedule, the lower the optimal dividend payout ratio.
   c. According to the text, a firm would probably maximize its stock price if it established a specific dividend payout ratio, say 40 percent, and then paid that percentage of earnings out each year because stockholders would then know exactly how much dividend income to count on when they planned their spending for the coming year.
   d. If you buy a stock after the ex-dividend date but before the dividend has been paid, then you, and not the seller, will receive the next dividend check the company sends out.
   e. Each of the above statements is false.

21. Which of the following statements is most *correct*?

   a. According to the asymmetric information, or signaling, theory of capital structure, the announcement of a new stock issue by a mature firm would generally lead to an *increase* in the price of the firm's stock.
   b. According to the asymmetric information, or signaling, theory of capital structure, the announcement of a new stock issue by a mature firm would generally lead to a *decrease* in the price of the firm's stock.
   c. If Firm A's managers believe in the asymmetric information theory, but Firm B's managers do not, then, other things held constant, Firm A would probably have the *higher* normal target debt ratio.
   d. There is no such thing as the asymmetric information theory of capital structure, at least according to the text.
   e. Statements b and c are both true.

22. Which of the following statements is most *correct*?

   a. According to the tax preference theory, investors prefer dividends and, as a result, the higher the payout ratio, the higher the value of the firm.

b. According to the "bird-in-the-hand" theory, investors prefer cash to paper (stock), so if a company announces that it plans to repurchase some of its stock, this causes the price of the stock to increase.

c. According to the dividend irrelevance theory developed by Modigliani and Miller, stock dividends (but not cash dividends) are irrelevant because they "merely divide the pie into thinner slices."

d. According to the information content, or signaling, hypothesis, the fact that stock prices generally increase when an increase in the dividend is announced demonstrates that investors prefer higher to lower payout ratios.

e. According to the text, the residual dividend policy is more appropriate for setting a company's long-run target payout ratio than for determining the payout ratio on a year-to-year basis.

23. Which of the following statements is most *correct*?

a. Stock prices generally rise on the ex-dividend date, and that increase is especially great if the company increases the dividend.

b. Dividend reinvestment plans are popular with investors because investors who do not need cash income can have their dividends reinvested in the company's stock and thereby avoid having to pay income taxes on the dividend income until they sell the stock.

c. In the past, stock dividends and stock splits were frequently used by corporations which wanted to lower the prices of their stocks to an "optimal trading range." However, recent empirical studies have demonstrated that stock dividends and stock splits generally cause stock prices to decline, so companies today rarely split their stock or pay stock dividends.

d. Statements a, b, and c are all false.

e. Statements a, b, and c are all true.

SELF-TEST PROBLEMS

1. Express Industries' expected net income for next year is $1 million. The company's target and current capital structure is 40 percent debt and 60 percent common equity. The optimal capital budget for next year is $1.2 million. If Express uses the residual theory of dividends to determine next year's dividend payout, what is the expected payout ratio?

    a. 0%   b. 10%   c. 28%   d. 42%   e. 56%

2. Amalgamated Shippers has a current and target capital structure of 30 percent debt and 70 percent equity. This past year Amalgamated, which uses a residual theory dividend policy,

had a dividend payout ratio of 47.5 percent and net income of $800,000. What was Amalgamated's capital budget?

   a. $400,000   **b.** $500,000   **c.** $600,000   **d.** $700,000   **e.** $800,000

3. The Aikman Company's optimal capital structure calls for 40 percent debt and 60 percent common equity. The interest rate on its debt is a constant 12 percent; its cost of common equity from retained earnings is 16 percent; the cost of equity from new stock is 18 percent; and its federal-plus-state tax rate is 40 percent. Aikman has the following investment opportunities:

          Project A: Cost = $5 million; IRR = 22%.
          Project B: Cost = $5 million; IRR = 14%.
          Project C: Cost = $5 million; IRR = 11%.

Aikman expects to have net income of $7 million. If Aikman bases its dividends on the residual policy, what will its payout ratio be?

   a. 22.62%   **b.** 14.29%   **c.** 31.29%   **d.** 25.62%   **e.** 18.75%

ANSWERS TO SELF-TEST QUESTIONS

1. no effect
2. dividends; capital gains
3. payout
4. capital gains; income
5. price (or value); information
6. volatile (fluctuating)
7. holder-of-record

8. ex-dividend; holder-of-record
9. payment; board of directors
10. dividend reinvestment
11. par value
12. clientele
13. more costly
14. treasury stock

15. b. A dividend increase could be perceived by investors as signifying poor investment opportunities and hence lower growth in future earnings, thus reducing g in the DCF model. The net effect on stock price is uncertain.

16. a. If investors are indifferent, firms should follow the residual theory. Thus, the smaller the optimal capital budget, the higher the dividend payout ratio.

17. c. A stock split will affect the par value and number of shares outstanding. However, no dollar values will be affected.

18. c. This is the Gordon-Lintner hypothesis. If investors view dividends as being less risky than potential capital gains, then the cost of equity is inversely related to the payout ratio.

19. b. Statement a is false; the proponents of this theory were Gordon and Lintner and empirical tests have not proven any of the dividend theories. Statement b is correct.

20. b. Statement a is false; the residual dividend policy calls for the determination of the optimal capital budget and then the dividend is established as a residual of net income minus the amount of retained earnings necessary for the capital budget. Statement b is correct. Statement c is false; a constant payout policy would lead to uncertainty of dividends due to fluctuating earnings. Statement d is false; if a stock is bought after the ex-dividend date the dividend remains with the seller of the stock.

21. b. The asymmetric information theory suggests that investors regard the announcement of a stock sale as bad news: If the firm had really good investment opportunities, it would use debt financing so that existing stockholders would get all the benefits from the good projects. Therefore, the announcement of a stock sale leads to a decline in the price of the firm's stock. In order to reduce the chances of having to issue stock, firms therefore set low target debt ratios, which give them "reserve borrowing capacity."

22. e. Statements a, b, c, and d are false, but statement e is true.

23. d. The statements are all false.

SOLUTIONS TO SELF-TEST PROBLEMS

1. c. The $1,200,000 capital budget will be financed using 40 percent debt and 60 percent equity. Therefore, the equity requirement will be 0.6($1,200,000) = $720,000. Since the expected net income is $1,000,000, $280,000 will be available to pay as dividends. Thus, the payout ratio is expected to be $280,000/$1,000,000 = 0.28 = 28%.

2. c. Of the $800,000 in net income, 0.475($800,000) = $380,000 was paid out as dividends. Thus, $420,000 was retained in the firm for investment. This is the equity portion of the capital budget, or 70 percent of the capital budget. Therefore, the total capital budget was $420,000/0.7 = $600,000.

3. b. Maximum BP_{RE} = NI/Equity ratio = \$7,000,000/0.6 = \$11,666,667.
       $WACC_1$ = 0.4(12%)(0.6) + 0.6(16%) = 12.48%.
       $WACC_2$ = 0.4(12%)(0.6) + 0.6(18%) = 13.68%.

We see that the capital budget should be \$10 million. We know that 60 percent of the \$10 million should be equity. Therefore, the company should pay dividends of:

Dividends = NI - Needed equity = \$7,000,000 — \$6,000,000 = \$1,000,000.
Payout ratio = \$1,000,000/\$7,000,000 = 0.1429 = 14.29%.

CHAPTER 14
FINANCIAL FORECASTING

OVERVIEW

Managers are vitally concerned with *future financial statements* and with the effects of alternative assumptions and policies on these *projected*, or *pro forma*, statements. The construction of pro forma statements begins with a *sales forecast*. On the basis of the sales forecast, the amount of assets necessary to support this sales level is determined. Although some liabilities will increase *spontaneously* with increased sales, if the sales growth rate is rapid, then external capital will be required to support the growth in sales.

Pro forma statements are important for two reasons. First, if projected operating results look poor, management can reformulate its plans for the coming year. Second, it is desirable to plan the acquisition of funds well in advance to insure that funds will be available when they are needed.

OUTLINE

Well-run companies generally base their operating plans on a set of forecasted financial statements. A sales forecast for the next five years or so is developed, the assets required to meet the sales target are determined, and a decision is made concerning how to finance the required assets. These forecasts represent the "base case" and are a standard by which to judge alternate forecasts.

■ The sales forecast generally begins with a review of sales for the past 5 to 10 years.

■ If the sales forecast is off, the consequences can be serious. Thus, an accurate sales forecast is critical to the well-being of the firm.

Any forecast of financial requirements involves (1) determining how much money the firm will need during a given period, (2) determining how much money the firm will generate internally during the same period, and (3) subtracting the funds generated from the funds required to determine the external financial requirements.

■ Two methods are used to estimate external requirements: the *projected, or pro forma, financial statement method* and the *formula method*.

The projected financial statement method involves projecting the asset requirements for the coming period, then projecting the liabilities and equity that will be generated under normal operations, and subtracting the projected liabilities and capital from the required assets to estimate the additional funds needed (AFN).

■ The first step is to forecast next year's income statement.
    □ A sales forecast is needed.
    □ Assumptions about the operating cost ratio, the tax rate, interest charges, and the dividend payout ratio are made.
    □ In the simplest case, costs are assumed to increase at the same rate as sales; in more complicated situations, cost changes are forecasted separately.
    □ The objective is to determine how much income the company will earn and then retain for reinvestment in the business during the forecasted year.

■ The second step is to forecast next year's balance sheet.
    □ All asset accounts can be assumed to vary directly with sales unless the firm is operating at less than full capacity. If the firm is not operating at full capacity, then fixed assets will not vary directly with sales, but the cash, receivables, and inventory accounts will increase in proportion to the increase in sales.
    □ Liabilities, equity, or both must also increase if assets increase—asset expansions must be financed in some manner.
    □ Certain liability accounts, such as accounts payable and accruals, will increase *spontaneously* with sales.
    □ Retained earnings will increase, but not proportionately with sales. The new retained earnings will be determined from the projected income statement.
    □ Other financing accounts, such as short-term debt, long-term debt, and common stock, are not directly related to sales. Changes in these accounts result from managerial decisions; they do not increase spontaneously as sales increase.
    □ The difference between projected total assets and projected liabilities and capital is the amount of *additional funds needed (AFN)*.

■ The third step is the decision on how to finance the additional funds required. Sometimes contractual agreements, such as a limit on the debt ratio, will restrict the firm's financing decisions.

■ One complexity that arises in financial forecasting relates to *financing feedbacks*, which are the effects on the income statement and balance sheet of actions taken to finance asset increases. Financing feedbacks are incorporated into the pro forma financial statements through additional calculations, or *passes*, of the projected income statement and balance sheet.

■ Once the pro forma financial statements have been developed, the key ratios can be analyzed to determine whether the forecast meets the firm's financial targets as set forth in its financial plan. If the statements do not meet the targets, then elements of the forecast must be changed.

Although forecasts of capital requirements are always made by constructing pro forma financial statements as described above, an approximation can be obtained by using a simple forecasting formula.

■ The formula is as follows:

$$\begin{matrix} \text{Additional} & & \text{Required} & & \text{Spontaneous} & & \text{Increase in} \\ \text{funds} & = & \text{increase} & - & \text{increase} & - & \text{retained} \\ \text{needed} & & \text{in assets} & & \text{in liabilities} & & \text{earnings} \end{matrix},$$

or

$$AFN = (A*/S)\Delta S - (L*/S)\Delta S - MS_1(1 - d).$$

Here, $A*/S$ = assets that must increase if sales are to increase, expressed as a percentage of sales, or the required dollar increase in assets per \$1 increase in sales; $L*/S$ = liabilities that increase spontaneously with sales as a percentage of sales, or spontaneously generated financing per \$1 increase in sales; S_1 = total expected sales for the year in question (note that S_0 = last year's sales); ΔS = change in sales = $S_1 - S_0$; M = profit margin, or rate of profits after taxes per \$1 of sales; and d = the percentage of earnings paid out in dividends (dividend payout ratio).

■ Inherent in the formula is the assumption that each asset item must increase in direct proportion to sales increases and that designated liability accounts also grow at the same rate as sales. Obviously, these assumptions do not always hold, so its results are not always reliable. Thus, the formula is often used as a supplement to the projected financial statement method.

■ The faster a firm's growth rate in sales, the greater its need for additional financing.
   □ Higher growth rates require managers to plan very carefully to decide if the additional financing needed is actually available to the firm. Otherwise, they may need to reconsider their projected growth rate.
   □ Dividend policy as reflected in the payout ratio also affects external capital requirements: the higher the payout ratio, the smaller the addition to retained earnings, and hence the greater the requirements for external capital. Dividend policy may be changed to satisfy

internal financing requirements, but this may have a negative impact on stock price and may be met with resistance from investors.

☐ The amount of assets required per dollar of sales, A*/S, is often called the *capital intensity ratio*. This factor has a major effect on capital requirements per unit of sales growth. If the capital intensity ratio is low, then sales can grow rapidly without much outside capital. However, if a firm is capital intensive, even a small growth in output will require a great deal of outside capital.

☐ Profit margin, M, also has an effect on capital requirements. The higher the profit margin, the lower the funds requirement, and the lower the profit margin, the higher the requirement. Thus, highly profitable firms can raise most of their capital internally.

The forecasting process is greatly complicated if the ratios of balance sheet items to sales are not constant at all levels of sales.

■ Where *economies of scale* occur in asset use, the ratio of that asset to sales will change as the size of the firm increases.

■ Technological considerations sometimes dictate that fixed assets be added in large, discrete units, often referred to as *lumpy assets*. This automatically creates excess capacity immediately after a plant expansion.

■ *Forecasting errors* can cause the actual asset/sales ratio for a given period to be quite different from the planned ratio. This situation can result in excess capacity.

If any of the above conditions apply (economies of scale, lumpy assets, or excess capacity), the A*/S ratio will not be a constant, and the constant growth forecasting method should not be used. Rather, other techniques must be used to forecast asset levels to determine additional financing requirements. Two of these methods include simple linear regression and excess capacity adjustments.

■ If one assumes that the relationship between a certain type of asset and sales is linear, then one can use simple linear regression techniques to estimate the requirements for that type of asset for any given sales increase. An estimated regression equation is determined which provides an estimated relationship between a given asset account and sales.

■ If a firm's fixed assets are not operating at full capacity, then the calculation for the required level of fixed assets will need to be adjusted.

☐ Full capacity sales is defined as actual sales divided by the percentage of capacity at which the fixed assets operated to achieve these sales:

☐ The target fixed assets to sales ratio is equal to the current year's fixed assets divided by full capacity sales:

$$\text{Full capacity sales} = \frac{\text{Actual sales}}{\substack{\text{Percentage of capacity at which} \\ \text{fixed assets were operated}}}.$$

$$\text{Target FA/sales ratio} = \frac{\text{Actual fixed assets}}{\text{Full capacity sales}}.$$

☐ The required level of fixed assets is equal to the target fixed assets to sales ratio times projected sales:

$$\substack{\text{Required level} \\ \text{of fixed assets}} = \left(\frac{\text{Target FA}}{\text{Sales ratio}}\right)(\text{Projected sales}).$$

Although the type of financial forecasting described in this chapter can be done with a hand calculator, virtually all corporate forecasts are made using computerized forecasting models. Most models are based on a spreadsheet program, such as Lotus 1-2-3. Spreadsheet programs are easy to construct for forecasts extending over several years, and they are useful for instantaneously recomputing projected statements and ratios when one of the input variables is changed.

SELF-TEST QUESTIONS

Definitional

1. The most important element in financial planning is the forecast of _____.

2. Those asset items that typically increase proportionately with higher sales are _____, _____, and _____. _____ assets are frequently not used to full capacity and hence do not increase in proportion to sales.

3. If various asset categories increase, _____ and/or _____ must also increase.

4. Typically, certain liabilities will rise _____ with sales. These include accounts _____ and _____.

5. _____ and _____ _____ are examples of accounts that do not increase automatically with higher levels of sales.

6. As the dividend _____ _____ is increased, the amount of earnings available to finance new assets is _____.

7. Retained earnings depend not only on next year's sales level and dividend payout ratio but also on the _____ _____.

8. The amount of assets required per dollar of sales, A*/S is often called the _____ _____ _____.

9. A capital intensive industry will require large amounts of _____ capital to finance increased growth.

10. The projected financial statement method assumes that the _____ of balance sheet items to _____ is _____ at all levels of sales.

11. The assumption of constant percentage of sales ratios may not be accurate when assets must be added in discrete amounts, called _____ assets, or when _____ of scale are considered.

Conceptual

12. An increase in a firm's inventory will call for additional financing unless the increase is offset by an equal or larger *decrease* in some other asset account.

    a. True   b. False

13. If the capital intensity ratio of a firm actually decreases as sales increase, use of the formula method will typically *overstate* the amount of additional funds required, other things held constant.

    a. True   b. False

14. If the dividend payout ratio is 100 percent, all ratios are held constant, and the firm is operating at full capacity, then any increase in sales will require additional financing.

    a. True   b. False

15. One of the first steps in the projected financial statement method of forecasting is to identify those asset and liability accounts which increase spontaneously with retained earnings.

    a. True   b. False

16. Which of the following would *reduce* the additional funds required if all other things are held constant?

   a. An increase in the dividend payout ratio.
   b. A decrease in the profit margin.
   c. An increase in the capital intensity ratio.
   d. An increase in the expected sales growth rate.
   e. A decrease in the firm's tax rate.

17. Which of the following statements is most *correct*?

   a. Suppose economies of scale exist in a firm's use of assets. Under this condition, the firm should use the regression method of forecasting asset requirements rather than the projected financial statement method.
   b. If a firm must acquire assets in lumpy units, it can avoid errors in forecasts of its need for funds by using the linear regression method of forecasting asset requirements because all the points will lie on the regression line.
   c. If economies of scale in the use of assets exist, then the AFN formula rather than the projected financial statement method should be used to forecast additional funds requirements.
   d. Notes payable to banks are included in the AFN formula, along with a projection of retained earnings.
   e. One problem with the AFN formula is that it does not take account of the firm's dividend policy.

SELF-TEST PROBLEMS

1. United Products Inc. has the following balance sheet:

Current assets	$ 5,000	Accounts payable	$ 1,000
		Notes payable	1,000
Net fixed assets	5,000	Long-term debt	4,000
		Common equity	4,000
Total assets	$10,000	Total liabilities and equity	$10,000

Business has been slow; therefore, fixed assets are vastly underutilized. Management believes it can double sales next year with the introduction of a new product. No new fixed assets will be required, and management expects that there will be no earnings retained next year. What is next year's additional financing requirement?

a. $0   b. $4,000   c. $6,000   d. $13,000   e. $19,000

2. The 1995 balance sheet for American Pulp and Paper is shown below (in millions of dollars):

Cash	$ 3.0	Accounts payable	$ 2.0
Accounts receivable	3.0	Notes payable	1.5
Inventory	5.0		
Current assets	$11.0	Current liabilities	$ 3.5
Fixed assets	3.0	Long-term debt	3.0
		Common equity	7.5
Total assets	$14.0	Total liabilities and equity	$14.0

In 1995, sales were $60 million. In 1996, management believes that sales will increase by 20 percent to a total of $72 million. The profit margin is expected to be 5 percent, and the dividend payout ratio is targeted at 40 percent. No excess capacity exists. What is the additional financing requirement (in millions) for 1996 using the formula method?

a. $0.36   b. $0.24   c. $0   d. -$0.24   e. -$0.36

3. Refer to Self-Test Problem 2. How much can sales grow above the 1996 level of $60 million without requiring any additional funds?

a. 12.28%   b. 14.63%   c. 15.75%   d. 17.65%   e. 18.14%

4. Smith Machines Inc. has a net income this year of $500 on sales of $2,000 and is operating its fixed assets at full capacity. Management expects sales to increase by 25 percent next year and is forecasting a dividend payout ratio of 30 percent. The profit margin is not expected to change. If spontaneous liabilities are $500 this year and no excess funds are expected next year, what are Smith's total assets this year?

a. $1,000   b. $1,500   c. $2,250   d. $3,000   e. $3,500

(The following data apply to the next three Self-Test Problems.)

Crossley Products Company's 1995 financial statements are shown below:

Crossley Products Company
Balance Sheet as of December 31, 1995
(Thousands of Dollars)

Cash	$ 600	Accounts payable	$ 2,400
Receivables	3,600	Notes payable	1,157
Inventory	4,200	Accruals	840
Total current assets	$8,400	Total current liabilities	$ 4,397
		Mortgage bonds	1,667
		Common stock	667
Net fixed assets	7,200	Retained earnings	8,869
Total assets	$15,600	Total liabilities and equity	$15,600

Crossley Products Company
Income Statement for December 31, 1995
(Thousands of Dollars)

Sales	$12,000
Operating costs	10,261
Earnings before interest and taxes	$ 1,739
Interest	339
Earnings before taxes	$ 1,400
Taxes (40%)	560
Net income	$ 840
Dividends (60%)	$504
Addition to retained earnings	$336

5. Assume that the company was operating at full capacity in 1995 with regard to all items except fixed assets; fixed assets in 1995 were utilized to only 75 percent of capacity. By what percentage could 1996 sales increase over 1995 sales without the need for an increase in fixed assets?

a. 33%   **b.** 25%   **c.** 20%   **d.** 44%   **e.** 50%

6. Now suppose 1996 sales increase by 25 percent over 1995 sales. How much additional external capital (in thousands) will be required? Assume that Crossley cannot sell any fixed

assets. Use the projected financial statement method to develop a pro forma balance sheet and income statement. Assume that any required financing is borrowed as notes payable. Do not include any financing feedbacks, and use a pro forma income statement to determine the addition to retained earnings.

a. $825   **b.** $925   **c.** $750   **d.** $900   **e.** $850

7. Use the financial statements developed in Self-Test Problem 6 to incorporate the financing feedback which results from the addition of notes payable. (That is, do the next financial statement iteration.) For purposes of this part, assume that the notes payable interest rate is 12 percent. What is the AFN (in thousands) for this iteration?

a. $28   **b.** $30   **c.** $20   **d.** $24   **e.** $36

(The following data apply to the next two Self-Test Problems.)

Taylor Technologies Inc.'s 1995 financial statements are shown below:

Taylor Technologies Inc.
Balance Sheet as of December 31, 1995

Cash	$ 90,000	Accounts payable	$ 180,000
Receivables	180,000	Notes payable	78,000
Inventory	360,000	Accruals	90,000
Total current assets	$ 630,000	Total current liabilities	$ 348,000
		Common stock	900,000
Net fixed assets	720,000	Retained earnings	102,000
Total assets	$1,350,000	Total liabilities and equity	$1,350,000

Taylor Technologies Inc.
Income Statement for December 31, 1995

Sales	$1,800,000
Operating costs	1,639,860
EBIT	$ 160,140
Interest	10,140
EBT	$ 150,000
Taxes (40%)	60,000
Net income	$ 90,000
Dividends (60%)	$54,000
Addition to retained earnings	$36,000

8. Suppose that in 1996, sales increase by 10 percent over 1995 sales. Construct the pro forma financial statements using the projected financial statement method. How much additional capital will be required? Assume the firm operated at full capacity in 1995. Do not include financing feedbacks.

   a. $72,459   **b.** $70,211   **c.** $68,157   **d.** $66,445   **e.** $63,989

9. Now assume that 50 percent of the additional capital required will be financed by selling common stock and the remainder by borrowing as notes payable. Assume that the interest rate on notes payable is 13 percent. Do the next iteration of financial statements incorporating financing feedbacks. What is the AFN for this iteration?

   a. $1,063   **b.** $957   **c.** $1,124   **d.** $927   **e.** $1,185

10. Your company's sales were $2,000 last year, and they are forecasted to rise by 50 percent during the coming year. Here is the latest balance sheet:

Cash	$ 100	Accounts payable	$ 200
Receivables	300	Notes payable	200
Inventory	800	Accruals	20
Total current assets	$1,200	Total current liabilities	$ 420
		Long-term debt	780
		Common stock	400
Net fixed assets	800	Retained earnings	400
Total assets	$2,000	Total liabilities and equity	$2,000

Fixed assets were used to only 80 percent of capacity last year, and year-end inventory holdings were $100 greater than were needed to support the $2,000 of sales. The other current assets (cash and receivables) were at their proper levels. All assets would be a constant percentage of sales if excess capacity did not exist; that is, all assets would increase at the same rate as sales if no excess capacity existed. The company's after-tax profit margin will be 3 percent, and its payout ratio will be 80 percent. If all additional funds needed (AFN) are raised as notes payable, what will the current ratio be at the end of the coming year? Ignore the effects of financing feedbacks on the income statement.

a. 2.47   **b.** 1.44   **c.** 1.21   **d.** 1.00   **e.** 1.63

11. The Bouchard Company's sales are forecasted to increase from $500 in 1995 to $1,000 in 1996. Here is the December 31, 1995, balance sheet:

Cash	$ 50	Accounts payable	$ 25
Receivables	100	Notes payable	75
Inventory	100	Accruals	25
Total current assets	$250	Total current liabilities	$125
		Long-term debt	200
		Common stock	50
Net fixed assets	250	Retained earnings	125
Total assets	$500	Total liabilities and equity	$500

Bouchard's fixed assets were used to only 50 percent of capacity during 1995, but its current assets were at their proper levels. All assets except fixed assets should be a constant percentage of sales, and fixed assets would also increase at the same rate if the current excess capacity did not exist. Bouchard's after-tax profit margin is forecasted to be 8 percent, and its payout ratio will be 40 percent. What is Bouchard's additional funds needed (AFN) for the coming year? Ignore financing feedbacks.

a. $102   **b.** $152   **c.** $197   **d.** $167   **e.** $183

ANSWERS TO SELF-TEST QUESTIONS

1. sales
2. cash; receivables; inventory; Fixed
3. liabilities; equity
4. spontaneously; payable; accruals
5. Bonds; common stock (or preferred stock, or retained earnings)

6. payout ratio; decreased
7. profit margin
8. capital intensity ratio
9. external
10. ratio; sales; constant
11. lumpy; economies

12. a. When an increase in one asset account is not offset by an equivalent decrease in another asset account, then financing is needed to reestablish equilibrium on the balance sheet. Note, though, that this additional financing may come from a spontaneous increase in accounts payable or from retained earnings.

13. a. A decreasing capital intensity ratio, $A*/S$, means that fewer assets are required, proportionately, as sales increase. Thus, the external funding requirement is overstated. Always keep in mind that the formula method assumes that the asset/sales ratio is constant regardless of the level of sales.

14. a. With a 100 percent payout ratio, there will be no retained earnings. When operating at full capacity, *all* assets are spontaneous, but *all* liabilities cannot be spontaneous since a firm must have common equity. Thus, the growth in assets cannot be matched by a growth in spontaneous liabilities, so additional financing will be required in order to keep the financial ratios (the debt ratio in particular) constant.

15. b. The first step is to identify those accounts which increase spontaneously with sales.

16. e. Answers a through d would increase the additional funds required, but a decrease in the tax rate would raise the profit margin and thus increase the amount of available retained earnings.

17. a. Statement a is correct; economies of scale cause the ratios to change over time, which violates the assumption of the projected financial statement method. Statement b is false; the points will not all lie on the regression line. Statement c is false; the AFN formula requires constant ratios over time. Statement d is false; the AFN formula includes only spontaneous liabilities, and notes payable do not spontaneously increase with sales. Statement e is false; the AFN formula includes the dividend payout, so dividend policy is included.

SOLUTIONS TO SELF-TEST PROBLEMS

1. b. Look at next year's balance sheet:

Current assets	$10,000	Accounts payable	$ 2,000
Net fixed assets	5,000	Notes payable	1,000
		Current liabilities	$ 3,000
		Long-term debt	4,000
		Common equity	4,000
			$11,000
		AFN	4,000
Total assets	$15,000	Total liabilities and equity	$15,000

With no retained earnings next year, the common equity account remains at $4,000. Thus, the additional financing requirement is $15,000 − $11,000 = $4,000.

2. b. None of the items on the right side of the balance sheet rises spontaneously with sales except accounts payable. Therefore,

$$\text{AFN} = (A^*/S)(\Delta S) - (L^*/S)(\Delta S) - MS_1(1-d)$$
$$= (\$14/\$60)(\$12) - (\$2/\$60)(\$12) - (0.05)(\$72)(0.6)$$
$$= \$2.8 - \$0.4 - \$2.16 = \$0.24 \text{ million.}$$

The firm will need $240,000 in additional funds to support the increase in sales.

3. d. Note that g = Sales growth = $\Delta S/S$ and $S_1 = S(1 + g)$. Then,

$$\text{AFN} = A^*g - L^*g - M[(S)(1+g)](1-d) = 0$$
$$\$14g - \$2g - 0.05[(\$60)(1+g)](0.6) = 0$$
$$\$12g - 1(\$3 + \$3g)(0.60) = 0$$
$$\$12g - \$1.8 - \$1.8g = 0$$
$$\$10.20g = \$1.80$$
$$g = 0.1765 = 17.65\%.$$

4. c.
$$0 = (A^*/S)(\Delta S) - (L^*/S)(\Delta S) - MS_1(1-d)$$
$$0 = (A^*/\$2,000)(\$500) - (\$500/\$2,000)(\$500) - (\$500/\$2,000)(\$2,500)(1-0.3)$$
$$0 = (\$500A^*/\$2,000) - \$125 - \$437.50$$
$$0 = (\$500A^*/\$2,000) - \$562.50$$
$$\$562.50 = 0.25A^*$$
$$A^* = \$2,250.$$

5. a.

$$\text{Full capacity sales} = \frac{\text{Actual sales}}{\text{\% of capacity at which FA were operated}} = \frac{\$12,000}{0.75} = \$16,000.$$

$$\text{Percent increase} = \frac{\text{New sales} - \text{Old sales}}{\text{Old sales}} = \frac{\$16,000 - \$12,000}{\$12,000} = 0.33 = 33\%.$$

Therefore, sales could expand by 33 percent before Crossley Products would need to add fixed assets.

6. e.

Crossley Products Company
Pro Forma Income Statement
December 31, 1996
(Thousands of Dollars)

	1995	(1 + g)	1st Pass 1996
Sales	$12,000	(1.25)	$15,000
Operating costs	10,261	(1.25)	12,826
EBIT	$ 1,739		$ 2,174
Interest	339		339
EBT	$ 1,400		$ 1,835
Taxes (40%)	560		734
Net income	$ 840		$ 1,101
Dividends (60%)	$504		$661
Addition to RE	$336		$440

Crossley Products Company
Pro Forma Balance Sheet
December 31, 1996
(Thousands of Dollars)

	1995	(1 + g)	1996	AFN	1996 After AFN
Cash	$ 600	(1.25)	$ 750		$ 750
Receivables	3,600	(1.25)	4,500		4,500
Inventory	4,200	(1.25)	5,250		5,250
Total current assets	$ 8,400		$10,500		$10,500
Net fixed assets	7,200		7,200[b]		7,200
Total assets	$15,600		$17,700		$17,700
Accounts payable	$ 2,400	(1.25)	$ 3,000		$ 3,000
Notes payable	1,157		1,157	+850	2,007
Accruals	840	(1.25)	1,050		1,050
Total current liabilities	$ 4,397		$ 5,207		$ 6,057
Mortgage bonds	1,667		1,667		1,667
Common stock	667		667		667
Retained earnings	8,869	440[a]	9,309		9,309
Total liabilities and equity	$15,600		$16,850		$17,700

AFN = $ 850

Notes:
[a]See income statement on previous page.
[b]From Self-Test Problem 5 we know that sales can increase by 33 percent before additions to fixed assets are needed.

7. d.

Crossley Products Company
Pro Forma Income Statement
December 31, 1996
(Thousands of Dollars)

	1st Pass 1996	Financing Feedback	2nd Pass 1996
Sales	$15,000		$15,000
Operating costs	12,826		12,826
EBIT	$ 2,174		$ 2,174
Interest	339	+102*	441
EBT	$ 1,835		$ 1,733
Taxes (40%)	734		693
Net income	$ 1,101		$ 1,040
Dividends (60%)	$ 661		$ 624
Addition to RE	$ 440		$ 416

*Change in interest = $850(0.12) = $102.

	1st Pass 1996	Financing Feedback	2nd Pass 1996
Total assets	$17,700		$17,700
Accounts payable	$ 3,000		$ 3,000
Notes payable	2,007		2,007
Accruals	1,050		1,050
Total current liabilities	$ 6,057		$ 6,057
Mortgage bonds	1,667		1,667
Common stock	667		667
Retained earnings	9,309	-24**	9,285
Total liabilities and equity	$17,700		$17,676
AFN =			$ 24

**Change in RE addition = $416 − $440 = -$24.

8. c. The first pass balance sheet indicates that the AFN = $68,157. This AFN ignores financing feedbacks.

Taylor Technologies Inc.
Pro Forma Income Statement
December 31, 1996

	1995	(1 + g)	1st Pass 1996	AFN Effects	2nd Pass 1996
Sales	$1,800,000	(1.10)	$1,980,000		$1,980,000
Operating costs	1,639,860	(1.10)	1,803,846		1,803,846
EBIT	$ 160,140		$ 176,154		$ 176,154
Interest	10,140		10,140	+4,430[a]	14,570
EBT	$ 150,000		$ 166,014		$ 161,584
Taxes (40%)	60,000		66,406		64,634
Net income	$ 90,000		$ 99,608		$ 96,950
Dividends (60%)	$ 54,000		$ 59,765		$ 58,170
Addition to RE	$ 36,000		$ 39,843		$ 38,780

Notes:
[a]Change in interest = $34,079(0.13) = $4,430.

Taylor Technologies Inc.
Pro Forma Balance Sheet
December 31, 1996

	1995	$(1 + g)$	1st Pass 1996	AFN Effects	2nd Pass 1996
Cash	$ 90,000	(1.10)	$ 99,000		$ 99,000
Receivables	180,000	(1.10)	198,000		198,000
Inventory	360,000	(1.10)	396,000		396,000
Total current assets	$ 630,000		$ 693,000		$ 693,000
Fixed assets	720,000	(1.10)	792,000		792,000
Total assets	$1,350,000		$1,485,000		$1,485,000
Accts. payable	$ 180,000	(1.10)	$ 198,000		$ 198,000
Notes payable	78,000		78,000	+34,079	112,079
Accruals	90,000	(1.10)	99,000		99,000
Total current liabilities	$ 348,000		$ 375,000		$ 409,079
Common stock	900,000		900,000	+34,078	934,078
Ret. earnings	102,000	39,843[a]	141,843	-1,063[b]	140,780
Total liabilities and equity	$1,350,000		$1,416,843		$1,483,937
AFN =			$ 68,157		$ 1,063

Notes:
[a]See 1st pass income statement.
[b]Change in addition to RE = $38,780 − $39,843 = -$1,063.

9. a. See the AFN line in the final column of the projected balance sheet above. This AFN is the result of the change to retained earnings due to the increased interest expense from the addition of notes payable.

10. c.

	Current Year	$(1 + g)$	1st Pass	AFN	2nd Pass
Cash	$ 100	× 1.5	$ 150		$ 150
Receivables	300	× 1.5	450		450
Inventory	800	+ 250[a]	1,050		1,050
Total curr. assets	$1,200		$1,650		1,650
Net fixed assets	800	+ 160[b]	960		960
Total assets	$2,000		$2,610		$2,610
Accounts payable	$ 200	× 1.5	$ 300		$ 300
Notes payable	200		200	+ 482	682
Accruals	20	× 1.5	30		30
Total curr. liab.	$ 420		$ 530		$1,012
Long-term debt	780		780		780
Common stock	400		400		400
Retained earnings	400	+ 18[c]	418		418
Total liab./equity	$2,000		$2,128		$2,610

$$AFN = \$\ 482$$

Notes:

[a]Target inventory/assets = ($800 − $100)/$2,000 = 35%.
Target inventory level = 0.35($3,000) = $1,050.
Since we already have $800 of inventories, we need:
Additional inventories = $1,050 − $800 = $250.

[b]Capacity sales = Sales/Capacity factor = $2,000/0.8 = $2,500.
Target FA/S ratio = FA/Capacity sales = $800/$2,500 = 32%.
Required FA = Target ratio × Forecasted sales = 0.32($3,000) = $960.
Since we already have $800 of fixed assets, we need:
Additional fixed assets = $960 − $800 = $160.

[c]Additions to RE = $S_1(M)(1 − \text{Payout ratio}) = \$3,000(0.03)(0.2) = \$18$.

The problem asks for the forecasted current ratio which is calculated as:
Forecasted current ratio = $1,650/$1,012 = 1.6304.

11. b.

	1995	(1 + g)	1st Pass 1996
Cash	$ 50	× 2	$100
Receivables	100	× 2	200
Inventory	100	× 2	200
Total current assets	$250		$500
Net fixed assets	250	+ 0[a]	250
Total assets	$500		$750
Accounts payable	$ 25	× 2	$ 50
Notes payable	75		75
Accruals	25	× 2	50
Total current liabilities	$125		$175
Long-term debt	200		200
Common stock	50		50
Retained earnings	125	+48[b]	173
Total claims	$500		$598
		AFN	$152

Notes:

[a]Capacity sales = Actual sales/Capacity factor = $500/0.5 = $1,000.
Target FA/S ratio = $250/$1,000 = 0.25.
Target FA = 0.25($1,000) = $250 = Required fixed assets.
Since Bouchard currently has $250 of FA, no new FA will be required.

[b]Addition to RE = $M(S_1)(1 - \text{Payout ratio}) = 0.08(\$1,000)(0.6) = \$48$.

OVERVIEW

About 60 percent of a typical financial manager's time is devoted to working capital management, and many students' first jobs will involve working capital. This is particularly true of smaller businesses, where new job creation is especially rapid. Therefore, working capital is an essential topic.

Working capital policy involves two basic questions: (1) What is the appropriate amount of current assets for the firm to carry, both in total and for each specific account, and (2) how should current assets be financed? This chapter addresses the first question, while Chapter 16 addresses the second.

OUTLINE

It is useful to begin by reviewing some basic definitions and concepts.

■ *Working capital*, sometimes called *gross working capital*, is defined as current assets, while *net working capital* is defined as current assets minus current liabilities.

■ The *current ratio*, which is calculated as current assets divided by current liabilities, is intended to measure a firm's liquidity. The *quick ratio*, which also attempts to measure liquidity, is calculated as current assets less inventories, divided by current liabilities.

■ The most comprehensive picture of a firm's liquidity is obtained by examining its *cash budget*, which forecasts a firm's cash inflows and outflows, and thus focuses on what really counts, the firm's ability to generate the cash inflows required to meet its required cash outflows.

■ *Working capital policy* refers to the firm's basic policies regarding target levels for each category of current assets and how current assets will be financed.

■ *Working capital management* involves the administration of current assets and current liabilities.

A firm's current asset levels rise and fall with business cycles and seasonal trends. At the peak of such cycles, businesses carry their maximum amounts of current assets.

■ There are three alternative policies regarding the total amount of current assets carried. Each policy differs in that different amounts of current assets are carried to support a given level of sales.
   □ A *relaxed current asset investment policy* is one in which large amounts of cash, marketable securities, and inventories are carried, and where sales are stimulated by the use of a liberal credit policy.
   □ A *restricted current asset investment policy* is one in which holdings of cash, securities, inventories, and receivables are minimized.
   □ A *moderate current asset investment policy* is between the two extremes.
   □ Generally, the decision on the current assets level involves a risk/return tradeoff. The relaxed policy minimizes risk, but it also has the lowest expected return. On the other hand, the restricted policy offers the highest expected return coupled with the highest risk. The moderate policy falls in between the two extremes in terms of expected risk and return.
   □ Changing technology can lead to dramatic changes in the optimal current asset investment policy.

■ Working capital consists of four main components: cash, marketable securities, inventory, and accounts receivable.

■ For each type of asset, firms face a fundamental tradeoff: current assets are necessary to conduct business, and the greater the holdings of current assets, the smaller the danger of running out, hence the lower the firm's operating risk. However, holding working capital is costly; so, there is pressure to hold the amount of working capital carried to the minimum consistent with running the business without interruption.

Cash is a nonearning asset. Excessive cash balances reduce the rate of return on equity and hence the value of a firm's stock. Thus, the goal of cash management is to minimize the amount of cash the firm must hold in order to conduct its normal business.

■ Firms hold cash for two primary reasons:
   □ Transactions balances are held to provide the cash needed to conduct normal business operations.
   □ Compensating balances are often required by banks for providing loans and services.

■ Two secondary reasons are also cited:
  □ Precautionary balances are held in reserve for random fluctuations in cash inflows and outflows.
  □ Speculative balances are held to enable the firm to take advantage of bargain purchases.

■ Most firms do not segregate funds for each of these motives, but they do consider them in setting their overall cash positions.

■ An ample cash balance should be maintained to take advantage of trade discounts and favorable business opportunities, to help the firm maintain its credit rating, and to meet emergency needs.

A cash budget projects cash inflows and outflows over some specified period of time.

■ The basis for a cash budget is the sales forecast and the level of fixed assets and inventory that will be required to meet the forecasted sales level.

■ Cash budgets can be created for any interval, but firms typically use a monthly cash budget for the coming year, a weekly budget for the coming month, and a daily budget for the coming week, or something similar.

■ A typical cash budget consists of three sections.
  □ The *collections and purchases worksheet* summarizes the firm's cash collections from sales and cash purchases for materials.
  □ The *cash gain or loss section* lays out the cash inflows and outflows, and the "bottom line" of this section is the net cash gain or loss.
  □ The *cash surplus or loan requirement section* summarizes the firm's cumulative need for loans and cumulative surplus cash.

■ If the firm's inflows and outflows are not uniform over the budget interval, say monthly, the cash budget will overstate or understate the firm's cash needs.

■ The cash budget can be used to help set the firm's *target cash balance*. This is accomplished by incorporating uncertainty into the budget, and then setting a target balance which provides a cushion against adverse conditions.

■ Computer programs, especially spreadsheet programs such as *Lotus 1-2-3*, are particularly well suited for preparing and analyzing the cash budget.

■ Note that the cash budget focuses on the physical movement of cash, and hence depreciation cash flow does not appear directly on the budget. It does, however, affect the amount of taxes shown.

Cash management has changed significantly over the last two decades as a result of interest rates and new technology.

■ From the early 1970s to the mid-1980s, there was a clear upward trend in interest rates which increased the opportunity cost of holding cash, and therefore, encouraged financial managers to search for more efficient ways of managing the firm's cash.

■ New technology, particularly computerized electronic funds transfer mechanisms, have improved cash management efficiency.

■ Cash management techniques encompass (1) cash flow synchronization, (2) using float, (3) accelerating collections, (4) getting available funds to where they are needed, and (5) controlling disbursements.

■ Synchronizing cash inflows and outflows permits a reduction in the firm's cash balances, decreases its bank loans, lowers its interest expense, and increases profits.

■ Net float is the difference between the balance shown in a firm's checkbook and the balance on the bank's records. A firm's net float is a function of its ability to speed up collections on checks received (*collections float*) and to slow down collections on checks written (*disbursement float*).

Several techniques are now used to speed collections and to get funds where they are needed.

■ A *lockbox plan* is a procedure which speeds up collections and reduces float through the use of post office boxes in payers' local areas.
  □ Customers mail checks to a post office box in a specified city. A local bank then collects the checks, deposits them, starts the clearing process, and notifies the selling firm that payment has been received.
  □ Processing time is further reduced because it takes less time for banks to collect local checks.

■ Firms are increasingly demanding payments of larger bills by wire, or even by automatic electronic debits.

Marketable securities typically provide much lower yields than a firm's operating assets, yet they are often held in sizable amounts.

In many cases companies hold marketable securities for the same reasons they hold cash.

While these securities are not as liquid as cash, in most cases they can be converted to cash in a very short period of time.

Marketable securities provide at least a modest return, while cash yields nothing.

William Baumol first recognized that the tradeoff between cash and marketable securities is similar to the one firms face when setting the optimal inventory level.
- ☐ His model suggests that cash holdings should be higher if it costs a lot and takes a long time to liquidate marketable securities, but lower if interest rates are low.

Inventory, which may be classified as raw materials, work-in-process, and finished goods, is essential to the operation of most businesses.

Inventory is greatly influenced by the level of sales. Since inventory is acquired before sales can take place, an accurate sales forecast is critical to effective inventory management.

Proper inventory management requires close coordination among the sales, purchasing, production, and finance departments. The sales/marketing department is generally the first to spot changes in demand. These changes must be worked into the company's purchasing and manufacturing schedules, and the financial manager must arrange any financing that will be needed to support the inventory buildup. Improper coordination among departments, poor sales forecasts, or both, can lead to disaster.

The goal of inventory management is to insure that the inventories needed to sustain operations are available, but to hold the costs of ordering and carrying inventories to the lowest possible level.

Inventory costs are divided into three categories: carrying costs, ordering and receiving costs, and the costs that are incurred if the firm runs short of inventory.
- ☐ *Carrying costs* generally rise in direct proportion to the average amount of inventory held. Carrying costs associated with inventory include cost of the capital tied up, storage and handling costs, insurance, property taxes, and depreciation and obsolescence.
- ☐ *Ordering costs*, which are considered to be fixed costs, decline as average inventory increase, that is, as the number of orders decrease. Ordering costs include the costs of placing and receiving orders.
- ☐ The *costs of running short* include loss of sales, loss of customer goodwill, and disruption of production schedules.

Inventory management also involves the establishment of an inventory control system. These systems vary from the extremely simple to the very complex.

■ One simple control procedure is the *redline method*. A red line is drawn inside the bin where the inventory is stocked. When the red line shows, an order is placed.

■ The *two-bin method* has inventory items stocked in two bins. When the working bin is empty, an order is placed and inventory is drawn from the second bin.

■ Large companies employ much more sophisticated *computerized inventory control systems*. The computer starts with an inventory count in memory. As withdrawals are made, they are recorded by the computer, and the inventory balance is revised. Orders are automatically placed once the reorder point is reached.

■ The *just-in-time (JIT) system* coordinates a manufacturer's production with suppliers' so that raw materials arrive from suppliers just as they are needed in the production process. It also requires that component parts be perfect; therefore, JIT inventory management has been developed in conjunction with total quality management (TQM).

■ Another important development related to inventory is *out-sourcing*, which is the practice of purchasing components rather than making them in-house. Out-sourcing is often combined with just-in-time systems to reduce inventory levels.

■ A final point relating to inventory levels is the relationship between production scheduling and inventory levels. Inventory policy must be coordinated with the firm's manufacturing and procurement policies, because the ultimate goal is to minimize total production and distribution costs, and inventory costs are just one part of the picture.

Carrying receivables has both direct and indirect costs, but it also has an important benefit-- granting credit will increase sales.

■ *Accounts receivable* are created when a firm sells goods or performs services on credit rather than on a cash basis. When cash is received, accounts receivable are reduced by the same amount.

■ The total amount of accounts receivable outstanding is determined by (1) the volume of credit sales and (2) the average length of time between sales and collections.

■ The investment in receivables, like any asset, must be financed in some manner.

Receivables must be actively managed to insure that the firm's receivables policy is effective. There are two commonly used methods to monitor a firm's receivables.

■ The *days sales outstanding (DSO)*, also sometimes called the average collection period (ACP), measures the average length of time it takes a firm's customers to pay off their credit purchases.
  □ The DSO is calculated by dividing the receivables balance by average daily credit sales.
  □ The DSO can be compared with the industry average and the firm's own credit terms to get an indication of how well customers are adhering to the terms prescribed and how customers' payments, on average, compare with the industry average.

■ An *aging schedule* breaks down a firm's receivables by the ages of the accounts, and it points out the percentage of receivables due that are attributable to late paying customers.

■ Both the DSO and aging schedule can be distorted if sales are seasonal or if a firm is growing rapidly. A deterioration in either the DSO or the aging schedule should be taken as a signal to investigate further, but not necessarily as a sign that the firm's credit policy has weakened.

The major controllable variables that affect sales are sales price, product quality, advertising, and the firm's credit policy. The credit policy consists of (1) the credit period, (2) credit standards, (3) collection policy, and (4) discounts.

■ The *credit period* is the length of time for which credit is granted. Increasing the credit period often stimulates sales, but there is a cost involved in carrying the increased receivables.

■ *Credit standards* refer to the strength and creditworthiness a customer must exhibit in order to qualify for credit.
  □ Two major sources of external credit information are available: credit associations and credit-reporting agencies such as Dun & Bradstreet and TRW.

■ *Collection policy* refers to the procedures the firm follows to collect past-due accounts. The collection process can be expensive in terms of both direct costs and lost goodwill, but at least some firmness is needed to prevent an undue lengthening of the collection period and to minimize outright losses.

■ The last variable in the credit policy decision is the firm's *cash discount policy*. Cash discounts attract customers and encourage early payment but reduce the dollar amount received on each discount sale.

■ Other conditions may also influence a firm's overall credit policy.

☐ It is sometimes possible to sell on credit and assess a carrying charge on the receivables that are outstanding, making credit sales more profitable than cash sales.

☐ It is illegal for a firm to charge prices or to set credit terms that discriminate between customers unless these differential prices are cost-justified.

Appendix 15A discusses the cash conversion cycle. The cash conversion cycle focuses on the conversion of operating events to cash flows.

■ The following terms and definitions are used:

☐ *Inventory conversion period*, which is the average length of time required to convert materials into finished goods, and then to sell these goods.

$$\text{Inventory conversion period} = \frac{\text{Inventory}}{\text{Sales per day}}.$$

☐ *Receivables collection period*, which is the average length of time required to convert the firm's receivables into cash, that is, to collect cash following a sale.

$$\text{Receivables collection period} = \frac{\text{Receivables}}{\text{Sales}/360}.$$

☐ *Payables deferral period*, which is the average length of time between the purchase of raw materials and labor and the payment of cash for them.

$$\text{Payables deferral period} = \frac{\text{Payables}}{\text{Cost of goods sold}/360}.$$

☐ *Cash conversion cycle*, which nets out the three periods just defined, and which therefore equals the average length of time between the firm's actual cash expenditures on productive resources and its own cash receipts from the sale of its products. Thus, the cash conversion cycle equals the average length of time the firm has funds tied up in current assets.

■ Using these definitions, the cash conversion cycle is defined as follows:

$$\begin{array}{llll} \text{Inventory} & \text{Receivables} & \text{Payables} & \text{Cash} \\ \text{conversion} + & \text{collection} - & \text{deferral} = & \text{conversion}. \\ \text{period} & \text{period} & \text{period} & \text{cycle} \end{array}$$

■ To illustrate, suppose it takes a firm an average of 72 days to convert raw materials and labor to widgets and to sell them, and it takes another 24 days to collect on receivables, while 30 days normally lapse between receipt of materials (and work done) and payments for materials and labor. In this case, the cash conversion cycle is 72 days + 24 days - 30 days = 66 days.

■ A firm should shorten its cash conversion cycle as much as possible without increasing costs or depressing sales. This would maximize profits, because the longer the cash conversion cycle, the greater the need for external financing--and such financing has a cost.

SELF-TEST QUESTIONS

Definitional

1. Current assets are also referred to as _____ _____.

2. _____ working capital is defined as _____ assets minus current _____.

3. The goal of cash management is to _____ the amount of _____ the firm must hold in order to conduct its normal business activities.

4. Precautionary balances are maintained in order to allow for random, unforeseen fluctuations in cash _____ and _____.

5. _____ balances are maintained to pay banks for services they perform.

6. Efficient cash management is often concerned with speeding up the _____ of checks received and slowing down the _____ of checks issued.

7. One method for speeding the collection process is the use of a(n) _____ system.

8. The difference between a firm's balance on its own books and its balance as carried on the bank's books is known as net _____.

9. Inventory is usually classified as _____ _____, _____ - ___ - _____, and _____ _____.

10. The goal of inventory management is to provide the inventory needed for operations at the _____ _____.

11. Storage costs, obsolescence, and other costs that _____ with larger inventory are known as _____ costs.

12. Ordering and receiving costs are _____ related to average inventory size.

12. Ordering and receiving costs are _____ related to average inventory size.

13. Inventory control systems that require suppliers to deliver items as they are needed are called _____ - ___ - _____ systems.

14. _____ _____ are created when goods are sold or services are performed on credit.

15. A firm's outstanding accounts receivable will be determined by the _____ of credit sales and the length of time between _____ and _____.

16. Sales volume and the collection period will be affected by a firm's _____ _____.

17. Extremely strict credit standards will result in lost _____.

18. Credit terms generally specify the _____ for which credit is granted and any _____ _____ that is offered for early payment.

19. The optimal credit terms involve a tradeoff between increased _____ and the cost of carrying additional _____ _____.

20. _____ policy refers to the manner in which a firm tries to obtain payment from past-due accounts.

21. Two popular methods for monitoring receivables are _____ _____ and the _____ _____ _____.

22. Credit sales may be especially profitable if a(n) _____ charge is assessed on accounts receivable.

23. _____ _____ are local groups which meet to exchange credit information.

Conceptual

24. Which of the following actions would not be consistent with good cash management?

    a. Increasing the synchronization of cash flows.
    b. Using lockboxes in funds collection.
    c. Maintaining an average cash balance equal to that required as a compensating balance or that which minimizes total cost.
    d. Minimizing the use of float.

25. A firm changes its credit policy from 2/10, net 30, to 3/10, net 30. The change is to meet competition, so no increase in sales is expected. The firm's average investment in accounts receivable will probably increase as a result of the change.

   a. True   b. False

26. An aging schedule is constructed by a firm to keep track of when its accounts payable are due.

   a. True   b. False

27. If a credit policy change increases the firm's accounts receivable, the entire increase must be financed by some source of funds.

   a. True   b. False

28. The costs of a stock-out do *not* include

   a. Disruption of production schedules.
   b. Loss of customer goodwill.
   c. Depreciation and obsolescence.
   d. Loss of sales.
   e. Answers c and d above.

29. The goal of credit policy is to

   a. Minimize bad debt losses.
   b. Minimize DSO.
   c. Maximize sales.
   d. Minimize collection expenses.
   e. Extend credit to the point where marginal profits equal marginal costs.

SELF-TEST PROBLEMS

1. The Mill Company has a daily average collection of checks of $250,000. It takes the company 4 days to convert the checks to cash. Assume a lockbox system could be employed which would reduce the cash conversion period to 3 days. The lockbox system would have a net cost of $25,000 per year, but any additional funds made available could be invested to net 8 percent per year. Should Mill adopt the lockbox system?

    a. Yes; the system would free $250,000 in funds.
    b. Yes; the benefits of the lockbox system exceed the costs.
    c. No; the benefit is only $10,000.
    d. No; the firm would lose $5,000 per year if the system were used.
    e. The benefits and costs are equal; hence the firm is indifferent toward the system.

(The following data apply to the next three Self-Test Problems.)

Simmons Brick Company sells on terms of 3/10, net 30. Gross sales for the year are $1,200,000 and the collections department estimates that 30 percent of the customers pay on the tenth day and take discounts; 40 percent pay on the thirtieth day; and the remaining 30 percent pay, on average, 40 days after the purchase. Assume 360 days per year.

2. What is the days sales outstanding?

    a. 10 days   b. 13 days   c. 20 days   d. 27 days   e. 40 days

3. What is the current receivables balance?

    a. $60,000   b. $70,000   c. $75,000   d. $80,000   e. $90,000

4. What would be the new receivables balance if Simmons toughened up on its collection policy, with the result that all nondiscount customers paid on the thirtieth day?

    a. $60,000   b. $70,000   c. $75,000   d. $80,000   e. $90,000

ANSWERS TO SELF-TEST QUESTIONS

1. working capital
2. Net; current; liabilities
3. minimize; cash
4. inflows; outflows
5. Compensating
6. collection; payment
7. lockbox
8. float
9. raw materials; work-in-process; finished goods
10. lowest cost
11. increase; carrying
12. inversely
13. just-in-time
14. Accounts receivable
15. volume; sales; collections
16. credit policy
17. sales
18. period; cash discount
19. sales; accounts receivable
20. Collection
21. aging schedules; days sales outstanding (DSO)
22. carrying
23. Credit associations

24. d. Management should try to maximize float.

25. b. No new customers are being generated. The current customers pay either on Day 10 or Day 30. The increase in trade discount will induce some customers who are now paying on Day 30 to pay on Day 10. Thus, the days sales outstanding is shortened which, in turn, will cause a decline in accounts receivable.

26. b. The aging schedule breaks down accounts receivable according to how long they have been outstanding.

27. b. Receivables are based on sales price which presumably includes some profit. Only the actual cash outlays associated with receivables must be financed. The remainder, or profit, appears on the balance sheet as an increase in retained earnings.

28. c. Depreciation and obsolescence are inventory carrying costs.

29. e. The goal of credit policy is to maximize overall profits. This is achieved when the marginal profits equal the marginal costs.

SOLUTIONS TO SELF-TEST PROBLEMS

1. d. Currently, Mill has 4($250,000) = $1,000,000 in unavailable collections. If lockboxes were used, this could be reduced to $750,000. Thus, $250,000 would be available to invest at 8 percent, resulting in an annual return of 0.08($250,000) = $20,000. If the system costs $25,000, Mill would lose $5,000 per year by adopting the system.

2. d. 0.3(10 days) + 0.4(30 days) + 0.3(40 days) = 27 days.

3. e. Receivables = (DSO)(Sales/360) = 27($1,200,000/360) = $90,000.

4. d. New days sales outstanding = 0.3(10) + 0.7(30) = 24 days.
   Sales per day = $1,200,000/360 = $3,333.33.
   Receivables = $3,333.33(24 days) = $80,000.00.

   Thus, the average receivables would drop from $90,000 to $80,000. Furthermore, sales may decline as a result of the tighter credit and reduce receivables even more. Also, some additional customers may now take discounts, which would further reduce receivables.

CHAPTER 16
FINANCING CURRENT ASSETS

Working capital policy involves decisions relating to current assets, including decisions about financing them. Since about half of the typical firm's capital is invested in current assets, working capital policy and management are important to the firm and its shareholders. In fact, about 60 percent of a financial manager's time is devoted to working capital policy and management, and many finance students' first assignments on the job will involve working capital. For these reasons, working capital policy is a vitally important topic.

OUTLINE

A firm's current asset levels and financing requirements rise and fall with business cycles and seasonal trends. At the peak of such cycles, businesses carry their maximum amounts of current assets. Similar fluctuations in financing needs can occur over these cycles, typically, financing needs contract during recessions, and
they expand during booms.

■ Current assets rarely drop to zero, and this fact has led to the development of the idea of *permanent current assets*. These are the current assets on hand at the low point of the year.

■ Seasonal current assets are defined as *temporary current assets*.

■ The manner in which the permanent and temporary current assets are financed is called the firm's *current asset financing policy*.
  □ The *maturity matching, or "self-liquidating," approach* matches asset and liability maturities. Defined as a moderate current asset financing policy, this would use permanent financing for permanent assets (permanent current assets and fixed assets), and use short-term financing to cover seasonal and/or cyclical temporary assets (fluctuating current assets).

☐ The *aggressive approach* is used by a firm which finances all of its fixed assets with long-term capital but part of its permanent current assets with short-term, nonspontaneous credit.

☐ A *conservative approach* would be to use permanent capital to meet some of the cyclical demand, and then hold the temporary surpluses as marketable securities at the trough of the cycle. Here, the amount of permanent financing exceeds permanent assets.

There are advantages and disadvantages to the use of short-term financing.

■ A short-term loan can be obtained much faster than long-term credit.

■ Short-term debt is more flexible since it may be repaid if the firm's financing requirements decline. Long-term debt can be retired, but this will probably involve a prepayment penalty.

■ Short-term interest rates are normally lower than long-term rates. Therefore, financing with short-term credit usually results in lower interest costs.

■ Short-term debt is generally more risky than long-term debt for two reasons.
  ☐ Short-term interest rates fluctuate widely while long-term rates tend to be more stable and predictable, and hence the interest rate on short-term debt could increase dramatically in a short period.
  ☐ Short-term debt comes due every few months. If a firm does not have the cash to repay debt when it comes due, and if it cannot refinance the loan, it may be forced into bankruptcy.

Different types of short-term funds have different characteristics. One source of short-term funds is accrued wages and taxes, which increase and decrease spontaneously as a firm's operations expand and contract. This type of debt is "free" in the sense that no interest is paid on funds raised through accruals.

Accounts payable, or trade credit, is the largest single category of short-term debt. Trade credit is a spontaneous source of funds in that it arises from ordinary business transactions. Most firms make purchases on credit, recording the debt as an account payable.

■ An increase in sales will be accompanied by an increase in inventory purchases, which will automatically generate additional financing.

■ The cost of trade credit is made up of discounts lost by not paying invoices within the discount period.
  ☐ For example, if credit terms are 2/10, net 30, the cost of 20 additional days credit is 2 percent of the dollar value of the purchases made.

☐ The following equation may be used to calculate the nominal percentage cost, on an annual basis, of not taking discounts:

$$\text{Nominal percentage cost} = \frac{\text{Discount \%}}{100 - \text{Discount \%}} \times \frac{360}{\text{Days credit is outstanding} - \text{Discount period}}.$$

☐ For example, the nominal cost of not taking the discount when the credit terms are 2/10, net 30, is

$$\text{Nominal percentage cost} = \frac{2}{98} \times \frac{360}{30 - 10} = 0.0204(18) = 0.367 = 36.7\%.$$

☐ In effective annual interest terms, the rate is even higher. Note that the first term on the right-hand side of the nominal cost equation is the periodic cost, and the second term is the number of periods per year. Thus, the effective annual rate is $(1.0204)^{18} - 1.0 = 1.438 - 1.0 = 43.8\%$.

■ Trade credit can be divided into two components: *Free trade credit* is that credit received during the discount period. *Costly trade credit* is obtained by foregoing discounts. This costly component should be used only when it is less expensive than funds obtained from other sources.

☐ Financial managers should always use the free component, but they should use the costly component only after analyzing the cost of this capital to make sure that it is less than the cost of funds which could be obtained from other sources.

☐ Competitive conditions may permit firms to do better than the stated credit terms by taking discounts beyond the discount period or by simply paying late. Such practices, called *stretching accounts payable*, reduce the cost of trade credit, but they also result in poor relationships with suppliers.

Bank loans appear on a firm's balance sheet as notes payable and represent another important source of short-term financing. Bank loans are not generated spontaneously but must be negotiated and renewed on a regular basis.

■ About two-thirds of all bank loans mature in a year or less, although banks do make longer-term loans.

■ When a firm obtains a bank loan, a promissory note specifying the following items is signed: the amount borrowed, the percentage interest rate, the repayment schedule, any collateral offered as security, and other terms of the loan.

■ Banks normally require regular borrowers to maintain *compensating balances* equal to 10 to 20 percent of the face value of loans. Such required balances generally increase the effective interest rate on the loan.

■ A *line of credit* is an informal understanding between the bank and the borrower concerning the maximum loan balance the bank will allow.

■ A *revolving credit agreement* is a formal line of credit often used by large firms. Normally, the borrower will pay the bank a commitment fee to compensate the bank for guaranteeing that the funds will be available. This fee is paid in addition to the regular interest charge on funds actually borrowed.

The interest cost of loans will vary for different types of borrowers and for all borrowers over time. Rates charged will vary depending on economic conditions, the risk of the borrower, and the size of the loan. Interest charges on bank loans can be calculated in one of several ways listed below.

■ *Regular, or simple, interest.* The interest payment is determined by multiplying the loan amount, or face value, by the stated interest rate. Principal and interest are then paid at the end of the loan period.

$$\text{Effective annual rate}_{\text{Simple}} = \frac{\text{Interest paid}}{\text{Amount received}}.$$

□ On a simple interest loan of less than one year the effective annual rate will be higher due to the compounding effect.

$$\text{Effective annual rate}_{\text{Simple}} = \left(1 + \frac{k_{\text{Nom}}}{m}\right)^m - 1.0.$$

□ Here k_{Nom} is the nominal, or stated, interest rate expressed as a decimal and m is the number of compounding periods per year (four for a quarterly loan or twelve for a monthly loan).

■ *Discount interest.* Under this method, the bank deducts interest in advance. The effective annual rate of interest is higher than the nominal, or stated, rate.

$$\text{Effective annual rate}_{\text{Discount}} = \frac{\text{Interest paid}}{\text{Face value} - \text{Interest paid}}.$$

☐ Alternatively,

$$\text{Effective annual rate}_{\text{Disount}} = \frac{\text{Nominal rate (decimal)}}{1.0 - \text{Nominal rate (decimal)}} \, .$$

☐ Effective annual rates on discount loans for less than one year have higher effective discount rates and are found using this formula:

$$\text{Effective annual rate}_{\text{Discount}} = \left(1.0 + \frac{\text{Interest paid}}{\text{Face value} - \text{Interest paid}} \right)^m - 1.0 \, .$$

☐ Here interest and face value are in dollars. A $1,000 loan at 12 percent for one month, discount interest, would have an effective annual rate of 12.82 percent.

$$\text{Effective annual rate}_{\text{Discount}} = \left(1.0 + \frac{\$10}{\$1,000 - \$10} \right)^{12} - 1.0 = 12.82\%.$$

■ *Installment loans: add-on interest.* Interest charges are calculated and then added on to the funds received to determine the face value of the note, which is paid off in equal installments. The borrower has use of the full amount of the funds received only until the first installment is paid. The approximate annual rate is double the stated rate, because the average amount of the loan outstanding is only about half the face amount borrowed.

$$\text{Approximate annual rate}_{\text{Add-on}} = \frac{\text{Interest paid}}{(\text{Amount received})/2} \, .$$

■ Compensating balances tend to raise the effective interest rate on bank loans.
  ☐ In general, this formula is used to find the effective annual interest rate when compensating balances apply and interest is paid at the end of the period:

$$\text{Effective annual rate}_{\text{Simple/CB}} = \frac{\text{Nominal rate (decimal)}}{1.0 - \text{Compensating balance(decimal)}} \, .$$

  ☐ The analysis can be extended to the case where compensating balances are required and the loan is based on discount interest:

$$\text{Effective annual rate}_{\text{Discount/CB}} = \frac{\text{Nominal rate (decimal)}}{1.0 - \underset{\text{(decimal)}}{\text{Nominal rate}} - \underset{\text{(decimal)}}{\text{Compensating balance}}} \, .$$

  ☐ It should be noted that when compensating balances or discount interest or both apply, the borrower must borrow a face amount significantly greater than the funds actually received. For a discount loan with a compensating balance, the face amount is calculated as follows:

$$\text{Face value} = \frac{\text{Funds required}}{1.0 - \frac{\text{Nominal interest rate}}{\text{(decimal)}} - \frac{\text{Compensating balance}}{\text{(decimal)}}}.$$

☐ If a firm normally carries cash balances with the bank, then those balances can be used to meet all or part of the compensating balance requirement, and this will reduce the effective cost of the loan.

Choosing a bank involves an analysis of the following variables:

Willingness to assume risks. Some banks are quite conservative, while others are more willing to make risky loans.

Advice and counsel. A bank's ability to provide counsel is particularly important to firms in their formative years.

Loyalty to customers. This variable deals with a bank's willingness to support customers during difficult economic times.

Specialization. A bank may specialize in making loans to a particular type of business. Firms should seek out a bank which is familiar with their particular type of business.

Maximum loan size. This is an important consideration for large companies when establishing a borrowing relationship because most banks cannot lend to a single customer more than 15 percent of the total amount of the bank's capital.

Merchant banking. Originally the term applied to banks which not only loaned depositors' money but also provided its customers with equity capital and financial advice. In recent years, commercial banks have been attempting to get back into merchant banking, in part because of their foreign competitors.

Other services. The availability of services such as lockbox systems should also be taken into account when selecting a bank.

Commercial paper, another source of short-term credit, is an unsecured promissory note. It is generally sold to other business firms, to insurance companies, to banks, and to money market mutual funds. Only large, financially strong firms are able to tap the commercial paper market.

■ Maturities of commercial paper range from a few days to nine months, with an average of about five months.

☐ Interest rates on prime commercial paper generally range from 1 ½ to 3 percentage points below the stated prime rate, and about 1/8 to 1/2 of a percentage point above the T-bill rate. However, rates fluctuate daily with supply and demand conditions in the marketplace, and since no compensating balance is required, the effective cost is even lower in comparison to bank loans.

☐ A disadvantage of the commercial paper market vis-a-vis bank loans is that the impersonal nature of the market makes it difficult for firms to use commercial paper at times when they are in temporary financial distress.

For a strong firm, borrowing on an unsecured basis is generally cheaper and simpler than on a secured loan basis because of the administrative costs associated with the use of security. However, lenders will refuse credit without some form of collateral if a borrower's credit standing is questionable.

Appendix 16A discusses procedures for using accounts receivable and inventory as security for short-term loans. Accounts receivable financing involves either the pledging of receivables or the selling of receivables (factoring). Credit can also be secured by business inventory. Blanket liens, trust receipts, and warehouse receipts are methods for using inventory as security.

SELF-TEST QUESTIONS

Definitional

1. In the maturity matching approach to working capital financing, permanent assets should be financed with _____ capital, while _____ assets should be financed with short-term credit.

2. Some firms use short-term financing to finance permanent assets. This approach maximizes _____ _____, but also has the _____ _____.

3. Short-term borrowing provides more _____ for firms that are uncertain about their _____ borrowing needs.

4. Short-term borrowing will be less expensive than borrowing long-term if the yield curve is _____ sloping.

5. Short-term interest rates fluctuate _____ than long-term rates.

6. _____ wages and taxes are a common source of short-term credit. However, most firms have little control over the _____ of these accounts.

7. Accounts payable, or _____ _____, is the largest single source of short-term credit for most businesses.

8. Trade credit is a(n) _____ source of funds in the sense that it automatically increases when sales increase.

9. Trade credit can be divided into two components: _____ trade credit and _____ trade credit.

10. Free trade credit is that credit received during the _____ period.

11. _____ trade credit should only be used when the cost of the trade credit is less than the cost of _____ sources.

12. The instrument signed when bank credit is obtained is called a(n) _____ _____.

13. Many banks require borrowers to keep _____ _____ on deposit with the bank equal to 10 or 20 percent of the face value of the loan.

14. Maturities on commercial paper generally range from _____ to _____ months, with interest rates set about 1 1/2 to 3 percentage points _____ the _____ rate.

15. A(n) _____ loan is one where collateral such as _____ or _____ have been pledged in support of the loan.

16. A(n) _____ _____ _____ is an understanding between a bank and a borrower as to the maximum loan that will be permitted.

17. The fee paid to a bank to secure a revolving credit agreement is known as a(n) _____ fee.

18. If interest charges are deducted in advance, this is known as _____ interest, and the effective rate is higher than the _____ interest rate.

19. With a(n) _____ loan, the average amount of the usable funds during the loan period is equal to approximately _____ - _____ of the face amount of the loan.

20. Commercial paper can only be issued by _____, _____ _____ firms.

Conceptual

21. The matching of asset and liability maturities is considered desirable because this strategy minimizes interest rate risk.

   a. True   b. False

22. Accruals are "free" in the sense that no interest must be paid on these funds.

   a. True   b. False

23. The effect of compensating balances is to decrease the effective interest rate of a loan.

   a. True   b. False

24. Which of the following statements concerning commercial paper is most *correct*?

   a. Commercial paper is secured debt of large, financially strong firms.
   b. Commercial paper is sold primarily to individual investors.
   c. Maturities of commercial paper generally exceed nine months.
   d. Commercial paper interest rates are typically 1 1/2 to 3 percentage points above the stated prime rate.
   e. None of the above statements is correct.

25. Which of the following statements is most *correct*?

   a. If you had just been hired as Working Capital Manager for a firm with but one stockholder, and that stockholder told you that she had all the money she could possibly use, hence that her primary operating goal was to avoid even the remotest possibility of bankruptcy, then you should set the firm's working capital financing policy on the basis of the "Maturity Matching, or Self-Liquidating, Approach."
   b. Due to the existence of positive maturity risk premiums, at most times short-term debt carries lower interest rates than long-term debt. Therefore, if a company finances primarily with short-term as opposed to long-term debt, its expected TIE ratio, hence its overall riskiness, will be lower than if it finances with long-term debt. Therefore, the more conservative the firm, the greater its reliance on short-term debt.
   c. If a firm buys on terms of 2/10, net 30, and pays on the 30th day, then its accounts payable may be thought of as consisting of some "free" and some "costly" trade credit. Since the percentage cost of the costly trade credit is lowered if the payment period is reduced, the firm should try to pay earlier than on Day 30, say on Day 25.

d. Suppose a firm buys on terms of 2/10, net 30, but it normally pays on Day 60. Disregarding any "image" effects, it should, if it can borrow from the bank at an effective rate of 14 percent, take out a bank loan and start taking discounts.

e. Each of the above statements is false.

SELF-TEST PROBLEMS

(The following data apply to the next three Self-Test Problems.)

A firm buys on terms of 2/10, net 30, but generally does not pay until 40 days after the invoice date. Its purchases total $1,080,000 per year.

1. How much "non-free" trade credit does the firm use on average each year?

    a. $120,000   **b.** $90,000   **c.** $60,000   **d.** $30,000   **e.** $20,000

2. What is the nominal cost of the "non-free" trade credit?

    a. 16.2%   **b.** 19.4%   **c.** 21.9%   **d.** 24.5%   **e.** 27.4%

3. What is the effective cost rate of the costly credit?

    a. 16.2%   **b.** 19.4%   **c.** 21.9%   **d.** 24.5%   **e.** 27.4%

4. Lawton Pipelines Inc. has developed plans for a new pump that will allow more economical operation of the company's oil pipelines. Management estimates that $2,400,000 will be required to put this new pump into operation. Funds can be obtained from a bank at 10 percent discount interest, or the company can finance the expansion by delaying payment to its suppliers. Presently, Lawton purchases under terms of 2/10, net 40, but management believes payment could be delayed 30 additional days without penalty; that is, payment could be made in 70 days. Which means of financing should Lawton use? (Use the nominal cost of trade credit.)

    a. Trade credit, since the cost is about 12.24 percent.
    b. Trade credit, since the cost is about 3.13 percentage points less than the bank loan.
    c. Bank loan, since the cost is about 1.13 percentage points less than trade credit.
    d. Bank loan, since the cost is about 3.13 percentage points less than trade credit.
    e. The firm could use either since the costs are the same.

(The following data apply to the next four Self-Test Problems.)

You plan to borrow $10,000 from your bank, which offers to lend you the money at a 10 percent nominal, or stated, rate on a 1-year loan.

5. What is the effective interest rate if the loan is a discount loan?

    a. 11.1%   **b.** 13.3%   **c.** 15.0%   **d.** 17.5%   **e.** 20.0%

6. What is the approximate interest rate if the loan is an add-on interest loan with 12 monthly payments?

    a. 11.1%   **b.** 13.3%   **c.** 15.0%   **d.** 17.5%   **e.** 20.0%

7. What is the effective interest rate if the loan is a discount loan with a 15 percent compensating balance?

    a. 11.1%   **b.** 13.3%   **c.** 15.0%   **d.** 17.5%   **e.** 20.0%

8. Under the terms of the previous problem, how much would you have to borrow to have the use of $10,000?

    a. $10,000   **b.** $11,111   **c.** $12,000   **d.** $13,333   **e.** $15,000

9. Gibbs Corporation needs to raise $1,000,000 for one year to supply working capital to a new store. Gibbs buys from its suppliers on terms of 4/10, net 90, and it currently pays on the 10th day and takes discounts, but it could forego discounts, pay on the 90th day, and get the needed $1,000,000 in the form of costly trade credit. Alternatively, Gibbs could borrow from its bank on a 15 percent discount interest rate basis. What is the effective annual cost rate of the lower cost source?

    a. 20.17%   **b.** 18.75%   **c.** 17.65%   **d.** 18.25%   **e.** 19.50%

Appendix 16A

(The following data apply to the next two Self-Test Problems.)

Douglas Industries needs an additional $500,000, which it plans to obtain through a factoring arrangement. The factor would purchase Douglas's accounts receivable and advance the invoice amount, minus a 4 percent commission, on the invoices purchased each month.

Douglas sells on terms of net 30 days. In addition, the factor charges a 14 percent annual interest rate on the total invoice amount, to be deducted in advance.

A-1. What amount of accounts receivable must be factored to net $500,000?

     a. $527,241   **b.** $515,464   **c.** $530,441   **d.** $525,367   **e.** $518,989

A-2. If Douglas can reduce credit expenses by $10,000 per month and avoid bad debt losses of 3.5 percent on the factored amount, what is the total annual dollar cost of the savings that results from the use of the factoring arrangement?

     a. $12,353   **b.** $11,076   **c.** $14,544   **d.** $13,767   **e.** $11,841

ANSWERS TO SELF-TEST QUESTIONS

1. permanent (long-term); temporary
2. expected return; greatest risk
3. flexibility; future
4. upward
5. more
6. Accrued; size (amount)
7. trade credit
8. spontaneous
9. free; costly
10. discount
11. Costly; alternative
12. promissory note
13. compensating balances
14. one; nine; below; prime
15. secured; receivables; inventory
16. line of credit
17. commitment
18. discount; simple (or nominal or stated)
19. installment; one-half
20. large; financially strong

21. b. The matching of maturities minimizes default risk, or the risk that the firm will be unable to pay off its maturing obligations, and reinvestment rate risk, or the risk that the firm will have to roll over the debt at a higher rate.

22. a. Neither workers nor the IRS require interest payments on wages and taxes that are not paid as soon as they are earned.

23. b. Compensating balances increase the effective rate because the firm is required to maintain excess non-interest-bearing balances.

24. e. Commercial paper is the unsecured debt of strong firms. It generally has a maturity from one to nine months and is sold primarily to other corporations and financial institutions. Rates on commercial paper are typically below the prime rate.

25. d. Statement a is false; the conservative approach would be the safest current asset financing policy. Statement b is false; short-term debt fluctuates more than long-term debt, thus, the greater the firm's reliance on short-term debt, the riskier the firm. Statement c is false; it makes no difference in the cost if the firm pays on Day 25 versus Day 30 in this instance. Statement d is true; if the firm can "stretch" its payables the nominal cost is 14.69% (the effective cost is 15.66%). Thus, the firm should obtain the 14% bank loan to take discounts as this is the lowest cost to the firm.

SOLUTIONS TO SELF-TEST PROBLEMS

1. b. $1,080,000/360 = $3,000 in purchases per day. Typically, there will be $3,000(40) = $120,000 of accounts payable on the books at any given time. Of this, $3,000(10) = $30,000 is "free" credit, while $3,000(30) = $90,000 is "non-free" credit.

2. d.
$$\text{Nominal cost} = \frac{\text{Discount \%}}{100 - \text{Discount \%}} \times \frac{360}{\text{Days credit is} - \text{Discount}}$$
$$\phantom{\text{Nominal cost}} = \frac{2}{100 - 2} \times \frac{360}{40 - 10} = \frac{2}{98} \times \frac{360}{30} = 24.5\% \ .$$

3. e. The periodic rate is 2/98 = 2.04%, and there are 360/30 = 12 periods per year. Thus, the effective annual rate is 27.4 percent:

$$\left(1 + \frac{k_{\text{Nom}}}{m}\right)^{12} - 1.0 = (1.0204)^{12} - 1.0$$
$$= 1.2742 - 1.0 = 0.2742 = 27.4\%.$$

4.   **c.**
$$\text{Effective rate on the discount loan} = \frac{\text{Interest paid}}{\text{Face value} - \text{Interest paid}}$$

$$= \frac{(\$2,400,000)(0.10)}{\$2,400,000 - (\$2,400,000)(0.10)}$$

$$\frac{\$240,000}{\$2,160,000} = 0.1111 = 11.11\%.$$

Credit terms are 2/10, net 40, but delaying payments 30 additional days is the equivalent of 2/10, net 70. Assuming no penalty, the nominal cost is as follows:

$$\text{Nominal cost} = \frac{\text{Discount \%}}{100 - \text{Discount \%}} \times \frac{360}{\text{Days credit is outstanding} - \text{Discount period}}$$

$$= \frac{2}{100 - 2} \times \frac{360}{70 - 10}$$

$$= \frac{2}{98} \times \frac{360}{60} = 0.0204(6) = 12.24\%.$$

Therefore, the loan cost is 1.13 percentage points less than trade credit.

5.   **a.**
$$\text{Effective rate} = \frac{\$10,000(0.10)}{\$10,000 - \$10,000(0.10)} = \frac{\$1,000}{\$9,000} = 11.1\%.$$

6.   **e.**   Approximate annual rate = $\$1,000/\$5,000 = 20.0\%$.

7.   **b.**
$$\text{Effective rate} = \frac{10\%}{1 - 0.15 - 0.10} = 13.3\%.$$

8.   **d.**
$$\frac{\$10,000}{1 - 0.15 - 0.10} = \$13,333.$$

$0.15(\$13,333) = \$2,000$ is required for the compensating balance, and $0.10(\$13,333) = \$1,333$ is required for the immediate interest payment.

9. c. Accounts payable:

Nominal cost = $(4/96)(360/80) = 0.04167(4.5) = 18.75\%$.

EAR cost $= (1.04167)^{4.5} - 1.0 = 20.17\%$.

Cost of notes payable: $0.15/0.85 = 17.65\%$.

Appendix 16A

A-1. a.
$$\text{Accounts receivable needed to factor} = \frac{\$500,000}{1 - \left(\dfrac{0.14}{12} + 0.04\right)} = \$527,241.$$

A-2. c. Monthly costs:

Commission = $527,241(0.04) =	$21,090
Interest = $527,241(0.14/12) =	6,151
	$27,241

Monthly savings:

Credit expense	$10,000
Bad debt losses = $527,241(0.035) =	18,453
	$28,453

The factoring arrangement will result in a savings of $28,453 − $27,241 = $1,212 per month, or $1,212(12) = $14,544 per year.